I AM AN
OIL
TANKER

Tracy Lee

I AM AN

OIL

TANKER

TRAVELS WITH MY RADIO

FI GLOVER

EBURY PRESS

First published in Great Britain in 2001

10 9 8 7 6 5 4

© Fi Glover 2001

First published by
Ebury Press
Random House
20 Vauxhall Bridge Road
London SW1V 2SA

Random House Australia (Pty) Limited
20 Alfred Street, Milsons Point
Sydney
New South Wales 2061, Australia

Random House New Zealand Limited
18 Poland Road, Glenfield, Auckland 10
New Zealand

Random House South Africa (Pty) Limited
Endulini, 5A Jubilee Road
Parktown 2193
South Africa

Random House UK Limited Reg. No. 954009

www.randomhouse.co.uk

A CIP catalogue record for this book is available from the British Library

ISBN 0091877865

Papers used by Ebury Press are natural, recyclable products made from wood grown in sustainable forests.

Jacket design by Ned Hoste @ 2H Design
Typeset by Textype, Cambridge
Printed and bound by MacKays of Chatham PLC, Kent

Contents

Acknowledgements

I have to say a huge thank you to all the people who agreed to be in this book and allowed me to tag along behind them whilst they were working and playing. In particular I'd like to thank Steve and Johnnie in Chicago for being a light at the end of the tunnel and Rose Willock on Montserrat for being an absolute star. I need to say a walloping thank you to my editor Hannah for putting up with loosely interpreted deadlines and always being enthusiastic, encouraging and wise. She's only about 14 – so I wish her the best of luck in the future through gritted, stained 31-year-old teeth. On a personal note, the back room boys and girls never get the credit they deserve in radio and without lots of very talented producers and editors I would never have been able to turn chatting into a career. So thank you to Sali Collins, Jon Zilkha, Karl Mercer, Jude Howells, Bill Rogers, Louise Cotton, Sandy Smith and Jo Phillips. And thank you to Liz Warner and Liz Molyneux for letting me loose on *The Travel Show* – which sadly is no longer. This book is also for everyone who ever listened to GLR and liked it, all twelve of you. Sadly that is no longer either. Shit. Is it me?

And ta very much to Gideon Coe too. He is still around, thank goodness.

To Mark
for being very very patient
and very very tall

1 Are you the girl on the radio this morning?

North California

There isn't a single part of the world where it is not possible to get a radio signal – except perhaps the tail end of Headley Hill Road in Hampshire where my dad lives and which exists in some kind of a radio-wave vacuum, reducing every programme to the sound quality of a food processor. In his house you can still get a huge choice of stations though – but if you *are* in his house trying this out you are a burglar and I'd like you to leave.

There are more than 35,000 radio stations in the world. And those are just the legal ones. Radio reaches more people than any other form of communication. It's matched in content only by the Internet – and that is filling up with radio stations too. Most people in this country own at least five radios in one form or another. Radio has been the tool of propagandists and evangelists – it has saved people's lives; it's made people millionaires; it can make you laugh and it can make you cry and it's full of people using clichés like that one. It can paint a picture in your mind that is unique to you, even though you are hearing what millions of others are hearing simultaneously. It can reduce people to quivering nervous wrecks, and it can make others show off just a little bit ...

'So you lick the girl's neck and then sprinkle a line of salt on the wet bit that you've licked and you slam the tequila and down, and lick the salt back off ...' Texan Bob pauses here to give me the kind of look you might project if you were auditioning for a part in a rather low-budget soft porn movie.

'... then you both suck the same piece of lemon ... and that's what we call a Texan Lick.'

This instant saliva-based cocktail may well be Texan Bob's own invention: I certainly haven't seen it on any bar menu and there was

1

something about the look in his eyes that meant I was never going to try it. If that is his chat-up line at 6 o'clock in the morning I didn't want to meet him around midday unless I was wearing one of those suits that protect you from the Ebola virus.

Texan Bob is six foot of denim – some stonewashed – with leather bits at various stages ... boots, belts and that string thing cowboys wear instead of a nice Sock Shop tie. It's all topped off with a stetson which he says he never takes off and so he can't wear headphones in the studio. I have no idea of his hair colour, how much he has left of it and what style it is formed into.

It's 6.18am on an already baking hot Tuesday morning and we are in Studio 1 at KZST in Santa Rosa, standing at a microphone opposite an American version of DLT called Brent Farris. He probably calls himself the Hairy Cheerio. This is Brent's Breakfast Show broadcasting across Sonoma County in North California and every Tuesday Texan Bob comes in to do a kind of comedy act with Brent who is at this moment fiddling around with some of the very expensive-looking radio equipment in front of him.

I have a passion for radio which – thank God and the bloke who let me on the BBC's Radio Training Scheme – I have been able to turn into a career. Sitting in a darkened room talking to yourself is not everyone's idea of a sane or comfortable way to earn a living, but it's how I have spent most of my working life with the (very) occasional sojourn into television.

On this particular morning in Sonoma County I'm missing radio quite a lot, because while Brent and Bob are making radio I am making TV – or a film for *The Travel Show* to be precise – and it's proving to be quite a laborious process. Matt, the director of the film, has decided that, instead of researching our destination from an office in Manchester with the help of 14 guidebooks, some websites and some suggestions from a bloke the series producer met once in a bar, we would come over to North California and, courtesy of the local radio station, ask the listeners where they think we should go.

It's a great idea and Brent and Bob said they would be happy to oblige and let us on to their breakfast show to take advice from the listeners of KZST. So there's me, Matt the director, Ben the producer, Pat the cameraman and Simon and his enormous range of booms on sound. We are all crammed into the main studio filming Brent and Bob and waiting for them to put out our request to their loyal listeners so that we can jot down all the suggestions and tour the region, safe in the knowledge that we are enjoying the best that the Valley has to offer.

I can understand that this doesn't sound like a laborious way to make a living. And *The Travel Show* was rarely laborious – it was a fabulous opportunity to travel round the world at someone else's expense (yours, actually – if you pay your licence fee), meet wonderful people, collect fridge magnets (124 so far) and the Brucey Bonus is that you get to have two passports so that later in life you can become a spy.

It's only proving a little tricky this morning because poor old Brent and Bob are having to do everything at least twice for the cameras so that the piece can be edited successfully. Given that this is a live radio programme, repeats are a little tricky to manufacture. It's also very early in the morning and everyone is a bit twitchy. I have never noticed how badly TV and radio actually get on when you expect them both to happen at the same time.

Brent's show is classic all American Breakfast Fare ... creamy deep voice, adverts, a few rocking tunes, adverts, traffic news, listeners' phone calls and then another advert chaser – and in this branded world you have to say the name of the station every time you open the microphone.

'Santa Rosa ... goooood morning ... this is the Brent Farris Breakfast Show on KZST ... It's another beautiful day in Sonoma county ... tops of 31 round Armstrong and lows of 25 on the coast. Traffic coming up ... and we have the BBC here today. I'll tell you why after these ...'

This is the present and the future of most radio – the majority of those 35,000 radio stations are music stations – pumping out the hits from Towers of Power all over the planet. It's a bit like Marmite – the ingredients are almost irrelevant and you seldom give them much thought, but if you spread it thinly it makes quite a tasty sandwich.

In every country in the world you'd be able to find something similar to Brent's breakfast fare – music and chat pushing along the time it takes until the next advert. This needs no explanation really but I will just point out that radio is big business. People do make extraordinary amounts of money out of what is essentially compressing the waves around us that create tides, breezes and all earthly patterns. And it's all happened very quickly.

*

3

In 1887 a German scientist called Heinrich Rudolph Hertz proved that electromagnetic waves could be sent through space. His name was then adopted as the measure of all radio frequencies before he went on to set up a chain of hire car companies.

I am joking there. I can't believe that he could have foreseen the importance of what he had discovered, although never having met him he may well have done. His scientific nous was then moved on a huge step further when Guglielmo Marconi managed to receive the first-ever transatlantic wireless signal sent from England to Newfoundland in 1901. The safety of ships at sea was changed forever as ship-to-shore communication became a possibility, using that wireless signal and Morse code.

So now the world had the knowledge of the waves and the wireless bit but not the thing that would make it possible to send voices and therefore enable Gary Davis and Dave Lee Travis to find work. Then in 1904 along came Sir John A. Fleming – a Brit – who developed a tube which could do just that. Just two years later an inventor called Lee de Forest enhanced this tube and created the first mechanism which could amplify voice transmissions. In the same year a Canadian inventor, Reginald Fressman, transmitted the first distant voice and music broadcast from Brant Rock, Massachusetts to ships at sea in the Atlantic. Radio as we now know it had been born.

I only include that list of men who shaped the medium because it strikes me that, apart from the greatness of what they did individually, the combined process was a truly international incubation: like a relay race across the world, the early pioneers had handed over batons of invention which gave the world its first real means of sending immediate wads of communication.

If you are fortunate enough to live in North California you have a lot of choice where your twiddling knob ends up. We didn't have to visit Brent and Bob – we chose to. There are 73 radio stations listed in the *San Francisco Chronicle* alone. All are local – 27 are on the AM dial and 46 on the FM. The *Chronicle* gives a brief explanation of what each of them pump out into the ether – nearly all of them sound intriguing.

For example, for our *Travel Show* film we could have gone to KEST, the Asian Personal Growth station in San Francisco. Palo Alto goes one better with the AM Palo Alto Personal Achievement, or we could have taken our chances with the generosity of San Francisco's residents at the 'Listener Sponsored' KPOO.

There are then dozens of music stations all carefully defined – 'contemporary rock', 'soft rock', 'rhythm and blues', 'urban contemporary'. These are carefully defined not only so you as a listener know which to plump for – the definitions are vital for the salesman to market the station, sell the ads and keep it all on air. In the interests of this film we have plumped for KZST which bills itself as 'adult contemporary'; I expect anything billed as adult to be rude and only available with a pin number or credit card, but this term simply means you get everything from Celine Dion to Oasis with a guaranteed sprinkling of Bryan Adams in the middle. Perfect for a *Travel Show* audience.

Brent and Bob's Tuesday Mayhem (the proper title of this show) goes out all over Sonoma, a lush verdant rich valley of wine and fruit stretching up into the vineyards of North California alongside its more famous neighbour the Napa. The Sonoma and Napa valleys are a bit like the Minogue sisters: Napa is Kylie – very well known, big in the eighties and with something to suit most tastes. Sonoma is Danni – in fact much prettier but not marketed quite as well. For all I know Sonoma may well have had the best-selling calendar of 1997, because Danni certainly did. It's sad that some useful piece of information like Pythagoras's theorem has been ditched from my brain in order to make room for that Danni fact.

We're still talking about the Texan Lick on air now and Bob is delighting in my shock.

'So let me get this straight, Bob, you go round licking girls' necks even if you haven't met them ...?'

'Sure, Fi, they love it. We do it all the time down at the line dance. You should come along ... you know how to line dance?'

'Errr, no.' This answer is a red rag to Texan Bob's Bronco Bucking Bull.

'She's never been dancin', Brent. I can't believe she hasn't been to a line dance – you've gotta come, I'll take you to the big ones we have, the Texan style ones ... they're *huge* ...'

'Yup – you've gotta take her dancin', Bob,' chimes in Brent.

I think a flicker of horror may have passed over my face.

It's not surprising that big business was quick to realise the potential of radio. America was probably leading the way just in terms of the amount of new stations that were cropping up. As well as the excitement in what was being created there was an understandable portion of fear too from the old media – newspapers.

Several experimental radio stations had sprung up in the States by 1920, the year of a presidential election. One station, KDKA in Pittsburgh, signed on by announcing the results of that election. Newspaper proprietors woke up to the fact that radio had just pre-empted their news – and once you had bought a radio set, that news was going to get into people's homes for free.

The press barons fretted away in their mansions, wrung their hands in consternation, their wives wondered what was preoccupying their time and making them pour extra large whiskies and come home even later from the offices. Am I getting a bit carried away here? Anyway the barons did what they always do – got out their wallets. They started buying up and setting up radio stations across the States.

The next big question was how to make radio pay and, after initial stabs at donations and subscription, it didn't take a board meeting to come up with the solution. Advertising. And now aside from the occasional national broadcaster, or listener-sponsored station, it's the adverts on radio that make it possible for you and me to phone in, play some time-consuming game with a lot of pauses in it – and win trips in planes and the occasional wad of cash.

I don't for one minute want to sound derisory about the money-making side of radio. It keeps radio alive. The downside, though, is that for all the choice of stations on your dial the content may not be that surprising – driven as it is by the need to keep within the demographics of the advertisers' desires.

I fully understand that you need to target an audience – that the man who drives a Mondeo, lives in Surbiton and has a kid with another on the way, who likes to mow the lawn at weekends and prefers Florida as a holiday destination may well enjoy Simply Red, new Eric Clapton tracks and a little something from M People. But who's to say that just occasionally he wouldn't like to crank his knob up to a Marilyn Mansun album track segued into a bit of Run DMC? The advertisers prefer to think that he doesn't, which helps them to convince their clients that they are wise to flog their products on the station that Mondeo man regularly tunes into.

*

Back in the KZST studio it's time for some of those ads. Car deals and cheap food outlets seem to be the staples of this station's sponsors which means that they believe their audience to be just a little under the income earning bracket of Mr Mondeo. All the ads have that jingly-jangly happy tune playing in the background and most seem to be voiced up by a very similar-sounding man.

While the cheery persuasive messages are playing I have to tell Bob that in fact we are going to go line dancing for the film but we have already decided which dance to go to and it's not one of his huge ones. He looks genuinely disappointed – maybe I have judged him too harshly, although the string tie is still causing me some problems.

Brent is busy pressing areas of his very hi-tech computer screen and the ads are followed by a weather report which tells us that our glow-in-the-dark Celtic skins are going to be burnt like a KFC chicken wing without the secret ingredients today. Brent's job doesn't look too taxing and he executes every change and movement with the air of someone who has been doing this for some time. He's like one of those cab drivers who like to drive with just the ball of their palm on the wheel, leaning back in the seat, other hand resting on thigh.

Some people can master the technological side of radio – all the faders that have to be pulled up or, as in Brent's more modern studio, the computer screens that key in the next bit of programming. I never could. The only time I had to 'drive a desk' was at GLR – the old BBC station in London. The result was not a slick affair. There were often a lot of pauses – which were fine really, it was the jingles that crashed into each other, the CD's that got played twice and the occasional studio that was left on air when whoever was in it thought they weren't.

One listener wrote to me to ask if I did it on purpose in an attempt to parody local radio. I wrote back and said yes.

Off air I ask Brent how long he had been waking up Sonoma county. He leans even further back in his chair, revealing quite a lot of middle-aged spread, and ruminates on the answer ...

'That'd be about seven years, Fi, before that I just ran the station.'

'And what kind of a show would you call your breakfast programme?' I hazarded a guess that the longer we talked about Brent the more he would like me. Another pause – accompanied by another expanse of girth emerging from the Hawaiian shirt.

'I'd say it's the number one rated show in Sonoma county, Fi.'

Turns out that Brent is a very big cheese in Sonoma. He does run the station and he also does another job somewhere in town that seems to involve lots of buzzwords that make it hard to work out which section of the Yellow Pages it would go into – something like Marketing Opportunity Realisation. He is very proud to point out that he gets up at 4.30 every day and is barely home before midnight. He looks very good on it too – though perhaps, like Bruno Brookes, the early morning starts will eventually take their toll and he'll go and set up whole radio stations on the Internet while making the occasional fishing programme for SkyTV.

I also get the feeling that Brent is very, very rich. If, like Bruno, he is planning to launch into Internet radio then he is a clever chap. Radio – with its buttons and twiddly knobs and white noise in between – is on the tip of a huge wave of change, courtesy of the Internet. I can probably go back to Dalston in North London and listen to Brent and Bob at home just by logging on with my modem.

Thousands of stations are already online – quite often at Five Live where I now work we get emails from people who are listening in Dubai or Canada. I find it very spooky. I've always used radio as a way to find my feet in a new place. It's reassuring to wake up at seven on the dot for a news bulletin – even if I can't understand what's being said. There's a certain way of speaking that newsreaders the world over use by which you can guess which are the sad stories and which are the funny ones. I like the feeling that I'm suddenly privy to everybody else's daily routines. I like trying to work out what the breakfast show bloke looks like, with his inevitable weather girl.

The ads always sound funny because you don't know where the Chicky Chick restaurant is and you've got no intention of popping down to buy your new season's separates in Ladies Fashions at the House of Style. But most of all I like the travel bulletins when you get a whole stream of new names and places flowing out at you:

'Out on Wacker it's busy backing up' and 'North Michigan through to the gold coast is trouble-free today' – all these are delivered over the theme tune to *ER* at one station in Chicago. It's a bold music choice as it makes me think that blood, guts and IC chem 3 tests are just about to start flowing.

I wonder if Internet stations will change radio for ever. I can't really answer this question at all right now. There are several huge leaps to be made in order for Internet radio to really catch on. First, you have to get used to listening to radio through a PC, although you can increasingly turn on your TV and log on through that, but you can't listen to Internet radio in your car while on the bus or out in the garden. If you do solve the technical side then you have to embrace a different mindset about why you're listening to the radio.

I think for most people the magic of radio has rather diminished and we take it for granted that it's on all the time somewhere. You might get up to it in the morning – catch a bit in the car, maybe have some regular show that you tune into. But not that many people get up and flick on the PC and say to themselves, 'I wonder what Israeli radio is putting out this morning – actually I did that yesterday, let's try Colombia today.' But it's an exciting prospect to be able to do that now, isn't it? Are we on the verge of global stations? Could Simon Bates come back and take over the world? I simply don't know yet and I'm probably the wrong person to ask anyway. I've never been any good at predicting big things – I thought Princess Diana would get back together with Charles.

Brent says that they are 'fully across the Net' at KZST. He says I would be able to listen to him at home in Dalston (I've told my parents it's Islington which crops up less on *Crimewatch UK*) but he is as mystified as I am about the extent that the Web will change the way we all listen. It's probably not the best time to be having this chat about such momentous things. The conversation is being snatched in between records and Bob and Brent's usual banter and Matt's directions to the crew. The lights on the phone bank just to the left of Brent are jangling away with people wanting to talk to him.

'So why do we have the BBC here today? Well, they're making a film for the Travel Programme and they need some tips on where to go in this beeeea-utiful county, So *come on!* Now's your chance – phone 'em up and tell 'em where to go.'

More lights flicker on the phone bank. Brent presses a part of his computer screen and pulls up a fader on the desk and one lucky caller is on air:

'Good morning, this is KZST you're on the air – what's your suggestion?'

The first call is from a guy who wants to know when the next balloon ride for charity is; the next is asking where the Annual Santa Rosa Kids Barbecue will be held and the third is in response to an appeal put out the day before when some farmer had begged the KZST listeners for a spare trailer as he was skint and his was bust. Sadly no one is calling for us – it's all Brent's usual daily fare which is understandably much more important to his listeners.

All of the them treat Brent like their best friend on air.

'How ya doing, Brent?'

'How are you today?'

'Yup Brent – just wanted to know ...' etc.

Wherever you are reading this you must have a local radio station where the same kind of thing goes on – where the genial host acts as some kind of entertainer cum Swapshop host cum confidante and becomes everyone's best friend without ever having met them. After all, you probably don't get to spend three hours a day with your best friend but you do with your radio presenters.

Brent obviously loves being the maypole around which everyone else is dancing. He has a big laugh which he isn't afraid to use, although it seems to come more readily when the red light is on than it does when we are all just chatting off-air. There's just a little of the Alan Partridge about Brent. I bet he opens a lot of fêtes and rodeos and has a stack of publicity photos already signed diagonally in the bottom right-hand corner: 'Keep Listening! Love Brent!' I bet it would be rather good fun to hang out with him for the duration of our stay in his valley.

The man with the trailer donated by another listener is still chatting away on air – he wants to thank all the listeners for bailing him out. He sounds young – maybe in his thirties – and he's got quite emotional about KZST's generosity and even though we have had nothing to do with the trailer escapade he ends up asking if we 'the BBC', as he puts it, would like to come out and see his farm. I know that for the purposes of *The Travel Show* a film that included an interview with a man whose business had been saved by receiving a trailer would not exactly fit into even the loosest remit of 'travel', so Matt shakes his head at Brent and asks him to put out another call for suggestions.

I wonder who else is listening to Brent and Bob this morning and if these two men actually like each other that much outside of the studio – there is a certain draughty frisson between them. I wonder if they've ever had a real SOS on their show. You still get them from time to time, don't you – in the middle of the charts Dr Fox will say 'Caroline on the M1 turn round immediately – get to a phone – call your mum urgently.' Terrible human curiosity makes you want to know why – what awful thing has happened that can't wait an hour or two?

Mr Hertz and the other boffins must be chuffed that their scientific prowess is still used to such effect. The BBC used to do loads of SOS messages after the main news bulletins including one during a chamber music concert from Savoy Hill:

'Here is an SOS message for Miss So and So – who is urgently requested not to take the white powder which was given to her in error by her doctor.'

There's a whole docu-soap in that one line.

Back on air Laura is the first caller to actually tell us what we want to hear – she says Armstrong Woods are the place to head for to see the enormous redwood trees and to sample what she calls 'the air and the scene'. She sounds genuinely pleased that the BBC are filming in her town.

'They must must must go to the Luther Burbank Gardens ... they are just so good ... and don't you have a cute accent? You should really go to the Luther Burbank Gardens – this time of year they are fabulous ... and if they do go, Brent, then let me know – I've always wanted to meet the BBC!'

And so it goes on as more and more of Brent's listeners light up the phone lines with their tips for our film.

Brent plays some records and Texan Bob and I have a chance to chat over our side of the table. He works in the marketing department, trying to flog KZST in among the 72 other stations in the county but had got himself Tuesday mornings with Brent where, as far as I could make out, they wind each other up a lot in the name of comedy.

I think Bob is probably a thwarted DJ himself. They are an international breed. People who go and work in radio stations in the sales department or accounts or on the competition desk but who have voodoo dolls of the main presenters and hope that enough pins will mean they all go sick at once and the saviour of the station is them.

Texan Bob had got lucky and hadn't needed all the pins. Now that he's stopped suggesting neck-licking ways to drink tequila he's quite growing on me. He's ever so keen to show us round the valley personally and I feel rather mean that I've been thinking dark thoughts about his intentions. Bob is obviously in love with radio too and I would imagine that Tuesdays are the highlight of his week. There is nothing jaded about his excitement every time the red light goes on and he is on air.

He reminds me rather of my cat who is, by pure chance, also called Bob and who gets so over-excited at the prospect of food that he starts eating it as it's falling out of the can. This results in most of the food remaining on top of his head. For the rest of the day all the cats in the neighbourhood follow him round licking his bonce. Poor Bob thinks it's because they like him.

Matt the director has finally managed to get all of his shots. He's got ones of Brent's hands and Bob's hat and those awful ones of me nodding like an imbecile at something Bob has said. We've got plenty of Brent's listeners telling us where to go and Brent himself has managed to get in a plug for a book he has written about Sonoma County. It won't be making the final cut but Matt doesn't point that out to him. It's just as well that we do have enough stuff because Brent is about to end his show and I don't think that we'd be very popular if we insisted on staying on air after 9 o'clock.

Another Hanson-esque song fades, there's a brassy climaxing station ident which seems to go on forever and then, with a big cheery goodbye and a round of applause in the studio, that is the end of the show.

Brent and I go for coffee after the show in the reception area where we sit underneath a great big picture of him. I tell Brent I've been listening to some of the biggies in American radio – Dr Laura and Howard Stern. He grimaces at the sound of both names. I say I'm amazed at what they can say – Dr Laura does a phone-in show to help people with their problems but is so unkind and patronising to them that I can't believe she helps very much and as for Howard Stern – well, he is obsessed with breasts and niggers – or at least he had been yesterday morning.

'Welcome to American radio,' says Brent cheerily. 'As long as people listen they'll get paid for it but we're not that kind of station.'

Brent suggests about four or five other stations that we should try tuning into while we are out filming during the week 'to get a flavour of us', he says. By this he means that you can hear Howard and Dr Laura wherever you are in the States – there is nothing North Californian about them. We chat a while longer but Brent says he has to go – to that other equally lucrative job somewhere in the marketing realms of Santa Rosa. I say my goodbyes and get given the inevitable T-shirt with KZST emblazoned across it.

On the way out of KZST's pristine headquarters I notice a photograph of one of the other presenters near the bottom of the stairs. One Leeza Gibbons – she does the Sunday Morning Chart Rundown. She's all teeth and hair and still very attractive. I know her from the British tabloids in the 1980s when she married one of our brightest soap stars, the talent known as Chris Quentin. He went back to the States with her because at the time she was earning a million dollars a year. It didn't work out and Chris came back heartbroken and penniless and made friends with Peter Stringfellow. I wonder how much they pay her at KZST now. I also wonder when she made the giant leap from Lisa to Leeza. If I was her and felt like a name change I might have looked a little more towards the surname department.

The line dance is held every week at the Bull Bar in Petaluma which has a huge bucking bronco machine positioned in the window. It puts fear into a girl's uterus. There are a couple of other bars on the street but otherwise it's big furniture shops and supermarkets shut for the night. The compulsory bunch of disconsolate youths are hanging around outside, presumably hoping that they will turn 21 by the end of the evening and be allowed to buy a drink. There is a uniform here – full dark denim for the boys. Denim with either yellow polka-dot T-shirts or rhinestoned white shirts for the girls. They all have long permed, dyed, crimped and streaked hair. Some of the boys do too. There aren't many places left in the world where the combination of yellow polka dots and a mullet are acceptable for an evening out.

We have been in and around the valley and county of Sonoma for a week now – we've filmed Armstrong Woods and marvelled at the girth of the redwood trees, we've tasted wines at the Fetzer vineyard and sampled their herb gardens. Very nice oregano. We've splashed about in the Vichy Spa in the hills on a day when the temperature gauge in the van hit 104 degrees and we've stuffed our faces in the restaurant of the Boonville Hotel which I can highly recommend. And all that is why *The Travel Show* is rarely laborious.

If you ever hear some TV idiot from a travel programme saying things like 'Oh, but it's really hard work when you're filming over there ... it's not like being on holiday you know', then send them a letter pointing out that they have disappeared up their own bottom and add something like 'Didn't I see you hosting a late-night quiz show on Central Cheltenham's latest cable TV station last month?' That'll get them where it hurts.

It's now our last night in North California but all through our stay here we have been accosted by people who heard us on Brent's Breakfast Show. The ranger who showed us round the woods greeted us like long-lost friends – one of the guests at the Vichy Spa had tuned in too and was delighted that she could put a name to the strange English voice. There used to be an ad on Capital Radio back in London in the early 1990s that simply said 'Radio Advertising Works'. Now I know it's true. Certainly the advertisers in North California have an audience on tap.

We listened to KZST as we were driving around with its easy listening tunes and smooth presenters and it kind of settled us into the valley. I took Brent's advice though and zoomed the dial across what North California offered and it provided a superb soundtrack to our trip – huge rocking breezy American tunes, Brent's own brand of cheeriness first thing in the morning and a crackling attempt to achieve more personally with Palo Alto Personal Achievement AM. In fact I couldn't really work out what was being achieved the evening I tried listening – I think it was money and how to cope with it but the interference meant that there were always going to be gaps in my knowledge and wallet.

The line dance is our finale for the film and the bar in Petaluma is now filling up.

'Where y'all from then?' shouts the barman as he makes three drinks at once.

'London.'

'London, Great Britain?'

'Yup – that's right.'

Isn't it funny how people ask you that? The likelihood of it being London, Alabama is surely quite small.

'Hey you're the pint-size one on the radio with Brent, aren't you?'

The coincidence of the barman recognising me from the radio is probably not that surprising, given that we have told the bar we are coming to film for the BBC and I am the one who arrived carrying a set of lights and asking to see the manager.

'Yup that's right, we've come to film a bit of line dancing,' I yell back, straining my tonsillitis scars.

One girl standing next to me says she heard us too:

'What does Bob look like?'

I tell her to have a guess.

'Mmmmmm ...Youngish – blond hair, big blue eyes ...'

How strange – this is her neck of the woods and it's her radio host and yet I'm the one with the answer. I don't want to ruin her radio dream so I just tell her she's pretty near the mark. It's not a complete lie – I can't tell her Bob's hair colour because he never did take his hat off.

'Ever line danced before?' The girl with an interest in Bob is asking me.

I shake my head mutely just in case that scar bursts and I turn into an *Omen* sequel.

'Well, it's real simple, honey ... just follow the caller and keep moving.'

Lots of things in life are simple – at different times in my life someone has told me that cricket, entering the single currency and dividing with fractions are simple. All those people lied. So you know that line dancing didn't go well. Those polka dots when moving at speed are really not helpful either. I kept having to be pushed back into the place I should have been in – at times the whole line was facing one direction while I was facing the other and even the band members were catching each others' eyes after my spectacular breakdancing impersonation in the 'turning' sequence. The whole thing actually turned out to be so bad that it was dropped from the final cut of the film. After it had got to the stage where people were openly laughing at me, I decided enough was enough and left the crew to do their pick-up shots.

I went back out to the car park, where the youths were still hanging and looking even more disconsolate, to have a fag and a drink because of course it's a bar in California and you can't smoke inside anywhere in the state. Over my solitary beer I couldn't help thinking that it would have been an awful lot more fun if we had gone to one of Texan Bob's huge line dances and indulged in a bit of belly-to-belly dancing. I might have been a bit better at it if I had been joined to a six-foot Texan by an umbilical cord. I bet old Bob would know everybody there and would probably have his own table in the VIP section (at the back by the toilets) as every local hero should.

It struck me that I had done this quite a few times before – sat outside in someone else's moonlight and thought up dreamy little mini-sagas about people whose radio presence had brushed over me in a foreign place. In all the countries I'd ever visited I'd always taken my little alarm clock radio with me and set it up by the bed, tuned it into someone else's radio station out of habit and drifted off to sleep or drifted into consciousness to the voices of a new place.

I'd had little daydreams about what all the hosts looked like. I'd found myself drawn to the pictures in the back of free glossy mags where local DJs posed with prize-winners at some local competition. I'd also found that radio provides a superb area of small talk with strangers. Quite often when you're making a film for TV you find yourself sitting opposite someone who you are about to pretend to be the best of friends with on screen. In fact, you don't know them from Adam – they are usually quite nervous, occasionally they are bored shitless.

'The Radio Conversation' had saved my ass and broken the ice quite a few times. Ask anyone in any country what their favourite radio station is and you're away ... more interesting than talking about the weather and less offensive than the minefields that are religion or politics – and somewhere in between in terms of interest. And everyone has a favourite station. No one has ever said to me, 'I don't listen to the radio.'

So over my fag (actually I'd had two by now) I got to thinking that maybe radio could be my passport round the world and maybe it was worth digging a little deeper into its international status. Maybe I should set out in search of the world's radio gems – just pitching up in strange places, tuning in and hanging out. I might find love and eternal happiness across a crowded microphone, someone who shared my addiction to the dial – I might meet someone who looked just as bad in a pair of headphones.

The Travel Show was facing an uncertain future – plans were afoot to find a new way of delivering travel to the demographics of BBC2. Something with 'more of a game show format' was being developed somewhere, so all of us were probably not long for the television world. I hadn't been inundated with other offers. The two weekly shows I was doing at Five Live were due to take a break for some sporting events and I was due an enormous amount of leave. In other words I wasn't that busy over the next couple of months.

And through that strange nepotistic world of media contacts there seemed to be a station or a host in every country who had a good story to tell. I already knew of one station in Montserrat that had talked a nation through a volcanic eruption; there was a bloke in Palm Springs who played nothing but Frank Sinatra on his station; there was a paranormal phone-in show coming out of a bunker in the Nevada desert; there was the married couple in Chicago who broadcast for six hours a night together; there were all those lifelines in war zones and private stories of grief and joy on the problem phone-in shows – there was so much to choose from already.

I wasn't all that interested in the huge figures of radio – the Sterns or the Dr Lauras. They had enough written about them and there were queues of journalists who had to fight through their PR people to get even the slightest quote. What I wanted to do was to hang around with the smaller fishes – the people who got phoned up about trailers and local barbecues and who had enough time to offer to show you round their home turf.

It also meant that I could share one of the great radio cock-ups with a truly international audience.

Dickie Arbiter is a man of great weight and gravitas. He has just retired as Press Secretary to the Palace (Buckingham, not Crystal) but before that he was an eminent broadcaster who regularly read the news on radio. It is said that one day he was handed a piece of copy just before going into the bulletin and understandably became a little flustered – so he announced the following to the nation:

'It's ten o'clock. I'm an oil tanker. Dickie Arbiter is ablaze in the Gulf.'

2

I'm feeling a bit grantic today

Austria to Belgium

In Colombia there is a station that has, through the pressure of the listeners, created a programme that you are unlikely to find in any other part of the world. The late-night music show on Memories Radio started out as your average mellow phone-in request show but built up a strange momentum. Usually the point of a request show is obvious: you phone up and ask for a tune that makes you happy or makes you think of some important moment in your life. Maybe you might phone and ask for a tune to be played for someone else who is also listening. It's unlikely that you would request a tune in the hope that the person it is for is still alive.

But that's what the listeners of Memories started to do. More and more people called in wanting to play tunes for loved ones who had been kidnapped by the gangs who trade in human life. Now the switchboard gets jammed every night with people desperate to believe that they can reach out to whatever grotty, hellish room their father or wife or child has ended up in while they wait for a beleaguered and corrupt police force to try to find them.

In Berkeley, California, shots have been fired at the studios of KPFA and a presenter has been dragged off air, screaming in protest at the proposed change in the ethos of what is one of America's few truly independent and left-wing radio stations. Staff were suspicious of a management suggestion that the station should try to get a bigger audience and lose some of its radical stance. They found themselves locked out, forbidden to talk about the troubles on air. Supporters pitched their tents outside the buildings and threatened to lynch the executive director. Joan Baez played a benefit concert for them. And all this in the land of free speech?

There is a station in Alaska with the widest 'reach' of any on earth but with fewer listeners than the local BBC station in Somerset. 'Reach' is the term used to signify how many potential listeners are out there within the area of that stations signal. Somerset Sound – and most other BBC local radio stations – probably are lucky to get up to 10 per cent of the potential audience tuning in. The Alaskan station gets 100 per cent. But then there are only three of them. Ha ha ha. Seriously, it would probably be cheaper to send out tapes than actually broadcast to their listeners – although they are all listening, there just aren't that many of them. A captive audience for advertisers though and if you are wise enough to advertise your range of thermal underwear on the radio then you must be able to wipe the competition.

These are just some of the things I have learned about radio since getting back from California.

Most of them have been garnered simply by typing in the word 'radio' on my search engine and scrolling through over two million results. This Internet radio thing does seem to have caught on. There are thousands of stations you can get through your PC speakers. Choose from Vatican Radio, which broadcasts its prayers and news in dozens of languages to hundreds of thousands of people, to Peninsula Radio which is broadcast only to the guests of the Peninsula Hotel in Hong Kong. I have had problems logging on to this one but I think it'll be worth it when I do. I'll keep you posted.

I have some sad news though. That second passport has been packed away – *The Travel Show* has been axed. So as well as spending the odd midnight hour listening to a squawky version of radio coming into my home via my very cheap laptop I have spent a week or so in the British Library, sitting on a wide leather chair in Humanities 2 section reading their collection of books on radio.

Key in the word radio to the libraries computer and you fare less well that on the Internet. It comes up with barely one hundred books. Not much for such a pervasive medium. Most are technical books; there's the occasional biography and a whole shelf of 'The Blue Book' which is the bible of radio contacts for the British industry. It's not a particularly interesting book for anyone who isn't working in radio, it's really just an encyclopaedia of contacts but it is worth a mention just because it lists Adrian Chiles' show on Five Live as being presented by Adrian Chives and thus called Chives on Saturday.

That made me titter a little bit, which caused all the brainy-looking silent people working alongside me in the British Library to look up. One of them tutted at me. This was his fifth tut of the day in my direction – the others caused by the fact that I was never any good at studying and get bored after about half an hour so I had been making frequent trips to the canteen and getting up and just having a wander round and, understandably, I was annoying this studious man.

So on the fifth and very loud tut I thought, 'Bugger this, what am I doing trying to research a medium that is – by its very nature – a loud form of communication, in a silent place? What am I doing reading about sound? I have to listen to it. I have to get off my butt – make one final squeak on the wide leather chair, put down the research books and go and physically tune in to radio.' I can't sit at home listening to it on my laptop either because I keep getting distracted by what you can type into your search engine and the results you get. Last night I tried 'turkey baster'. Best not to ask why but it came up with 31 results – and that wasted one hour of good research time.

I have thought a lot about why I like radio though – and why it has become such a big part of my life. On a professional level I get to have lots of fun working with bright-minded people, in a job that is never the same from one day to the next. I have had the pleasure of interviewing some inspirational people, meeting personal heroes and being reduced to tears by Jeffrey Archer. It made me a stronger person. But I can't just leave it at that. On a personal level, I have an addiction to radio. I like the soundtrack it gives my day, I love the choice that you get sweeping across the dial ... I like the pictures it creates in my head. I love the ponderous documentaries about vegetables on Radio 4 with all their pauses and crafted background sounds, but then I love Five Live more with its cheek and pace.

I like Radio 1 for when I'm feeling a bit lacklustre; there isn't a bad mood that can't be cleared by Mark and Lard. I choose Capital when I'm happy to live in London, soothing Magic when I'm not. Radio 2 is corking at the weekends if only for Paul Gambaccini's opening line, 'Saturday is our day ...' which he has been saying for years. I still believe he means it – he's just talking to me.

There's a pirate station that pumps out from one of the tower blocks in Hackney that we get on a Saturday night. It's just on the edge of GLR's frequency – but sometimes it's alright. Bit shouty and techno – but if I ever graze across it is makes me feel like I'm a real living hard-edged Londoner. Of course I'm not – I'm from Slough and have alarmingly soft edges.

Which would you rather be – if you ever had to make the choice – deaf or blind? Blindness would scare me more. Deafness would upset me more. There is something intensely comforting about the human voice, something remarkably stimulating and mood changing about music and the spontaneity of bright comic minds that I would truly miss. Remind me of all this if you see me bashing my way down the street with a white stick cursing my misfortune.

With so much radio out there it's hard to choose which bits to grasp. I have hit on a way to work my way round some little bits of the globe. I'm not going to go to the stations that might have made the biggest headlines – or the ones that have been written about before. I'm going to go on personal recommendation – and on sheer personal curiosity – and see where that takes me.

This means going back to some places I've visited before and didn't have time to explore what I'd heard. And taking a chance on other people's tastes for the rest. And I know where I'm going to start – Vienna. This is because a very nice sound recordist I had worked with last summer told me once about a station called Blue Danube Radio. He said he thought that it was originally set up to broadcast to UN executives in Vienna and to help them with their language skills. He said it was funny because they tried to explain English to the Austrians, French to the Germans and all those combinations to each other – on air, every day. That was good enough for me – a station with a little bit of a different agenda and something to get my teeth into. And Vienna feels like a good place to start – a civilised place, a cosmopolitan hub and only a cheap flight away.

The man in front of me in the queue to get on Buzz's flight to Vienna today, though, is probably not thinking about radio as he insists on stopping to have a chat with the stewardess.

'What kind of plane is this?' he asks the startled girl.

I'd respect her a lot if she says 'One with wings' but she doesn't and with a smile reminiscent of one of the American Synchronised Swimming team informs Mr Plane Spotter of its make and model.

This seems to reassure him – although I'm finding it slightly worrying. Apparently though it is a new type of quieter airplane and this is what he wanted to know.

So we get to our seats – all 12 of us, in a plane big enough to seat at least 200. This is the real joy of low-cost airlines – because so many of them are launching at the moment, if you play your cards right and go in the first couple of weeks, then no one else seems to know about them and you get a club class feeling of space for £19.50. This means that I can move away from the businessman who is sitting next to me and insists on looking at the contents of his handkerchief every time he blows his nose – which is frequent. Despite this, travelling to Vienna is an attractive proposition – it is after all a city that has given us an ice-cream dessert that people at dinner parties fight over, some whirly biscuits, and a hit by Ultravox that was kept off the number one slot by Joe Dolce.

That's churlish, isn't it? What about housing the talent of Mozart, nurturing a Hapsburg empire and coating veal in breadcrumbs to create the Austrian Schnitzel? Given all that, it's really not fair for the businessman to be taking the British Phlegm Allowance to Vienna in exchange for their gifts to the world. And that's before we even get to Blue Danube Radio.

I am intrigued by the notion of BDR – usually stations that are set up for educational means are a trifle on the dull side and if I was to look at the ethos of this one on paper, I think I would imagine it to be a bit like tuning into a constant Teach Yourself a New Language tape. For some reason I never found that woman on the ads very convincing when she promised I could learn Uzbekistani in just four days.

I have discovered that there is an urgency about getting to Vienna as well, which has added a certain frisson to my trip. I have only a week in which I can indulge in the delights of programmes with names like *Be My Guest*, the *Softsound Cafe* and a DJ called Hal Rock. At the end of the week Blue Danube will be no more – it will become the somewhat scarily titled Fear FM.

The flight is just about long enough to digest the printouts of the website for BDR that I whipped off the computer that morning. Hence I already know the names of their shows, and a bit more about the station's inception.

Twenty years ago the government decided to part with some of its funds in an attempt to create a radio station that would try to integrate the many languages of Europe and therefore build up the vocabulary of the many executives who would be visiting the UN in Vienna and other illustrious international bodies that had chosen the Hapsburg capital as their headquarters. The idea was to create a high-quality news and music station that would bring all those briefcase-carrying people together and act as an entertainment as well as an information haven.

As English speakers are notoriously bad at grasping other languages and as English, German and French all have their own strange idioms, the idea of a programme to explain some of these was born. *Passport* is what the BDR people now call this show. The *Passport* team consists of different language speakers who try to explain what things like 'raining cats and dogs' means and when it is appropriate to use it. Every day there is a phrase – today's is 'Easy Does it' – and on the web page you can get a translation of this and things like 'this house costs an astronomical amount', which suggests that Austria is also on the verge of a housing explosion that will mean only the very rich city whiz kids will be able to afford more than a one-bedroom fleapit in a strange part of town. Just in case you feel the need to know how to say this in German it is: *Dieses Haus kostet eine astronomische summe.*

Apart from aiming to keep people understanding each other in the estate agents and bars of Vicnna, the web page suggests that Blue Danube Radio is a station dedicated to ticking the listening boxes of as many people as possible – so as well as the staple fare of news in the handily titled *Today at 6* and the usual Breakfast and Drivetimes there is a country music show, a bit of solid interviewing in *Be My Guest* and that *Softsound Cafe* crops up a lot … Somchow I can't get Sad Cafe out of my mind when I see that title. Whatever happened to them?

I have brought a number of other printouts from the Web with me to try to piece together something of a route for my trip, which you will be glad to know does not start and finish in Vienna. Since deciding on my random way of selecting radio stations around the world to visit, it turns out that everyone has a suggestion to make.

There is an Argentinean jazz station of some interest to aficionados and there is an Icelandic one that is all female. About thirty people have insisted that I try to meet Howard Stern and a very nice man called Peter Hanington who works on the *Today* programme tells me that he has a friend in Beirut who works for the *Financial Times* and has just done a small piece about a minute radio station run by UN peacekeeping troops in Southern Lebanon. Now that sounds like a bit of a peach and by my reckoning I could spend a week in Vienna, then with little bother and cost fly down to Beirut the week after.

Over the past few years people have written evocative numbers in Sunday colour supplements about the old faded beauty of Beirut and how much it's 'coming on'. There is said to be a fashion in holidays every year in the same way that there is in hem lengths – once upon a time it was Puerto Banus, then came Florida, last year it was Zanzibar, this year it is Beirut. It doesn't mean much to those outside the poncier parts of the travel industry, but it does mean that if you want to get there before a lot of people called Xavier who have complicated facial hair, then you need to get a move on.

So I have taken Peter up on his offer to put me in touch with his *FT* friend – who is called Gareth Smyth – and I have sent him an email to see if he could perhaps accompany me down to where the UN station is in the former Occupied Zone. Feeling pretty confident that at least some wheels are in motion, I have to concentrate on what Vienna and Blue Danube Radio might have to offer.

All the other passengers on this flight to Austria have nodded off to the gentle drone of the aircraft. It's an early evening flight and the stewardesses look knackered too – they have probably hopped back and forward over the bulk of Europe at least four times already today. Two of them are leaning against the metal containers that make up the galley kitchen discussing the delights of the various different hotels they have to stay in abroad. It doesn't make the job sound very attractive. The joys of flitting over to the glamorous capitals of continental Europe have obviously palled with the realisation that the job is more about staying in poky rooms next to the generator, alarm calls at 5am and heavy-set Saudi Arabians trying to chat them up on the Dubai run.

I wish I had the guts to ask them lots of questions, but they don't look like they would value the interruption. For instance, is it true that if you flush an airplane loo while you are still sitting on it you will get sucked into the vacuum and not be able to get out? A friend of mine once told me that he got round the smoke alarms in the toilets by lifting up the sink plug which also created a vacuum – therefore dragging the smoke away. Is it true that stewards and stewardesses use the oxygen masks to cure their hangovers? And did the captain have a special button that releases airplane waste into the sea? They are burning questions born of spending too much time on planes.

Depending on whether you place air miles above family unity, my sister and I were very lucky as my dad moved out to Hong Kong when we were very young and we got to spend a disproportionate amount of time travelling out to see him. In those days the flight stopped off four times – usually in Frankfurt, Tehran, Delhi and Bangkok. It was an exotic trip to be making when only five years old and was the perfect age for long-haul travel. I seem to remember being perfectly happy in what was a huge seat for a tiny girl – the air stewardesses looked impossibly glamorous and I was content to collect all the mini pepper sachets throughout the flight and draw pictures of what I thought the plane looked like.

My sister always used to have a go at me for not being able to colour 'up to the edges' in my early drawings. She was absolutely right – the colours were always very bright but if there was an outline you could guarantee that I would have coloured over it, or not up to it or just made it look very messy. She likes to use this as a greater metaphor for my life now. And she is probably right. If she was going on a trip round the world it would be organised with precision. She would not head off with a bit of a plan, a few contacts, the email address of a man called Gareth in Beirut and a lot of fluff at the bottom of her suitcase.

That same sister and I used to pretend that we were travelling by ourselves on those early Hong Kong flights, so we would constantly ignore my mother. We must have made her look very silly and almost mad to the other passengers. She gave up coming out to Hong Kong in the early 1980s and I don't think she has got on a plane since. So the seeds of travel were sown early.

I still get a thrill at feeling so grown up on planes when I'm travelling alone. It seems to be the very epitome of girl independence and even though I have other trappings of a post-feminist life (job, debt, two cats, too many choices) it's the flying that always makes my bosom swell with pride. I'm also particularly fortunate in having grown to no more than dwarflike proportions in adult life so not only do you get the best dresses in the Kookai sale but you also find that airline seats are reasonably comfortable. And I actually like the size of airline meals. When else in life do you choose to eat a Bakewell Tart pudding these days?

Yet again I'm standing behind Mr Plane Spotter as we leave the plane. Now even though there has been complete and delicious silence for the last 45 minutes of the flight, he stops to tell the air stewardess that the plane was not as quiet as he would have hoped. She's obviously had worse complaints so she very politely says she'll pass the message on – and then she winks at me – which is some feat considering the amount of frosted glaze on her lids. What on earth did Mr Plane want to travel in? A glider? Perhaps he had taken the name 'Buzz' airlines a little too seriously and is waiting for the launch of 'Gentle Hum', the low-cost airline from the Noise Abatement Society.

*

Like an acne-ridden teenager, Vienna appears a lot sexier at night. You
drive through vast streets lined with grand hotels, all with matching
concierge standing to attention outside. The streets all have names that
suggest the street namer fell asleep and leant on his fifteenth-century
keyboard, looked up and thought 'Oh, that'll do ...' so you have
Argentinierestrasse, Landesgerichtsstrasse and Franzensbruckenstrasse.
In the eighteenth century the then wife of the British ambassador, one
Lady Mary Wortley Montagu, wrote that she was disappointed with
Vienna because of the crowded way it had been built:

> the streets are very close, and so narrow one cannot observe
> the fine fronts of the palaces.

Fortunately for the twenty-first-century visitor the streets are now
Japanese-tour-operator-coach-sized and the proportions are big. The
Ringstrasse gives you your bearings – a kind of early M25 which orbits
the main centre of the city, and as you sweep along it gives you the
opportunity to 'wah' and 'woooh' at a succession of impressive
Hapsburg buildings. Neoclassical and baroque and huge and clean, this
was a city of wealth and in many ways it still is. Now its court is largely
one of executives and UN officials who, judging from the portraits of the
Hapsburgs which you will find in many school history books, are not as
good looking as previous Viennese citizens.

In order to be close to the radio station I have booked myself into the
Triest Hotel – which is in the south of the city on one of the main
arteries of the Weidner Haupstrasse. It's described in some piece of
tourist literature as 'Conran designed' and a 'temple of style'. I am a
complete sucker for beautiful pictures in brochures that suggest I am
going to be able to live temporarily in a world of freshly pressed linen
and colour-coordinated bedside lamps.

I'm reading a book by a lady called Mai Ghoussoub in preparation for
getting to Beirut – it's a compilation of stories about women and how
they coped with the wars there – and it in she says:

> I have always cherished the anonymity of hotel rooms. In their
> square bastions of similarity, their depersonalised and serviced
> rooms, my isolation fills me with a soothing detachment ...

I couldn't have put it more eloquently myself.

Hotels give you a fabulous opportunity to check your own troubled life in at the front desk and live a kind of parallel existence for a while. No one need know who you are or why you're there. Your time is your own, even though the bathrobe is not.

My sister and I made a promise to each other at about the age of 15 and 16 respectively that if we didn't manage to find happiness with suitable jobs, boys and children later in life then we would end up living in a hotel, preferably on Cap d'Antibes in the South of France, where we would have neighbouring suites and wear Joan Collins style wigs and full make-up in the midday sun and saunter through the lobby with our little poodles in the morning. We could eat our way through room service of an evening and become known to the staff as 'those mad little Glover sisters'. Sadly we hadn't really thought through the cash side of things and as it turned out that we weren't heiresses to an empire like that Woolworth's girl it really wasn't on the cards.

We can of course still go for the wigs and pooches. Ideally I would like the wig to be bigger than the dog. Proportions are everything.

I should confess something to you about choice of accommodation for this trip: I never went backpacking and don't intend to start now. It may be deeply unfashionable to say this but the idea of sharing dormitories, taking train journeys of longer than eight hours and competing over illnesses just never appealed. There are three types of backpacker. The first are the people who like simplicity, enjoy travel, are interesting about it and don't have pots of money. They are nice. The second type are not getting any sex at home and the less said about them the better. And the third type have way too much money, usually have a place at St Andrew's University next autumn and thought *The Beach* was a great book. They have conversations like this:

'Well, of course you know Jamie had terrible Dengue fever in Thailand.'

'It can't have been as bad as Clarissa's amoebic dysentery ... she lost four stone in two weeks when she went through Laos.'

'Oh yup, Laos – awful hygiene – did find a place to stay for two pounds a night though ...'

'Jamie, what did we pay? I think it was only one pound, wasn't it? ... And you'll never believe who we bumped into ...'

Why should you rate countries so highly on their ability to have a totally fucked economy, usually helped by the West's paying only for very cheap labour, and in the same breath almost celebrate serious disease as if it were some kind of travel prize that you had won, a bit like air miles or a free upgrade?

I sat next to a boy at a party once who announced that in his gap year he was off to Mozambique. That is the same Mozambique that has just been terribly flooded. I asked him if he was going to help with the aid effort and he said no – he was going to stay with some people running a luxury hotel over there.

'But the country is at a standstill,' I said. 'There is disease everywhere, people are still having a rough time.'

To which he replied, 'Oh I just know I'm going to get bilharzia the moment I step off the plane ...'

Well, why on earth are you going then? To take up a doctor's time if you do get ill? To brag about it when you get home? To buy some nice souvenirs – probably still a little damp, but hey – that's authentic for you! And of course this bloke was loaded and proceeded to have a conversation about just how cheap it would be when he got there, and how much he was looking forward to meeting some 'different' people. I presume he meant 'slightly less rich, but still with a bolt hole in Gloucershire'.

And apart from all that there are more practical things that have stopped me from stepping off the beaten track. I need to have my legs waxed at least every fortnight in order to prevent people on the beach from thinking that evolution is slipping backwards. So it is that the Triest gets my business.

The hotel has one of those heavy doors that may be designed to keep unwanted riffraff out as well as the Austrian winters. Inside it's all hushed and marbled with smooth clean lines and just the one tropical flower in place of the overflowing candelabra of lilies so beloved of the grander hotel chains.

Minimalist staff are a must here as well. The receptionist looks like she may well be a close personal friend of Kate Moss and Meg Gallagher but I could forgive her that, as her English is far better than my German. Apparently Johnny Depp has stayed at the Triest and liked it very much. This isn't saying much these days as you seem to be able to guarantee that every hip hotel in the world has either entertained him, Liz Hurley or the Dalai Lama.

Whoever stayed in my room last has left a London phone number on the note pad by the bed. I'm tempted to phone but I don't want to wake Patsy up. Hotels like the Triest always say things like 'styled for the individual' – as opposed to all those ones designed for Siamese twins – but there are a lot of similarities with other 'individually styled' hotels. For example the mini-bar will have kettle chips or grissini sticks rather than a packet of Walkers; the little bottle of wine will have a cork in it not a screwtop; and you will want to nick all the toiletries and probably a small piece of 'desk furniture', i.e. the blotter, or the rather nice clothes brush and shoe-cleaning kit.

Nicking things from hotel rooms is an international pastime and if, like me, you feel guilty if you take the half-used bottles of shampoo then console yourself – most people are much, much worse. The Ritz Hotel in London announced a guest amnesty a few years ago when they tried to encourage previous occupants to hand back the lamps, rugs, shower curtains, footstools and small chairs that people had managed to conceal in their luggage. I'm not sure how many people owned up and returned the goods but it made for a great little news piece and it does set you thinking about how you could get away with a 16-foot rug concealed about your hand luggage.

I guess if you travel with all those matching Louis Vuitton trunks like Joan Collins and Elton John then you could pack up your whole suite including the boy who brought you breakfast and the concierge would be none the wiser. I once asked the manager of one of the Hilton hotels in Bangkok how many people did try and take the fluffy bathrobe home with them despite the polite warnings telling you not to and he rolled his eyes and said. 'About one in three people.'

Did he bother to chase them all up? He said they usually looked at the size of the person's bill and if they had been a big spender in the hotel they let it pass, if they had been in a standard room they wrote and asked for it back but if, horror of horrors, they had been in an economy room or part of a tour then they whipped it off the credit card bill straight away – at a cost of $100. The trade price was less than $20.

Anyway, most things in the Triest seem to be nailed down so it was going to be the Molton Brown shampoo and body wash that I would be taking home rather than the rather fetching spindly chrome desk lamp.

To avoid the high possibility of Blue Danube Radio not being on the TV after the porn channels I have come prepared with a new purchase from Stansted's duty free – it's one of those wind-up radios that the entrepreneur Trevor Baylis made which revolutionised the listening habits of millions of people across the world who didn't have access to electricity. Although I'm sure that Trevor didn't decide to design it so that it fits in with top-whack European hotels he did this by accident and it's looking good perched on the cherry wood bedside table.

The only trouble with the exciting new wind-up radio is that it doesn't have entirely clear dials so you don't really know what frequency you are on except that it is somewhere between 102 and 106. BDR is either broadcasting a marathon mix of top tracks or some oom-pah-pah folk music probably performed by people with long plaits. I think it might be the latter.

The FM dial is otherwise pretty standard European fare: Robbie Williams is everywhere with 'She's The One' and two stations are giving me Billy Joel. It's good to know that Christie Brinkley's divorce settlement is still being drip fed by royalties and the fruits of her ex-husband's labours are being enjoyed by thousands of Austrians on their way home from work. If they have less than perfect English I wonder what they think he's singing about in 'Uptown Girl'.

When John Inverdale was presenting the *Drivetime* programme on Five Live he did a phone-in one afternoon about the best of the worst musical malapropisms which was won hands down by one gentleman who had heard a group of foreigners singing quite happily to Bob Marley's classic 'Jammin'. It had miraculously turned into a homage to a closer Europe with 'We're Germans ...' The same guy also thought that the Bob Dylan classic went:

The ants are my friends
They're blowing in the Wind
The ants
They're blowing in the Wind.

Blue Danube Radio is far easier to identify in the morning. The Breakfast Show is the only one on the dial to be broadcast in English and today's host is telling me in between records about words of wisdom he has found in some handy book, probably designed as a stocking filler but an essential tool of the early morning DJ. Today's DJ is called Duncan.

'Air,' he intones, 'is like sex; you don't notice it until it's not there.'

'It's darkest before the dawn,' he continues in a droll fashion, 'so if you want to nick anything that is the time to do it.'

It's a comforting pleasure to wake up in a strange city as a tourist but to find yourself part of other people's daily routines – and this is what tuning into the local radio station does for you. Thousands of Viennese must be shaken from a decent night's kip by the ramblings of Duncan on BDR. It's a good feeling to know that I'm one of them.

Routines go out of the window on holiday – or when you're working abroad. That lack of routine is part of what makes it great to be away but drives lottery winners insane. No alarm clock, no school run, no start time at work etc. In order to keep this routine going back home you probably rely a bit on radio if you listen of a morning. If you find yourself being able to guess which Mystery Year Simon Mayo is playing his tunes from, then you know that all of the aforementioned are running very very late.

Breakfast radio is the staple of any station and it gets the biggest audience – it is the ballast in the day's output. Commercial stations run their biggest competitions between seven and nine; the newsmakers of Westminster clamber on to the airwaves in Britain to tell us things they think we should know and for most listeners their daily radio allowance is used up by nine.

I can't remember the last time that I didn't switch on the radio as soon as I woke up. Breakfast radio is my early morning grouting – it sets the day in motion, reassures me that nothing truly terrible has happened overnight or, if it has, reassures me that I am now going to learn a bit about it. Because of this kind of human link, breakfast DJs often become the nation's favourites. Career-wise, breakfast shows are the most sought after for those reasons. Lifewise, they are crap.

Having to get up at four in the morning is truly terrible. I only managed it for a couple of years at GLR. Some people seem to be unaffected by the fact that it is still the middle of the night and your blood sugar level is at zero. I just couldn't function. The only plus was that it's one of the few times the roads in Central London are clear, apart from Christmas and when a princess dies. But even being able to drive in fourth gear round Marble Arch wears off after a while.

Duncan's just fading out of a Tina Arena track and then it's a neat segue into The Eurythmics. BDR's music is quite loud and rocking, the jingles by comparison are quite soft and understated. Perhaps this is to do with 'the change' that is coming and the fact that they may not be known as BDR for much longer. Maybe they think that if they stop using their name it will become easier to start using a completely different one the week after next.

The bulletins are two tone – English and German – and then three tone – English, German and French – so they take some time. Much of the news is dominated by the arrival of Jorg Haider on the international political scene. Jorg comes with the prefix 'far right politician' on the bulletins back in Britain. He is famous for making comments about liking some of Hitler's policies and not wishing Austria's borders to let anyone else through. He's a slick character, though, and his success in his own province has brought him to greater power in Austria's national government.

Otherwise it's house fires and Viennese bureaucracy. The jewel in the crown of the show is the arrival of the *Passport* team to explain today's mysterious language barriers. The lady doing the Passport for the day is obviously so familiar to the listeners that she needs no introduction and she remains fixed in my head as Miss Passport.

Duncan seems to enjoy this part of his show enormously. His enthusiasm is catching, so I stop trying to extract mutant hairs from my chin with the help of the magnified bathroom mirror and end up sitting on the bed staring into space, listening with the kind of concentration that my fourth-form French teacher Miss Cooper could only have dreamt I would one day have ....

'What do you have for us today then?' he asks.

'The word Duncan is "forthwith" ... that's "forthwith" ...'

I'd never thought of that as a particularly tricky word before. If you think about it, it could be a little confusing as there are no two-withs or three-withs – we just go straight in at four.

Duncan is giving me the opportunity to learn what the German word is for an animal being pregnant. We also have 'is that the long-term vision ...?' and 'to trade in futures'. If those are today's handy phrases then you can tell what kind of audience they are targeting, except for the pregnant animal bit.

The Triest has Blue Danube Radio on in reception and the dining room so I can carry on listening to Duncan while having breakfast. Given the high style of the hotel it's a good sign that they feel BDR is in keeping with the needs of its clients. I wonder if any of the businessmen chomping through their breakfast are secretly thinking 'I'm going to use that forthwith word today and really impress them with my grasp of English.'

I'm secretly hoping that Blue Danube Radio is in a state of terrible flux over its impending changes – that there are presenters having hissy fits all over the place about the cruel style of management that is demanding the end of *Passport* as the world knows it. This will prove that radio is full of passionate people whose principles remain strong against the advancing might of ratings analysts and focus groups. I want to watch a little bit of radio history being made as the first and last Linguaphone-style radio station melts into a soft rock future.

The first thing I must do is tear myself away from the Triest.

In 1979 when BDR was set up there were 40,000 internationals in Vienna. Most worked for Western companies that came to Vienna because it was as close as they could get to the still curtained-off east. Like ex-pats anywhere I should imagine that the perks were rather good and the pay not too bad either. I should imagine as well that there were either a lot of bored wives sitting around in plush apartments in Vienna, or an awful lot of wives who were only seeing their husbands once or twice a month. This might explain the proliferation of underwear shops in the centre of Vienna.

There's no one in them but there are a lot of very well-dressed women stopping for a gaze. They might be looking at their own reflections and checking that their YSL Touche Eclat has done the business for the morning but there's a rich lawyer driving to work in his BMW somewhere who has either very generously bought a pair of $100 pants for his loved one or has reaped the benefit of her own purchasing power.

Even though it is late spring and things in Europe are starting to warm up, the Viennese ladies are displaying scant regard for the work of PETA and other animal welfare organisations – there are fur-trimmed mules, fur-trimmed T-shirts and probably fur-trimmed thongs available in the highly polished window displays. In fact some of these women probably think Peta is the name of a maid they once had. They have highlights in their hair to match the streaks in their mink and the odd one has the ultimate on coordinating accessories – a small poochy dog who has been bought not to clash with the essential shopping outfit. Maybe at the end of their canine days they will become a handy shopping bag or in the smaller examples, a spectacle case.

*

St Stephen's tower can be seen from everywhere in Vienna – a sharp pointy thing with a roof that has a distinctly Seventies curtain design on it. It's blackened by wear and tear, but has the familiar things that every large cathedral has to have. Renovation works going on up on the roof, large clusters of noisy schoolchildren looking for somewhere to go and have a fag, and an old man who has seen the light and is now wandering around with a cardboard placard advising people to do the same. This never really works as a marketing ploy does it? Why would you want to convert to or embrace a religion that seems to condemn you to looking miserable and cold and makes people walk past you very quickly. You can't really see the boardroom chats in high-ranking advertising agencies:

'Well, Gunter, we need to get more people into the church – any ideas?'

'We could go for the all-out TV campaign, or the humorous radio ads – or perhaps a bit of direct mail that offers you the chance to go to Bethlehem at Christmas and feel good inside ...' suggests Gunter tentatively.

'No, I like the old man with tabard wandering around actually ... what about using a catchy phrase – something like "Atheism Isn't Working".'

'Mmmm.' Gunter is not convinced.

The cathedral is in the middle of a pedestrianised precinct and yes, I know that the precinct was probably pedestrianised after the cathedral was built, but there are none of the cloisters or graveyards of say Winchester or Canterbury. Sadly I have spent so long looking in the windows of the jewellery and pant shops that I am running a little bit late. I leap into a cab just behind the square and in my very best tourist-German ask for the Funkhaus on Argentinierstraase where Blue Danube Radio lives.

'Aaaah! Blu Danuba Rar-deo ...' shouts the cabbie, pointing at his stereo.

'Aaaah! Yes!' I shout back.

'Kunt tree! Kunt tree! ... is gud.'

Mmmm. A bit trickier.

'Kunt tree musik ... I like ...'

Ahh. Country music – of course. I feel I'm going to get a bit stuck on a conversation about the new crossover generation of Faith Hill and Shania Twain, so I fall into terrible *Allo, Allo* style German, nodding and shouting.

'Das is good, ja.'

'Veeeery good, Blu Danuba!'

I hate to tell him that soon the country show might bite the dust and as he isn't a bilingual, go-getting young German who likes modern music he'll not be welcome to stop on the dial at Fear FM. Sometimes having no language skills is a bonus. With a bit more nodding and shouting we get to the headquarters of his favourite station.

The Funkhaus is a kind of mini South Bank for television production and radio, and has the dodgiest lifts in the world. I'd arranged to meet Robin Lee who is one of the senior producers there. She's American and greets me with the firm handshake you would expect of a native of Chicago. She has the manners and helpfulness to go with that greeting.

'Hi, Fi – I'm Robin – err, I've temporarily forgotten why you're here ...'

'I sent an email about coming to visit you for this book I'm writing?'

'Ohhh yea ... of course ... well, how can we help, do you want to look round, do you want to chat to people ... the studios on air are downstairs, we're in the middle of moving things right now – busy time – you know about the changes ... everyone's a bit on edge today ...'

Robin has that way of looking you so directly in the eye that it's almost painful – she's blonde and petite and you get the feeling that she has more energy than is strictly required in most human beings. And although she says that she is very hassled right now, she looks like she is handling it just fine.

Robin used to be on the stage. She toured with *Phantom of the Opera* and still walks in a way that suggests her mother put her in a leotard and dancing shoes when she was very young. There seems to be a different kind of uniform going on in the Funkhaus compared to the fur-trimmed elegance of central Vienna – this is dominated by denim, combat trousers and quite a lot of cardigans. Robin is wearing numbers one and three in this list. She is incredibly helpful and within five minutes she has introduced me to three presenters and another producer and has embarked on the story of Blue Danube Radio.

'BDR was meant to be quite educational and you know – kind of newsy but a good listen at the same time. Most of the people who work here come from other parts of Europe – we all speak at least two languages. We are funded in part by a licence fee – but you know all this is going to change, right?'

We both do a slight raising of the eyebrows at this stage. It's a sympathy eyebrow raising – not a quizzical one.

'Yup – I heard about all that.'

'We're going to become FM Fear,' she sighs.

'What ... Fear as in "I'm shit scared of this station" or Fear as in the one after three and before five in German?'

Robin pauses for one second and then gives a right royal hearty laugh. I've been waiting to crack that shit joke for weeks and I knew I was going to blurt it out too soon – I can't believe no one has cracked it before but I guess that they are all so fluent in German that they no longer see the humour in pronouncing things strangely and giggling at the double entendre that it creates in English. I have a long way to go in terms of European integration.

In fact the licence fee bit is not going to change. That will still be paid but it's part of the reason why BDR is going to cease to exist. Robin tells me that the ratings are not that good for BDR, and the Director General along with other Very Important People in Radio has decided that they really do need a station that reaches out to the younger audience. The last new channel that was launched for the younguns was back in 1967.

By this time we are in the lift going down to the studios. Radio stations have a thing about putting their on-air studios miles away from the production offices – maybe to give the DJs time for a bit of inspiration on the walk down to their bunkers. So while computers are whirring and the ashtrays are overflowing upstairs, Hal Rock who is on air at the moment is contained some four floors down.

Hal Rock (real name, I believe) is on air at midday and he is the head presenter of BDR – this is his term not mine. He looks not unlike Marvin Gaye in his heyday and has a voice like coffee creamer. He is practically chainsmoking Marlboro lights in his studio which looks out on to a snow-covered garden.

There are no CD cases scattered around the studio as it's all on a computer, so his job has been made easier by just having to press a part of the screen when he wants to speak, mix, stop or pause. It's his job along with the other DJs to present that air of calm and happiness to the listeners while all around him people are upset or worried by the changes. He is doing a very good job. I had imagined that the staff of BDR might be slightly wary of talking openly about what was going on at their station but far from it – they all seem more than happy to air their grievances and fears. Perhaps this is because they know their station and their audience better than their managers think. After all, Hal gets to talk to his audience every day.

In between the Bryan Adams and the incessant station ident, Hal tells me about the idea for the new sound of Fear FM.

'It's got to be "non pedagogic",' says Hal.

This is met by a very blank look from me. 'Sorry, I'm not really with you there.'

'Well, I think they mean that there can't be any more education – have a listen to the promo coming up, it's meant to explain it to our listeners ... see what you think.'

The promo consists of someone putting on a headmistress kind of voice and getting her 'pupils' to repeat basic English phrases after her. It ends with her saying 'and now the news in English' in a voice like Christine Hamilton's. It is deeply patronising.

There is no explanation as to why they are doing this but I guess it is trying to say 'this is the usual shit you have been listening to on BDR and coming up is some really good new stuff on FM Fear.' They are repositioning themselves in the market and seeking out that typical catchment audience known to the marketers as 'German under 30s who like their music but don't really care about the news that much'.

Hal doesn't look impressed. Part of the problem seems to be that the consultation period involved before making the changes may not have involved consulting the employees that much. Hal says there are meetings every day about how the new station is going to sound and how they should all embrace the delights of more music and less pedagogic-ness, but they don't seem to be convinced.

I daresay that there have been a lot of focus groups so beloved of media organisations before new formats have been decided upon. I don't know how they work their Austrian focus groups but they are probably quite similar to the ones in UK radio. These involve asking a 'cross section' of people to listen to shows and come along and share their thoughts over biscuits and tea and the occasional glass of wine in some meeting room in West London. By cross section they mean black, white, rich, poor, old, young, male and female. And it can be as blatant as that.

GLR used to do quite a few of these, one of which came up with the conclusion that the people who would listen to us doing the Breakfast Show were probably people who would like to buy the *Daily Star* but felt they should get something a bit more worthy. You could take that either way really. Our only comfort was that people probably don't tell the whole truth when they are sat in a room full of strangers. Just watch

Question Time. We always found it rather strange that our futures could be judged on the contrived criticisms of a bunch of invited guests.

Radio never seems that hard to work out when you're doing it, or when you are listening to it – and although you can throw all the money and production in the world at a show, its success will ultimately depend on whether the person doing it is likeable/knowledgeable and hopefully intelligent and funny with it. Endless discussions about whether the weather should go before the travel or which newspaper people would buy if the show was a newspaper will not halt falling ratings. And trying to second guess what a whole new audience will feel about a station suddenly told to change its sound is, I believe, nigh on impossible.

I felt a lot of sympathy for Hal and his colleagues. But they didn't seem to need my sympathy. I had expected to begin this radio journey in a station of chaos – where people were fighting for their jobs, where the passion of radio had stirred them into action – I wanted demonstrators and angry listeners bashing down the doors, I wanted people burning free station car stickers on braziers outside. What I had found were a load of very professional radio people feeling a bit dejected but carrying on regardless.

Perhaps this is the effect of living in Vienna as an international. You feel no great loyalty or fury either way. It's a very nice place that you are staying in for a while. As Hal says, crimes against the person are very low here. Crimes against radio stations wouldn't even show up. But there is something rather interesting about the ultimate reason why all this change is happening. The word 'accountability' crops up here.

Aside from the focus groups, the listening figures themselves are a bit of a problem for BDR because they are only allowed to count the number of citizens who are listening to the station – i.e. visiting businessmen at the Triest, people like me and others passing through Vienna don't count, which I think kind of goes against the ethos of why it was set up in the first place.

When I point this out to Robin, she gives me one of those 'well, I couldn't possibly comment' looks. It seems astonishingly daft to set up a station for executives visiting Vienna as 'internationals' and then to ask everybody who isn't an international if they listen to that station. If back in Britain the government set up a station for, say, Turkish people visiting relatives in Leicester, and then asked everybody else in Leicester who wasn't Turkish if they listened to it, I think I know what the answer might be. Robin is ahead of me on that one though.

'It's because of the licence though – internationals don't have to pay it.'

And this is the key. All those hotel-living, tax-exempting 'internationals' are getting the benefit of a radio station aimed solely at them without having to pay a penny, whereas that nice young German speaker who wants more up-to-date tunes and less 'forthwith' lessons is paying away and not getting it back. Once that is explained it's hard to see how BDR survived so long, apart from the fact that Vienna has done very well out of pleasing its international community so far and I should imagine would not want to lose its place on the international stage as a centre for commerce and trade.

I ask Hal if he's worried about losing his job.

'No – they've been good about that – some of the more specialised programmes have gone but they've guaranteed us contracts for another year so we won't be out on the streets.'

So there's no chance of a DLT-style on-air resignation and the opportunity for a budding sub-editor to write the headline 'Rock's Off'. But the entire success of the new station is down to how it sounds on air and it's a hard job to leave a station on a Friday by saying 'This is Hal Rock on Blue Danube Radio' only to arrive on Monday with a 'This is Hal Rock on Fear FM', knowing that unless you have had a sudden and disturbing drug-induced personality change over the weekend you are actually exactly the same person.

Hal didn't start out life as a DJ. He left London in 1991 and went to Vienna to learn another language and one of his friends pointed out an ad for the News Editor of BDR in England and sent it to him while he was there. He didn't get the job as NewsEd – 'News wasn't really my thing' – but he did literally bump into the station manager in a corridor as he was leaving and she said come along and file things. So he did. She also said that he didn't have the right kind of voice for radio so he couldn't expect to get on air. She must have been the only deaf station manager in the world as Hal has the kind of voice that makes Simon Bates sound rough. And whatever you thought of Simes he did have a lovely dulcet tone to him. So Hal worked his way up through the *What's On Guide* and now here he is – 'Head Presenter'.

'So would you ever go back to London?'

'God no,' he says.

Hal is quite unashamedly zealous about the delights of Vienna.

'It's clean and it's safe,' he states. 'You don't get any trouble here –

crimes against the person are very low ... you just don't have to worry –
and it's just got that kind of quality of life that you can't get in England
any more.'

'Does it ever get a bit dull?'

'Well, it depends what you mean by dull.'

'You know, a bit ... erm ... claustrophobic.'

'No not at all – you've got the restaurants, the opera, we get lots of
bands here ... and within a couple of hours you can be anywhere in
Europe – if you want to go skiing for the weekend you just get in the car
and you go.'

'And what's the down side?'

'Well ...' Hal ponders for while.

Robin pipes up from the corner, 'They're very rude in the shops – and
they can't queue. If you ever get the beginnings of a queue, by the time
there are twenty or so people it's turned into a mess ... and the Viennese
can seem a bit arrogant – like they don't really care, you know?'

I wonder whether this might just be Robin's view, having come from
a country that excels at the veneer of public service – she has got to that
thought before me.

'I find it weird when I go back to the States now – everyone's so, you
know ... friendly and all "have a nice day" and stuff but I still reckon
they're bad about it here.'

'Yeah – and they're really morbid too,' says Hal. 'Austrians like
nothing more than a good funeral.'

'They've got this thing here called "grantic",' says Robin who's getting
quite into the downside of her home-from-home now. 'It means kind of
grumpy – a bit moody – that's what Austrians are – they're a bit grantic.'

By this time Hal has got to the news bit of the programme which
involves quite a few different voices, first English, then French and
finally German. The last two come from a different studio but the
English bit comes from Sarah in Hal's studio. The lead story is now about
a fireman who has been arrested on suspicion of starting several blazes
himself while off duty. Sarah is slightly worried about the contempt
involved in this story. She used to be a journalist in England where the
laws are quite tight – that's why if Mr Fireman lived in, say, Lincolnshire
the story you would hear on the news would be something like:

'A fireman has been arrested on suspicion of arson. The 28 year old is
being held at Such and Such Police Station. Last week two houses in the
village of Niceplace were burnt to the ground. No one was injured in the

fires but the cost of rebuilding the houses has been set at 150 thousand pounds.'

But because Austria doesn't have the same laws as we do, she has to read the following:

'A 28-year-old fireman has been arrested on suspicion of arson. The 28 year old who works for the Vienna Fire Service was involved in putting out two house fires last week in one of the southern districts of the city. These fires were found to have been started deliberately. The chief fire officer said it was not the first time a fire officer had started blazes himself – but it was an appalling waste of time and posed a grave danger to the public.'

Now if you were listening at home you would be pretty convinced that they had got the right man and already proved that he was responsible, i.e. he's a guilty man already, isn't he? I can understand her concerns. The rest of the news is less contentious and when the red light goes off in the studio we are all sitting in, it means we have about ten minutes to chat while the trilinguists get on with the news in French and German.

Hal is by now on to his fifth fag and I feel it's time to let him get on with the rest of his show. He's got to introduce some piece about the seven deadly sins and as that may involve saying more words in a minute than he has done in the last sixty I think it's time to go. Robin offers me the tour of the production offices and says she'll help me find something to do this evening from the Blue Danube Radio *What's On Guide*.

Upstairs is the production office which is filled with surprisingly happy people. I had expected everyone to be gloomy and showing physical signs of disturbance at the changes going on around them. I thought they might be a little bit more 'grantic' but I guess that if their jobs are guaranteed and they get to stay in this civilised city for at least another year then perhaps I'm overestimating the effect that a management turn may have on a person's life.

Robin is busy rummaging through a pile of papers in order to find that essential evening selection. There is a Maria Callas Masterclass on at the State Opera – which I know that I should go to but I'm not sure I can afford the ticket – I can't stand opera anyway and so I justify my lack of interest on the grounds that I am going to deny a true opera fan the chance of a lifetime. I'd probably leave at half time and I'm still coughing up ridiculous amounts of phlegm and wouldn't last an aria without clearing the lungs. As you can tell from this, I feel bad that I didn't choose that one. Some theatre company is doing a production of *Blithe Spirit* – even Robin scowls at that one.

'No, I don't really go for *Blithe Spirit*.'

'It's not the choice of play I'm scowling at,' says Robin.

We exchange the international look that says 'Oh dear, amateur dramatics' and move on.

'There's *Mozart the Musical*?' she says.

Now that's more like it. Close harmonies and a story that I know without the translation. I feel a plan coming together. When she shows me the ad for it I'm hooked because it's not just *Mozart the Musical* – it's *Mozart! The Musical*. You know that exclamation mark is going to make all the difference.

Now I'm tempted to ask Robin to come with me to the show because I think she's probably quite a good laugh, but she's starting to look like she wants to be busy with something else so I chicken out. It's a very British thing isn't it? That 'I don't want to impose' feeling. I'm going to have to work harder at what the Americans probably call 'reaching out' to people. Maybe it's time to buy one of those management books you always find at airport bookshops – you know, the 'How to Travel Round the World without Appearing Really Stuffy', written by a Professor in Interpersonal Relationship Development Skills from the University of Wisconsin.

But by the time I have had this wish, Robin has scuttled off to fix something else. She's probably thinking, 'I wish that British girl had asked me to go with her – after all the trouble I've gone to ...' Anyway, one of the other producers, Katya, seems keen to chat so we go and sit in the reception area and muse about the way forward for BDR.

'I can't be bothered to go to any more meetings about it,' she sighs. 'We're all on rant duty right now. We'll just have to see how it all turns out anyway. There's no point in all this endless speculation ... Did you know that one of the managers said that they didn't want any speech programmes after seven in the evening because "no news happens at night anyway". I mean, can you believe that? Burglars'll be fine from now on, won't they?'

Katya is one of those girls who, because of their natural beauty, you wish you could hate but end up liking because they're really nice too. She came to Vienna almost by chance in that it was a journey of love – her first boyfriend here had a bike, a flat and 'he was OK for a while' but, although the romance didn't last, Katya liked Vienna and came back to work at Blue Danube Radio.

It turns out that she is not the only member of staff to come to Vienna for the love of a man and not the love of the city. The newsreader fell in love with an Austrian and two of the other producers are married to Viennese men. No wonder the underwear shops are doing such good business. Katya gives me an almost exact copy of Hal's Guide to Liking Vienna A Lot ...

'It's so clean, it's so safe ... It's only a couple of hours to most other places in Europe and the work is good.'

I ask if it doesn't involve an awful lot of stories about bureaucrats and strange departments in the overstaffed UN.

'Oh no, you actually get to meet people here – because the city is so small and because the politicians get out and about you can actually get the big interviews instead of endless quotes from advisers. You know, the ministers do genuinely have their meetings in some of the coffee houses and you can just phone them up and find things out. I did Tony Blair the other day – now that wouldn't have happened back in England, would it?'

'And during the Kosovo stuff, the army was really good about keeping the journalists informed. I went out with them on a couple of their missions – they're really fun and they don't mind answering questions. You just can't imagine some regiment letting you hitch a ride on their tanks back home, can you?'

No, not unless you are Margaret Thatcher and it's a photo opportunity. I'm not surprised though that Katya has got to see the friendlier side of the UN troops – I should think they imagine all their Linda Lusardi calendars have come at once when Miss Adler phones up and says 'Can I come on a mission with you lot, please?'

I bring up the topic of Jorg Haider – head of the far right Freedom Party. He is in full swing in Vienna at the moment and this is the height of the controversy about his election – other European countries are threatening to withdraw communications with Austria if Mr Haider's fully elected minions are given posts in the government. Nice, civilised, lingerie-wearing Vienna is up in arms about this man who did once advocate the education policies of Hitler and wants the borders into Austria to have the friendliness of Checkpoint Charlie.

'No one wants him here,' says Katya. 'People are a bit embarrassed that he has been elected – his supporters aren't here – they are in his province but he just got so many votes – that's why he's in such a strong position.'

'What's he like?'

'Well, he's attractive – that's the other problem. He's got the Porsche and the looks and the wife and the money. And he just lies very well. That's what's a nightmare for journalists – you know you'll sit down with him and say "Well, you did say this and that" and he'll just look you straight in the face and say "No, I didn't." So then you end up having a ridiculous argument like a couple of three years olds along the lines of "Yes, you did", "No, I didn't" and you just don't get anywhere. Oh and he's got these cards too ....'

'Cards?' I have a vision of him shuffling a pack and doing a few bar-room tricks.

'Yup, he actually uses cards when he's on TV debates and stuff. He writes down the main point and starts flashing it at people and, well, I guess it just makes things seem easier to understand. It's quite a neat trick.'

Now although this sounds absurd, I can see Katya's point: despite all the media training that our politicians – and presumably the ones in Austria – get, it still doesn't seem to be able to cure these people of the drivelling party line that emerges from their mouths when asked a very simple question like 'Where is the money coming from?'

I guess that if William Hague got the odd NOBO board out in the House of Commons, people watching at home might stick with it instead of flicking back to the menu to see when the next edition of *Ready Steady Cook* is on. By the way, at the moment on British TV, if you have a digital box, it's on four times a day and one of them is the special *Celebrity Ready Steady Cook*.

'How are people going to get rid of Jorg, then?'

Katya says that he'll probably just prove to be so rubbish at actually doing anything that he'll go of his own accord. So far he hasn't had to prove that he can handle budgets or dictate policy – and it's not like people have welcomed him with open arms in Vienna. 'Some of the protests here have been huge – well huge for here. Thousands have been marching to the government buildings and you don't often see that here. I think people are truly angry that the rest of the world thinks Austrians are all hot-under-the-collar right-wing fascists.'

'Have any of the marches got a bit out of hand?' I ask, hoping for tales of Viennese ladies throwing their mink-coloured pooches at the Freedom Party offices in disgust.

Katya chortles away. 'Errr, not exactly ... it's still pretty civilised –

everyone marches very properly and if there are people on bicycles they stick to the cycle paths and I even saw some demonstrators last week stopping off at the recycling bins and putting their drinks cans into the right containers before rejoining the march.'

Up against that kind of steely (recyclable) resolve, Jorg surely doesn't stand a chance – even with the cards.

Mozart! The Musical is on at the Theatre de Wein. I'm worried about the exclamation mark now. Imagine if Cameron had called it *Les Miserables!* subtitled 'Not really that depressing – in fact it's quite a laugh!' Can they really make Mozart's miserably short life into something humorous and worthy of that punctuation. Or is this the dark humour that Robin was referring to? Is it all going a bit grantic? The theatre that the musical is on at is, rather handily, just round the corner from my hotel, which once again usefully preserves those kitten heels from further snow damage. By seven o'clock in the evening Vienna seems to be a city full of people snugly ensconced in basement bars nursing enormous beers that British pubgoers can only envy from afar.

Hal and Katya are right: it does feel safe and clean and civilised. Very, very civilised. *The Musical!* is popular and it turns out that I got one of the last tickets. The Theatre de Wein is a beautiful gilded affair with many private boxes, and people have dressed up for the occasion. Even those who come straight from the office have managed to coordinate their work wear with the kind of jewellery that magazines tell you 'can spruce up any outfit'. While the orchestra tunes up and everyone else is chatting away to their companions, I realise that I'm not sure how much longer I want to stay in Vienna. Like having a cab waiting outside with the meter ticking, I am already thinking about moving on.

Nice as it is checking into my individually styled hotel and lazing around listening to the radio, I must make sure my trip begins to take shape. So far it could only be described as linear really. I know that at some point I have to get to America – land of free speech, the highest paid jocks in the world and also someone called Art Bell.

Art is a radio phenomenon and has been recommended to me by several people at work as a must-hear on any trip around radio stations. He broadcasts some kind of paranormal phone-in which people say is truly weird – it's full of alien encounter stories, conspiracy theorists and gun-toting nutters. Art works out of his own studio in a town called

Parumph in Nevada. This I have gleaned from his website which has a webcam where I have watched his picture jerk from a sitting to a standing position over the course of an hour while he is broadcasting the show.

He sounds perfect as an example of what exists on the fringes of the dial. But before even thinking about booking transatlantic crossings I have to make sure that Beirut is fixed. Gareth – my only contact there – is proving to be a gem and has sent an email confirming that he can sort out a trip to the radio station run by the troops in Southern Lebanon for the week after next. He is even going to hire a car and drive me down there. He says that it's best not to go alone. So far, so good. He sounds responsible, sensible, full of initiative and his grammar and spelling are both impressive.

However, I am a little concerned that he keeps on telling me that Southern Lebanon, the former Occupied Zone, is 'perfectly safe'. I have ended each of my emails with teeny weeny queries about bloodshed, *intifadas*, shelling by Israel and general mayhem in the Middle East. After all there must be a reason for the peacekeeping force being there. I get the feeling that Gareth is a more hardened hack than I am.

The chattering has subsided as the lights go down in the theatre. Watching a film in a language you don't know invariably gives it more gravitas – all those French films can't be good but the subtitles do give them an intellectual edge, don't they? I'm hoping the same goes for foreign musicals.

Mozart! opens promisingly. Lots of women come on in beautiful ornate costumes and huge wigs and the man sitting next to me has moved his foot off my handbag which will save both of us a lot of embarrassing tugging and pulling in the interval. The piece on stage has loads of rollocking numbers with big bass lines but I'm having problems working out where we are in terms of the plot as I don't understand the lyrics and am only armed with the phrase 'this house costs an astronomical amount'.

It's a splendid performance in terms of scenery and spectacle, the costumes are wonderfully chintzy and the wigs become almost cartoon-like. I find it slightly strange, though, that they all keep bursting into song with startled looks on their faces – don't they know that they're about to go into another big number? So when all the ladies of the court are fussing around the little Mozart boy and the courtiers are strutting at the back, I'm still trying to work out what it is that has led them into this latest big number – they are probably belting out some deep and thought provoking lyrics but because of the rocktastic beat I can't help think that they're probably singing:

> *Wolfgang's a genius!*
> *He has all the hits!*
> *He's really good!*
> *We love him to bits!*

There are some pretty fancy dance routines just before we go into half time and, as my basic German has completely let me down, I am now keeping myself amused by my own imaginary lyrics – I reckon I'm pretty close to the truth with the next blockbusting hit routine:

> *Watchout Wolfgang Amadeus!*
> *Looks like the big one's jealous!*
> *But I prefer the wig to these hats!*
> *If I sing louder, maybe I'll end up in Cats!*

TV and films spread the word about foreign places and make you feel comfortable in places you've never been before. I already feel that I know Chicago through the emergency room antics of *ER* – and if I ever go to Dallas I will undoubtedly feel heartened in the knowledge that, if I am stuck for somewhere to eat in the evening, I can always try getting a table at the Cattleman's Club. Please don't disillusion me and tell me that JR's favourite lunching place is a work of fiction.

I guess that musicals work in the same kind of way. You are pretty much guaranteed the same experience all over the world. Big staging, big hits, sad bit in the middle and sprightly boys in the chorus who would rather be in Westlife. I'm sure that *Mozart!* will make it's way to the West End and on to Broadway where the same kind of people, if not exactly the same people, who are in the Theatre de Wein will applaud loudly at the short life of one of the world's great musical prodigies.

The applause was almost deafening at the end of the show – a full five minutes of clapping with a bit of a standing ovation in the front that faltered a bit by row 23. I joined in all the way but I couldn't help feeling a bit let down. Not by Vienna or its talented performers or its resigned but committed radio people – but by a slight combination of all three. It was all a bit clinical. I was getting a bit grantic.

*

And so the next morning turned out to be my last morning in Vienna. It should have been morning four out of about six, but for a message that I picked up on my mobile on leaving the theatre. It was from a very nice lady at the BBC who said that a ticket for the England–Rumania game at Euro 2000 had just become available and would I like it? I don't suppose it comes as anything new to you that free tickets are made available to corporations and sponsors and the like – it's not news to me either but it is new to actually be offered one.

Contrary to public perception, life in radio or TV is not one big freebie. Actually it probably is if you are a big TV star, but in radio the level of free offers usually stretches to a few CDs and the occasional invite to the launch of a new *Musical!* in the West End. Obviously I don't usually get offered sports tickets because I'm not a sports journalist, but because Five Live is the BBC News and Sports network they do float around from time to time. I believe that Frank Warren had been due to attend the game but had to pull out at short notice. Something about a row he had with Mike Tyson. It will be the first and last time in my life that I can say I've been invited anywhere instead of Frank. I'm ashamed to say that I grasped the offer with unseemly ferocity and booked myself on to a flight from Vienna to Brussels for that afternoon.

I've emailed Gareth to explain that I'll be with him in Beirut a little later than planned – I've stopped asking him about the safety of the Occupied Zone now and simply put a query about clothing as a final PS on my note to him. I did include a weak gag about flak jackets, though – because, you never know, he might email back saying 'Of course you have to wear a bullet proof vest', in which case I will know that his interpretation of the word safety is very different from mine. I have time for just one last Viennese treat so I decide to go and look at some poo.

Going down a sewer is not something that you often see advertised as a tourist attraction around the globe – probably because shit is shit the world over. But here in Vienna some entrepreneurial people saw an opening in the market. In an attempt to cash in on the success of *The Third Man,* they have gained access to the very sewer where the escape scene was shot.

It's amazing how a little bit of celluloid glamour can last for years in the tourist industry. One of the finest examples I ever saw was in Puerta Vallarta – a resort on the west coast of Mexico. Puerta Vallarta was put on the international travellers' map by Richard Burton who went there to film *Night of the Iguana*. He was having an affair with Liz Taylor at the time – she followed him there, and so did the paparazzi.

Richard bought a house in the town, in one of the back streets, a spacious affair with wide views out to sea from the roof terrace. Then he bought a house over the road for Liz and connected the two with a pretty little bridge over the road. This was decades ago and both Richard (obviously) and Liz haven't lived there for years. But it is still called the Liz Taylor B&B and Museum and when we were there in 1998 you could go on a tour of the house, even if you didn't want to stay there.

The term 'museum' was a loose one. Hardly any of the original fittings were left and on every surface there were photos of Liz which on closer examination turned out to be nothing more than pictures cut out of magazines and stuck in frames. You could still pose for photos in front of the bar – but little of the magic of the previous occupants remained. The lady who gave us a tour very proudly pointed out in the kitchen that 'although the hob you see here is the original one Liz Taylor cooked on, the microwave is a more recent addition.'

For my sewer tour I turn up at the appointed street corner where there is a kiosk and a rail of grey jackets standing next door to it. There are a couple of guys sitting around smoking and wearing similar jackets. They are the tour guides. I am told by one of them – Joseph – to put a jacket on and pay for my ticket and wait until the manhole cover in front of the kiosk is opened up. I'm sniffing the air, trying to work out just how bad this is going to be.

We wait for a couple more curious tourists to turn up and Joseph says we're ready to go. The manhole cover comes off and we all nervously start descending the rather slippery staircase down to the sewer. The steps look a bit wet but I don't want to cling on to the handrail just in case some little piece of fluid (piss, basically) has managed to spurt up and land there. I reckon that it doesn't matter how much I wash my hands afterwards that bit of wee might have managed to get inside my skin and then I'm obviously done for and will die a horrible death from some strange urine-carried disease.

That starts a terrible train of thought because what about all those airborne viruses that are bound to be living down in the sewers with only pee and poo for company? Oh my God. What is the point of doing this? I might as well be off to Mozambique for a bit of bilharzia inhalation.

The sewers are huge – I was expecting to have to crouch down but in fact the tunnels are at least seven foot high and once my eyes have got used to the half light I can see that in fact they are beautifully cobbled. We take a few twists and turns in the damp darkness and come to a bridge where you can see the water (and things) streaming down a massive open tunnel below. Joseph is doing a nice line in film anecdotes – apparently Orson Welles refused to go into the sewers until perfume had been poured in further upstream. That would be an incentive to get it right in the first take.

The smell and the darkness are becoming rather oppressive and we're all huddling together looking down tentatively at the bits of bog roll floating down below. There's a flower stuck to one of the pipes going up the wall. How has that survived a flush so successfully? Joseph is explaining to us that this is the worst time of day to do the tour because the loos of the city are quite busy after breakfast. I had never thought of it that way.

Suddenly the lights all go out and a siren sounds ... I panic and start trying to run past the equally scared German tourist who is standing behind me.

'Alarm! Alarm!' Joseph shouts. 'There's a man in the sewer!'

We all peer down through the darkness – I'm expecting to see someone flailing around in the murky water but we can't see anything.

The lights flicker back on and there's a massive crack which sounds like a gun being fired. I know that I screamed. And I also know that I nearly added to the contents of the sewer.

There is indeed a man in a long trenchcoat down below. He's standing to the left of the sewer tunnel and he does have a gun. He is waving it up at us. There is more shouting but by this time I am rooted to the spot. It's only when the German tourist gets out her camera that I realise this is part of the tour. This is their re-creation of the film. Fear is now replaced by the feeling of being a complete twat. The man runs off under the bridge we are standing on and everyone starts a kind of nervous laughter. There is much chest clasping. I think Joseph has realised that I am not his best customer in terms of nerves and he comes round to the front of the group to lead me out of the tunnel.

'It's making you scary, yah?'

I nod, rather too vigorously.

'It's realistic, yah?'

Nod.

'We go to the big river tunnel now – follow me.'

'OK,' I squeak. 'Is that the end of the tour?'

He laughs. 'No more big bangs! Just a bit of talking now, nearly there.'

Quite literally there is light at the end of this tunnel and we walk into what seems like an underground beach. This is where the river flows underneath the city – the water is lapping gently at the stone floor that we are standing on but it's not roaring past like the shitty version was and the stench has lifted. This tunnel is a huge vaulted cave by comparison and the point of stopping off here is so that Joseph can talk us through a macabre slide show projected on to the opposite wall showing the syringes and condoms and wigs and small animals that have turned up in the sewerage system.

The Q&A session is thankfully short and we are soon free to climb the stairs up to the manhole cover to sweet-smelling freedom. I'm so glad I made the effort. Just so you don't have to.

All I have left to do in Vienna is pick up my one bag from the Triest and head to the airport. There's time for one last wind on the wind-up radio and from the bunker at the Funkhaus Duncan is once again amusing the Viennese on their way into work. By now I feel that he is a close personal friend of mine and I, for one, will be very sad to come back to Vienna and find that I am no longer being welcomed into the Blue Danube world of language skills, soft sounds and gentle British innuendo.

I'm sure that the German-Under-30s-Who-Like-Music-and-Not-News will be well served eventually and the ratings will soar and the focus groups will crow with delight over their warm wine about how much better the station is. But there aren't many places left in the worldwide radio dial that appeal to such a niche market as BDR has been doing.

In the incessant desire to please more of the people more of the time, today he's telling the listeners of Austria about the Welsh language – it's good to know that Welsh jokes travel. He starts off by explaining how difficult it can be to understand some of the longer place-names in the land of Shirley Bassey, but it turns out that what he is doing is cleverly preparing the ground for a joke. It's not the funniest joke in the world but it's good to hear it again ...

'So there are two Austrian blokes driving along in Powys and they can't understand the road signs and get a bit confused so they decide to stop at a restaurant in the next town and ask one of the locals for help ...'

Duncan pauses here to laugh at something said off mike by the girl in the studio with him. I have no idea what it was and to be honest it doesn't add to the flow of the piece. When he comes back he finishes the gag although he has to repeat all that stuff I've just written down. Anyway we join him again when they're in this restaurant ...

'Could you help us please?' says Lost Austrian No. 1.

'We need to know exactly where we are,' chips in Lost Austrian No. 2.

The girl leans over the counter and says 'BUR-GER KING, OK?'

And just as I'm almost out of the door Duncan delivers a peach. He's talking to someone about how health services have improved and reveals the startling fact that 'many people – including women – died in childbirth'.

I could have lied to you about why I was then going to get on a plane and head to Brussels. I could have pretended that I always intended to go and spend some time with the team from Five Live at Euro 2000. But you know that if I hadn't been offered a freebie I probably would have gone straight to Beirut.

However I can loosely claim that there is a radio purpose to this trip. For the duration of the tournament Radio Five Live have set up mini radio stations in Belgium and Holland. The aim being to provide a service for fans travelling to and from the games – information about tickets, times, squads, injuries, accommodation, general help and a bit of banter I should imagine too.

They have done this by prevailing on the local radio authorities to lend them a frequency in both countries. I know that this has not been an easy task, having heard various people in charge of the operation muttering their way around Television Centre back in London for several months before I embarked on my trip. Not only does the mini station, called the 'opt out', provide its own little programmes on a daily basis but it then pumps out Five Live on the borrowed frequency for the rest of the day. And it's on FM which is more than it is back home. This is quite a historic achievement. Imagine if a German station had asked the government if they'd mind lending them Radio 3's frequency for a couple of weeks during Euro 96? I'd be surprised if the answer would have been yes.

I don't think that the BBC has any spare frequencies either – there seems to be much sniping about the ones they already occupy. Maybe there is a cupboard somewhere in Television Centre marked 'Radio Stations – Spare, Please Put Them Back After Use' which has simply been forgotten about while people rush around creating new directorates, polishing Peter Sissons's head and fighting to keep the sports rights. So I can put the 'just' in justify for this little sojourn into Belgium on account of the fact that I can bring you a sparkling little insight into how outside broadcast teams work.

I know. This must be one of my weakest links ever.

3 I am Frank Warren

Belgium to Beirut

'Use your fucking legs – they get 25 thousand quid a week each you c***!'

This spirit-bolstering comment comes from the bloke in the England shirt standing behind me in row 7 of the Stade du pays de Charleroi. It's two minutes to go until full time and Romania have probably just taken their country into the quarter finals of Euro 2000, courtesy of some nifty passing and a penalty created by Philip Neville. The £50,000 a week England player on the receiving end of such perspicacious advice is David Beckham, who looks a little tired by this stage of the game, and I'm not surprised.

It's a muggy hot night in Charleroi and it's just about to be the end of a rollercoaster tournament for Kevin Keegan's team that has seen them lose to Portugal, win against Germany and be threatened with expulsion from the whole thing if there is any more trouble from the hooligans. I am feeling rather guilty now because, as you know, by this time I am meant to be in the war-scarred heat of Southern Lebanon listening to the output of a tiny radio station set up to entertain the soldiers of a UN peacekeeping force.

I should not be in a very good seat in the ground sitting next to Steve Cram and behind that excitable girl who presents *Blue Peter* whose name I always forget. It is only because this is a prime BBC ticket and I should be Frank Warren that I am sitting next to Steve Cram. Utterly charming and still looking like a 24 year old, he is being very kind and is talking me through every inch of the game, like a private commentary service with added swear words.

All around me are thousands of England fans with their heads in their hands. One guy who had four little crosses of St George painted on his face has tears or sweat rolling down his face, creating the impression that someone has just planted a comedy red and white pie on his face.

For the last two minutes there's a roar every time England touch the ball, but there's not a single ounce of lucky breaks left in the pot and the whistle goes.

It's not exactly England's finest hour. Rumania 3, England 2 – the three lions have been silenced. By this I don't mean to make some deep metaphor about England's insignia, I mean that the three blokes standing two rows below in full fancy dress lion costumes have slumped in their seats and stopped cheering. What is it about football fans that the hotter the temperature the more clothing they wear, yet on a freezing cold day in the pissing rain at St James Park there are lots of blokes with naked torsos?

'They deserved that,' says the guy to my left. Other people are experimenting with forms of language from the more colourful end of the palette. As we all stand there the Rumanian fans in the stadium are going berserk – there's a sea of gold and blue motion from their end – hugging, screaming, shouting, waving. The three other stands are motionless. Thirty thousand England supporters are wishing, like Cher, that they could turn back time.

As we all trudge out of the stadium there's a terrible air of despondency. The stadium in Charleroi is right slap bang in the middle of a residential area – during the game in between the corners of the stands you could see some of the merry Belgian residents having barbecues on their balconies and enjoying some of the finest views of the pitch. Now they're just watching hordes of upset and peed-off English fans head off into their town – and they may well be wondering what will happen later on tonight.

Having been out of the news loop in Vienna I have only seen a few pictures on Austrian TV showing thugs with three lion shirts on, throwing plastic chairs around and getting squirted with a huge water cannon. These were followed by some pictures of hundreds of fans sitting in the same square with their hands tied behind their backs – it looked like school assembly gone wrong. Presumably in between these two events a lot of arrests had been made

And somewhere in this huge mêlée is a very nice man from the BBC called Gordon Farquhar who I've arranged to meet by the burger bar at the entrance to the green section of the stadium. The Charleroi authorities have helpfully strung up some green balloons at the exit so that people know where to go – a bit like a kiddies party. As well as wandering around looking for the green balloons Gordon is one of the team from Radio Five Live over here for the tournament. His official title is the Sports News Correspondent – for the purposes of this trip he has been on 'hoolie watch', as it's called within the Five Live team.

Gordon has become affectionately known as The Brigadier because of his upstanding nature, officer-like stature and command of the situation. We've arranged to meet outside the stadium to walk back into town to meet the rest of the news team who have been watching the game on TV in their hotel. There is a horrible lack of natural justice in the fact that they have been working their bollocks off for the last two weeks in the name of English football and have not managed to get tickets to the game, whereas I have been swanning around in beech-wood hotel bedrooms and have managed to swing one.

We finally bump into each other in the crowd around the green balloon entrance. It's only about a ten-minute walk into town and we pass hundreds of fans being herded on to buses that will take them straight out of town to the car parks, or to the train station where they'll head back to Brussels or Ostend. Gordon says the Charleroi authorities don't want anyone staying in the town unless they are going to be safely tucked up in bed in the next hour.

His job is not an enviable one. It basically involves a lot of walking around and looking out for trouble – a bit like a school prefect after lights out but a whole lot more dangerous. What he's looking for is the first sign of trouble flaring up. If it does, then he has to report it and stick with it until it's over. It's not exactly a job spent in the best company.

'You're constantly looking out for the worst kind of people,' he says with a grimace, 'people who'll knife you, people who sing "No Surrender" and don't even know what it's about, people who are just plain evil.'

He says he'll have to do a tour of the railway stations a little later on to make sure that nothing is going off but it's quieter tonight than it was for the England–Germany game and he's not expecting anything too untoward. I ask about how the 'opt out' station is going and if it's on air at the moment. Gordon says I'll have to wait until tomorrow to see it in action – he thinks it's been quite a success although there's no real way of knowing. No one has the time to stand outside the ground asking pissed-off England fans if they've been listening to Five Live on Belgian FM.

Tonight Charleroi is looking rather pretty. Roads of neat, terraced houses stretch out from the stadium with the occasional cafe on the corner. There is no traffic – all the roads have been closed off. The cafes are doing big business but only in cokes and kebabs. No booze is allowed within a certain radius of the stadium. Some of Charleroi's residents have put their chairs out on the pavements and are watching as we all walk past. From their nods and stern looks I can sense that they aren't saying 'There go those marvellous upstanding English people – what a shame they are going.'

Charleroi itself is a post-industrial town in the heart of the Pays Noir – the Belgian Black Country. My indispensable guidebook, purchased at the airport in Vienna, puts it another way: 'The approaches are hardly inviting – belching chimneys dot the horizons, beside which rise grass covered slag heaps.' The belching chimneys are a result of the fact that Charleroi lies in the heart of Belgium's industrial geography – iron foundries, coal mines and glass works.

As a nod to its history the Musée du Verre is the only thing in town that the guidebook recommends. Apparently if you have any kind of an interest in glass then this will fascinate you – early glass, contemporary glass, Roman and Venetian glass are all contained in a building at the National Institute of Glass. I'm very clumsy so I doubt I'll make the trip. It's rather ironic that a town so dedicated to its glass has been entertaining English, German and Portuguese fans with plastic beer beakers in the main square.

Charleroi is said to be a bit on the rough side now – the demise of industry leading to inevitable bitterness and unemployment. But it's hard to judge that opinion tonight as the town has been invaded by 15,000 far more bitter people.

I ask Gordon about the hooligan problems and he confirms part of the story that goes with the Austrian TV pictures. More than 400 England fans have been treated to a special weekend break in some of Brussels finest jail cells and on Sunday UEFA issued the final warning – any more trouble and the team, along with their highly paid legs, can all go home. Now Philip Neville has saved them the trouble.

Gordon is pretty peed off though. According to him it's really not been as bad as everyone back home has been making out. Gordon says the whole story is far less dramatic – and that his job as a radio correspondent has been made a little tricky by the fact that everyone back home thinks that they are an expert on what has happened here.

*

Nothing at all happens on our walk back into town. No trouble, no fights – just a spooky silence due to the lack of cars. The hotel that the Five Live team are staying at is just a couple of minutes' walk from the main square, the Place Charles II. It's called the Socatel and if I was a heat-seeking missile then I wouldn't have needed Gordon, or even a map.

The tiny bar inside the hotel must be at least 95 degrees. Belgium has been experiencing a heatwave for the last week and if the hotel did have air con it had turned into more con than air tonight. My colleagues who usually look so calm and collected in the cool studios of Television Centre are all dripping with sweat. They too look like they have just done 90 minutes on a pitch with some balletic Eastern Europeans.

Victoria Derbyshire, co-presenter of the Breakfast Show, has been over here for the whole tournament. She looks genuinely very upset at England's demise and is nursing a beer at the bar with Hayley Valentine, one of the producers. Charlie Whelan, ex-spin doctor turned football pundit, has been here the whole time too. Tonight he is sporting an England shirt whose nylon nature is probably not helping his personal heat situation.

Jon Zilkha is the man in charge of the whole news operation for the station and looks like he hasn't seen a bed or a razor for at least a week. Gary Wisbey is the SM (studio manager) who is in charge of all things technical and last but by no means least is Peter Allen. Peter is the *Drivetime* presenter and a radio legend who normally looks like the well-groomed terrier of the newsroom. Tonight he looks like someone has taken a blowtorch to him and put him into the same kennel as an angry bull mastiff.

Peter's just come back from doing a tour of the town to check for trouble with a huge man called Mark Sandell. Mark's job is to do 'hoolie watch' with Gordon. He, Gordon and Jon are something of hooligan veterans, having covered previous football tournaments together. There must be something particularly bonding about having bottles thrown at you in Lens, Marseille, Rome and now Belgium. Despite the result of the game there's still a lot of laughter going on in the bar.

Five Live has had a difficult evening because back in London at Television Centre – where the station is based – a generator blew up about an hour before the game was due to start and everyone had to be evacuated from the building. Hence all the team over here had to talk bollocks for 45 minutes before the match, otherwise the airwaves would have gone rather quiet. Peter says it was truly bollocks. Along with that – and to help pass the time – they have all been trying to think of what the collective noun for a bunch of Five Live journalists should be. The winning entrants are a 'freeload' from Peter and a 'superfluity' from Gordon.

Jon, Gordon and Mark decide who's going to go where for the last 'hoolie watch' of the night.

'Bloody rubbish' is Charlie's verdict on the evening.

'I just can't believe it's ended,' says Victoria. 'What are we doing for Breakfast?' she asks Jon. This is not a polite social request for details of where to eat croissants. It's Jon's task to sort out who does what for the link-up to the Breakfast Show the next morning. There then follows what has to be the most laid-back and well-lubricated planning meeting I have ever had the good fortune to witness. Given that it is by now approaching midnight, none of the team shows any particular signs of dismay at the fact they will all have to be up again in about five and a half hours' time.

'You do the six o'clock, Victoria, Charlie can do the seven and you can both do eight.'

By this he means that Victoria will go on air, from the studio in Charleroi, to chat through the night's event with Julian who will be asking the questions from London.

'What's the studio like here?' I ask Jon.

He just laughs. 'Well, you can come and see it tomorrow morning – Mark can walk you up. It'll be a historic moment – the last ever Five Live FM opt out from Charleroi – tears may have to be shed ...'

Everyone laughs sarcastically at this last comment.

Welcome to the world of the high budget Outside Broadcast. When Judge Jules and all those Radio 1 DJs decamp to Ibiza for the summer I'm sure that they do it in style. Perhaps if Sue MacGregor ever leaves the *Today* studio she may have her own personal Winnebago, but most radio people don't. There are quite a few OBs I've done that may help to prove this point. I can't actually think of one that doesn't. The finest, though, was at the South Bank Centre when I was doing the afternoon show at GLR.

I have no idea why we decided to go to the South Bank Centre but I arrived there on a very windy rainy day to see that the mixing desk and outside studio had been set up on one of the balconies overlooking the Thames. Crash barriers had been erected to keep the crowds at a suitable distance so that the noise didn't interfere with the interviews. The show was on air at one o'clock. By 1.10 just the one person had turned up – and that was Simon Hughes, MP, the first guest. Not a single other member of the public showed up.

As the afternoon progressed the crash barriers started to rattle a bit more and the publicity photographs blew away in the stiff breeze. The stiff breeze turned into a thunderstorm at about 2 o'clock and the engineers back in the studio had to take over and play records for about twenty minutes because the noise of wind on the microphones was too much to bear. At 3.50, just before the show ended, one solitary person came to stand behind the crash barrier.

'Are you the girl from *Tomorrow's World*?' he shouted.

'No, I'm Fi Glover,' I shouted back.

'Steve? What kind of a name for a girl is that?'

By this time Mark and Gordon have gone off for a last trip round the town centre and the railway stations to see if any last England hangers-on are causing any trouble.

'I doubt there will be any,' says Jon. 'They're too fed up and too hot, I should think.'

If the Belgium police had had any sense about them they should simply have banged up any troublemakers for a night in the Socatel – by the morning they would have been so dehydrated with the heat that they wouldn't have had the strength to raise a David Beckham finger, let alone a plastic chair.

'Wait 'til you get upstairs,' says Hayley. And she's not wrong. One last round of white Belgian beer and everyone slopes off upstairs. Hayley and I bump into a very tired-looking Peter Allen wandering around on the fourth floor, staring angrily at his plastic key card.

'Doesn't work,' he says.

'It happens all the time Peter – you have to go downstairs and ask them to reset it.'

Peter says an unbroadcastable word and ambles off down the corridor.

The next morning I'm off to the makeshift media centre which has been set up in a room above a cafe, overlooking the main square in Charleroi. There's absolutely nothing that would suggest there had been a football match the night before as Charleroi's residents go about their morning routines.

I recognise the Place Charles II from the pictures on TV. It's a smallish circular square – if that makes sense – with cafes all around and streets leading off down the hill. They're the kind of cafes where you imagine it would be nice to while away a morning reading the papers and drinking too much coffee – perhaps on a weekend mini-break with your loved one. It's the kind of sunny place where you could chat happily about future plans, joint pensions and confess at last that you don't like his mother very much.

Charleroi has a darker to side to it, though – one which the guide books don't mention. Do you remember the case of Marc Dutroux? He was responsible for the kidnap, rape and murder – by slow starvation – of several children in Belgium. He had houses all around Belgium, some in Charleroi. The case caused an international outcry, not just because of the sad and horrific nature of his crimes but also because a mixture of police incompetence and corruption emerged in the enquiry into the case.

In one of those terraced back streets, no more than a mile away from this square, the police eventually searched one of Dutroux's houses and found large quantities of children's clothing. The clothes were put on display so that parents whose little angels had never been found might be able to identify perhaps a T-shirt or a skirt and put two and two together to make a horrible four.

I've only learnt this terrible fact this morning from an idle chat I had with Mark on the way up here. Is it a form of city racism to view a place badly for the crimes of one of its citizens? So many tourist spots across the world are actually scenes of crime. From battlefields to executioners' blocks to bridges over rivers to houses of serial killers. In fact, some of London's finest tourist attractions, the Tower of London and the London dungeons, celebrate early human rights abuses, now with the added opportunity to buy a nice tea towel with a summary of English history on it.

Does the passing of time make any sense of evil dissipate? I don't know. Does evil hang around in the atmosphere? Many people say they can sense the badness of a place. If I'm told where it is then I probably can too. If I were to go and stand in Cromwell Street in Gloucester then I could probably sense something, even though Fred and Rosemary West's house is gone. I believe they have planted trees and paved over the end of the road in an attempt to help people forget. But would I sense that evil if I didn't know what had happened there?

I'd heard the tail end of a documentary on Radio 4 about Dutroux's crimes. It was a brutally shocking piece of radio. The reporter spoke to one of his victims who had been caged and raped by him – held in the basement of one of his houses. She spoke of how she almost had a sense of gratitude to her captor when, at last, he led the police to her. I imagined her prison to be in a run-down, litter-ridden back street in some miserable town where the sun never shone. A road where half the houses were boarded up anyway, where cars stood on bricks. But it may well have been here in Charleroi with its pretty cobbled streets and neat terracing – those houses I thought were so appealing last night. Once you know a fact like that it's hard to let it go, it's hard not to let it taint the way you feel about a place.

One of the cafes on the side of the square has become home to Five Live. On the ground floor it's a typical European cafe with its long bar, glistening coffee machines behind it, a couple of old men already ensconced at tables in the window. But upstairs it departs from the norm. Upstairs is a whole bloody radio station. The 'media room' that they are using is actually the spare room above the cafe – and it's a sea of wires and lights and little black boxes and empty fag packets and piles of papers and people.

In what used to be the kitchen off the back of the room Gary – the engineer – is busy twiddling buttons on a mass of equipment spread out over the work surfaces. I presume that he is actually keeping everything on air. On the top of the old cooker he has another series of boxes and microphones and a tiny TV that is showing the people sitting at the table in the middle of the room. This is so that he doesn't have to peer round the door in order to see them giving him various hand cues for pieces and tapes into the programme.

Victoria and Charlie are sitting at the table with Jon Zilkha and Hayley – they've all been there since six. I can't hear the output of Five Live – it's just in their headphones. Occasionally, out of the blue, one of them starts speaking in response to a question from Julian Worricker who's hosting the show back in London.

'Sure, it's sad to be going – but after last night I don't think many people would say that we deserved to stay,' says Victoria.

There's another long pause.

Charlie laughs at something said back in London.

'Don't be ridiculous,' he says.

That could be a retort to so many things, it's not even worth trying to explore the options.

Neither Victoria or Charlie have much to add that would cheer up Kevin Keegan but at least they can report that there was no violence last night and most England fans have already left the country with their own personal disappointment. Given that none of this lot could have had more than five hours' sleep they are remarkably perky. Victoria has even managed a colour-coordinated outfit and perfectly applied make-up. Someone should clone that girl's liver. When they do I'd like to be first in the queue.

As soon as it hits nine o'clock in London the headphones come off and it's time for a hot seat change. In Charleroi this is when the 'opt out' begins. Back in London Nicky Campbell is starting his phone-in show which is about England's exit from the tournament and Charlie needs to stay on to do a bit of that with Kevin Miles – one of the team from the Football Supporters Association.

You might imagine listening back in England that Kev and Charlie are sitting in some carefully ordered studio in order to do this phone-in, but in fact they are both banished to the balcony with lip microphones (those little ones that sports commentators use which sit under your nose and make you look like you're holding an ice-cream cone permanently to your mouth). They have to go and stand outside to do their bits because the table is needed for the opt out. Presumably Gary has pushed some button in his kitchen which means that if you are listening in Belgium you suddenly get this programming rather than the Campbell phone in.

'And a very good morning to you – this is Nick Garnett in Charleroi. It's ten o'clock and it's time to pack up your bags and buy some cheap cigarettes and head home. This is our last broadcast from the centre of Charleroi and the end of Five Live on FM in Europe. We banked on getting all the way to Rotterdam but we haven't – so let's just hope that Eurostar is running on time today ... We can get you there, travel coming up, we hear from Stansted where thousands of fans are arriving back and we'll also hear what Charleroi really thought of *les Anglais* ...'

Nick Garnett is usually Five Live's regional journalist in Manchester but this was actually his idea to do the opt out and so he gets to present it.

The first piece is an update about the returning fans at Stansted – half way through the coverage is lost, so Nick has to pick up ...

'We seem to have lost Kate Williams at Stansted so the problems continue, don't they. We'll carry on by taking a look at the English papers with Charlie Whelan ...'

A couple of frantic hand signals from Nick and Charlie steps off the balcony, sits down at the table and slips seamlessly into discussing newspaper coverage

'Of course they didn't have that long to prepare their papers ... *The Times* goes with "England's dreams are shattered" – well, that's a good one isn't it?' he says sarcastically. 'The *Mirror* has got "wet eyed Shearer" – they're trying to do a Gazza there – I don't know if he is crying ... There's also a story in the *Sun* here that I like – "Belgian Mayor Blames English for Turkish Riot" – this is the Mayor of Brussels who says that it is all the fault of the England fans that the Turks ran through the streets brandishing bottles and knives. Well, what do we think of the mayor?' He pauses. 'I can't repeat it on air ...'

Charlie has made a pretty successful mid-life career change into broadcasting. Having exited politics in not perhaps the way he imagined, he has probably annoyed his enemies (of which I believe there are just a few) by becoming a sought-after pundit. I first met him in a garden outside the Savoy Hotel where he was attending some press awards and we were meant to be doing a photo shoot for a programme that we were all about to launch – *Sunday Service* on Five Live.

He scared me. Not just because of his choice of a rather beige lounge suit but because he came with this aura of being Charlie Whelan – ex-press secretary to Gordon Brown and a man who was famous for shouting and swearing at people if he didn't get his way. Him, me and Andrew Pierce – the other presenter of *Sunday Service* – stood rather uncomfortably next to each other. It was a photograph that was meant to say 'We're all great mates – have a listen to our fantastic programme.' The result was a picture that made Charlie look a little drunk, Andrew look a little cold and me look like a young boy in drag.

Thankfully the programme has been a bit more of a success. Charlie, as it turns out, is not scary at all. He probably won't thank me for saying this but he is like a big, cuddly Alsatian – warm, affectionate but occasionally given to biting the hand that feeds him.

'Do you think Keegan can survive?' Nick is asking Charlie.

'Well, I think he will, just because you can't think of anyone else who could do the job right now ...'

They do a bit of chat and with some more hand signals out to the balcony Kevin Miles puts his lip mike down and swaps places so that Charlie can go back to the phone-in. Gary cues up a piece that Victoria has done with a BBC correspondent. By 'cues up' I mean that he loads the relevant bit of audio into one of his machines and looks up at the TV screen in the kitchen for the hand signal from Nick – at some point Nick flails an arm in the air which I guess is the cue.

Have you ever watched *Frasier* and wondered how on earth Frasier's phone-in show within the programme stays on air? It really wouldn't in a real-life radio station – and neither should this one. For a start Frasier spends more time talking to Ros, his producer, than he does to any of his callers. So if it was a real radio show you would simply hear silence while he was doing this – which wouldn't really add to the flow.

People walk in and out of his studio all the time – which you would hear – and he never has to talk 'up to the hour'. This is the bit when DJs or presenters have to waffle away for 30 seconds or so in order to hit the news bang on time – at exactly 10 o'clock or whatever it is. Continuity announcers have to do the same thing on TV up to the BBC *News at Ten*. At home you see the clock with its little seconds hand ticking up to the top and some poor bloke or lady has to make the phrase 'and now the BBC *News at Ten* with Michael Buerk' last either two seconds or five seconds depending on when the last programme ended. Frasier, though, can simply sign off at any time – and he never trails the programme after him, which is always a sign of an ungenerous broadcaster.

This 'opt out' shouldn't stay on air just because it seems an impossibility that what looks like a room full of electrical junk is actually a fully fledged radio station. If you start thinking about how radio works, and you don't have a degree in engineering, then it seems unlikely that it ever does. It is a fantastic achievement that a few bits of metal and some electromagnetic waves, which are usually controlling tides in the Pacific, can turn a chat round a messy table into something that fills a whole frequency.

Of course it's this simplicity that means I get to hear a dozen or so pirate stations 'going out over North London' every weekend in Dalston. All the pirates need is an aerial and an amp stuck on the top of a tower block – height means a better signal – and you are in business. What I can't work out though is how they manage to target a certain frequency. The two most powerful ones in our area are just off GLR's 94.9 point on the dial and 93.5, which is where Libby Purves and the rest of Radio 4 live. I can understand wanting to be near the first one – because quite a lot of GLR's audience would probably enjoy some innovative dance tunes of a weekend, but I can't understand how many Radio 4 people would want *Book at Bedtime* to come with a nosebleedin' speed garage beat.

Belgians waking up this morning may well be as dismayed to find what is on one of their spare frequencies. Their police and the authorities here are getting a bit of a slamming. Kevin Miles is still talking about the hooligan problem and the way it's been portrayed:

'It was billed as being World War Three. We ended up without any serious injuries, the police reported twenty panes of glass broken – a couple of cars damaged, that's all. You would have thought it was the worst violence football had ever seen ...'

Ah, perhaps Kevin has underestimated the significance of breaking twenty panes of glass in a town which only gets into the guidebooks for its Musée de Verre. It might be something they take rather badly.

'I had this conversation with a German journalist,' Kev is saying, 'and he said if you're writing a story about a motorway you'll write about the couple of bad crashes there have been on it, not about the hundreds of thousands of cars that drive quite safely by. You wouldn't conclude that the whole motorway should be shut down just on the basis of a couple of bad crashes – so it is important to have a sense of proportion. There were probably 20,000 England fans in Charleroi that day and there were maybe 200 involved in that incident in the square ...'

Nick looks at the clock next to him – he's almost at the end of his last-ever opt out – somewhere in about twenty minutes' time whatever was being pumped out on RTBF's regional frequency will be making a return to normal programming after the strange *les Anglais* have stopped telling them how bad the Mayor of Brussels is. It's odd to think that there probably are more Belgians listening to this than England fans. From the actions of their police and the man with the water cannon, they don't think this is just a little isolated problem.

Apparently The Belgian authorities had been a little resistant in granting the BBC this frequency and needed some persuading. It was one of two frequencies that the 'opt out' station has been on. England played in Eindhoven before Charleroi so the station and the news team started off with their wires and microphones in Holland – which they said was really rather cool and pleasant.

I've got this little feeling that very few of this team will be making a return trip to Belgium in order to spend their vacations soaking up *La Belgique*.

'Well, that's about it from Charleroi. We're going to pack up our bags and head home too. It's the rather premature end of Five Live FM – hopefully we'll be back with another Five Live abroad – maybe next time it'll be in Japan. Just remember, though we may be the donkeys of Europe, we did beat Germany this week.'

Bless us. We got the booby prize.

'It's time now to return to Nicky Campbell's phone-in, which today is about one thing and one thing only ...'

Gary fades up the London output which quite seamlessly starts with a female caller saying, '... and they should be strung up and shoved in a cupboard where they can't get into any more trouble ...'

Nick puts his papers in the bin and Gary emerges from the kitchen – and that is that. To my knowledge no national station has ever taken over the airwaves of another by mutual consent. Sadly this piece of radio history seems to have passed everyone else by – Kevin and Charlie are still out on the balcony, Jon is on the phone trying to work out who can go home today and Mark is rummaging around in the kitchen trying to find his comedy football hat that he left there the night before. I offer to take a photograph of the momentous event.

Nick gets out a digital camera: 'Use this one – and have a look at some of those, they might give you an idea about what we've been up to ...'

The picture I take is of Nick looking knackered, sitting at a table with a huge ashtray in front of him and Mark walking through the picture at the back with his enormous squashy football-shaped hat on. I don't think that the BBC will be wanting to use it when they pitch to the Japanese for the opportunity to run a radio station in Japan for the duration of the World Cup. I just can't imagine what the caption would be. Perhaps 'Smoking Can Seriously Damage Your Head'.

Judging from the photos Nick has stored on his camera there has been some celebrating earlier on in the tournament. There are a lot of pictures of various members of the team dressed up in some of the more ridiculous merchandising from Euro 2000 – St George sunglasses and more of those hats. People in certain areas of the government would pay good money for the ones of Charlie – and I am happy to make those available. Then there's one of Nick with what looks suspiciously like a Spice Girl.

'Is that Sporty Spice, Nick, what on earth were you doing with her?' I ask him.

Nick's eyes go a bit dreamy.

'Mel C ... oh Mel C was wonderful ... basically she was supposed to be singing last night at the game. We had seen it in one of the tabloids last week so we hassled the record company into making her available. Then UEFA said to her you can't drive your limousine up to the ground for security reasons so you'll have to get on the bus, to which her people said "Er ... she's actually worth more than any England player on the field." So they said OK you can go in with the press on one of their shuttle buses – to which they said basically "Piss right off." So after a lot of to-ing and fro-ing her people said, "Well, if we do get her into the ground, how will we get her on to the pitch?" They said we'll give you front row seats and she can clamber over the hoardings and make her way on to the pitch with her guitarist. As you can imagine they pulled out of it immediately ...'

There then follows a discussion around the table about whether Mel C was being a bit prissy and starry with quite a few voices saying that she should have just gone for it anyway and what happened to the good-time girl from Liverpool image so carefully honed over the past few years. The jury remained out.

There are shots of the other 'media room' they used before they came here. The room we're in at the moment is apparently a luxurious option. In Eindhoven Nick says that the facilities were even worse:

'We were camped out in this attic above a bar which was basically just a storeroom for lots of Christmas decorations – really dusty. It was a dreadful dreadful place – cockroaches, rats, you name it – it was crawling around there. It had the most extraordinary light fitting – shaped like a great big bottom – made of plastic. We were trying to nick it but we couldn't find a box big enough to put it in.'

Mark Sandell has by now put the comedy football hat down.

'God, you should have seen the size of the cockroaches – you should have seen Gordon's face when he came back in after seeing them, he said he thought he saw a jockey trying to dismount from one of them.'

Mark is about six foot six and I wouldn't have thought that he would be scared by even the largest of cockroaches. One of his feet could bring heartache to several cockroach families.

I ask Nick if he knows how many people actually listened to the opt out.

'We've got no idea – Kev's getting quite a few phone calls after we gave out his FSA number here but we've got no way of knowing how many people tuned in or just found it on the dial by chance ... I don't suppose we'll ever know. It's more about the concept though – we've just proved that it can work. The next time there's a big sports event or a news event or anything that has legs, we know that we can set something up in two hours and then demolish it in ten minutes like we're going to do today.'

Charlie has finished on the phone in and says he's off for a wander round town.

'Need a bit of fresh air I think,' he says, picking up the sunglasses with the cross of St George across both lenses. I can't believe that he ever attended conferences or political tournaments with Gordon Brown where you could buy souvenir sunglasses that are quite so tacky – how his life must have changed. Maybe I'm wrong and he has a whole collection of T-shirts with slogans like 'Eastern European Economic Stability Conference 99 – It Rocks! ' and 'Euro – the Final Countdown!'

There's an air of something approaching sadness in the room. It may just be that everyone is knackered.

'It's just been bloody good fun really,' says Nick.

'Is that the look of a man who's had bloody good fun?' I ask, pointing at Gary.

Gary has his chin on his hand and looks like someone has just told him that although it's all over he's still got to dismantle all the equipment, pack up about 74 silver boxes' worth of cables and microphones, return endless bits of lost property to various BBC persons around the town and then drive home to London. That's because someone just has.

'The hours that he has had to work have been horrendous,' says Nick, nodding towards Gary.

'It's not that, Nick, it's working with you,' says Mark.

'Bastard,' says Nick. 'I gave him a hand cue today – OK, it was after the tape had started but I did cue him – and that was a first.'

'That's not a hand cue, Nick,' says Gary rather wearily.

Gary has been getting a fair amount of piss taken out of him during this trip because he and Paul Greer, another one of the journalists here took a trip to see the graves at Ypres a few days ago. Obviously it is a place with an awesome amount of tragic atmosphere and while they were looking around, Gary explained how, having lost both his parents quite early on in his life, he now lived every day to the full. Paul paused for a perfect moment before quipping.

'So this is living life to the full is it, Gary?'

Now a couple of times a day Paul phones Gary while he is knee deep in cables and stress and simply asks, 'Are you still living life to the full then?' It would be a good moment for Paul to phone now.

In among all this there is one man who is still working – Jon. The man who is always on the phone.

'It's been quite surreal sometimes,' Jon says. 'Like when we've been stuck up in the attic in Eindhoven or here above the cafe. No one walking past has realised that a whole radio station is on air up there. They were going to come and see what we were doing – the Belgian authorities – but no one ever showed up ...'

His phone goes and he leaps to it.

The Brigadier arrives, looking rather pleased with himself. He has just checked out of the Socatel. It's going home time for everybody here and, for Gordon, Euro 2000 turns into another notch on his outside broadcast bedpost. I want to ask him about what he'd said last night about radio versus TV. It's a conversation people in radio are always willing to have because we are treated rather like the poor relation in the media family. TV is the shining, go-getting younger brother who gets all the glory and wins all the prizes.

How many endless surveys have you read with titles like 'TOP TEN TV MOMENTS OF ALL TIME' or 'THE 10 FUNNIEST TV SHOWS EVER' or just TV – TELL US SOMETHING ABOUT IT AND WE'LL REPRINT OLD PHOTOS AND QUOTES'. TV gets all the coverage, whereas radio gets far more listeners. It's been going for longer and there isn't a world event that it's missed. So it seems a little unfair.

'The problem with TV,' says the Brigadier, 'is that you can be right in the middle of the action and take all these tight shots of what's going on around you and it's always going to look frightening – you know the kind of shots when people come running up to the camera and shove it around a bit. At home you feel like they're punching out at you. The TV cameras can't show the two hours beforehand where you got the impression that something was about to happen, or the fact that you have seen one or two nasty characters – but that everyone else is just having a beer and shaking hands with the other teams fans. And now, the only image of the whole thing will be those mad ten minutes, caught on camera – for ever more.'

Many, many world events have been captured by just one TV image – and rightly so. Quite simply the visual image has that power. The students standing in front of the tanks at Tiananmen Square, the victims of drought in Ethiopia, President Kennedy being shot. They all cropped up in one of those pre-millennial surveys. All last a lifetime in your mind from the moment you see them.

In my corner entitled 'RADIO IS IMPORTANT TOO' I'd like to point a little thing out. Think about the question 'Where were you when you heard that JFK had been shot?' The key word in that sentence is 'heard'. You see, you probably did hear it on the radio first. And then you saw it on TV and that makes you think that TV brought the news to you. But it didn't. Radio doesn't have the power to place a lasting picture in your mind, probably because it asks you to make that picture up yourself. But it's there as the unsung hero of so many huge moments in history. Chamberlain's speech relayed from 10 Downing Street in September 1939 when, after detailing the nature of negotiations with Germany and the insistence by Britain that they leave Poland, he said, 'And I have to tell you no such undertaking has been received and that consequently this country is now at war.' Imagine the impact of that one voice on so many lives. All these enormous things belong to our ears. So when is someone going to do a bloody survey about it?

I bet you heard about the death of the Princess of Wales on the radio. It was a Sunday morning and I should imagine you switched on the radio in bed ... or in the car, or someone else did and then they phoned you. I got a call about four that morning – I was meant to be doing the Breakfast Show at Five Live. I'd had the radio on as I was getting up at 3.45 to get ready – I heard that she had been injured, no more than that.

Ken Murray was the editor on duty. He called to say that they reckoned she had died and that I'd not be needed. I spent a spooky hour or so assuming that she had died, while watching all these correspondents on TV struggle not to let on that they thought that too. They had to wait for the official green light to say that. And yes, of course I went to the TV as soon as I heard the news because, love radio as I surely do, I still want pictures to go with it sometimes.

Gordon and Mark are by now piling up their stuff into the car to drive back to Brussels. They do seem delighted to be leaving. I ask them if they'll all miss each other when they get home.

Gordon nods. 'The team worked really well – if you were just filming stuff as it goes along it would be funnier than anything you'd see on telly – any sitcom, any play – it's just the banter that goes on. Obviously it's crap when you try and repeat it to people back home but it keeps us happy over here.'

'Do you know what?' says Gordon after climbing into the passenger seat. 'I think I may have experienced some chafing on our final late-night tour of Charleroi.'

Mark thinks about this as he pulls out from the slip road on to the motorway.

'Shall I follow signs to the Ring then, Gordon?'

71

*

Mark drops me off at the airport – which hasn't changed much in 24 hours. Gareth is going to meet me off the plane at the other end in Beirut – I have finally managed to have a conversation with him instead of all the emails. I didn't mention safety at all. But that doesn't mean that I'm not thinking about it. Now I know that Beirut is peaceful these days – that is why it is 'coming on' so well for the discerning traveller. It's still the Southern Lebanon bit that I am worried about. The UN station there is in a village called Tibnin, a few kilometres away from the Israeli border and in the heart of what has been the Occupied Zone. It has been effectively a war zone for two decades.

The radio station has been set up as a bit of welcome light relief for the soldiers there and I don't want to be foolish enough to think that, just because I am visiting that part of the world to seek out entertainment, this somehow makes me immune to passing bullets. Some journalists choose to seek out strife and war and report on it. They do it well. Presumably Kate Adie, John Simpson and Michael Nicholson choose hotels for their ability to withstand gunfire and shelling – not on the basis of colour-coordinated linens and individual styling. And therein lies the essential difference between what they do and what I do.

I wonder why everyone on this flight is going to Beirut. We are a disparate lot, crammed into a departure area at Brussels airport. Two families with about seven kids between them, two very beautiful young Lebanese women with their somewhat older husbands, and the rest are businessmen with world-weary faces and identical black suitcases on wheels with those pull-out handles. You know the suitcases I mean. They are cabin-luggage sized – about 1ft by 2ft with an extendable handle so that you can pull them along behind you. And they are always black. Now that to me seems a design flaw.

In this airport alone there must be at least 10,000 of those cases all being trundled along behind people – all have a flapping check-in label on them, and all of them the same colour. It must be terribly difficult to keep track of which one is yours. They are the scourge of the modern traveller. On the ever-increasing walkways that you have to run along to catch your plane there is always some idiot who seems to forget that they are pulling a little block of leatherette along behind them. They blindly turn corners whenever they want to, they trip up old people on the walkways, they run into your heels in the queue – they are a nuisance.

People should have indicators and rear-view mirrors attached to them. Or like me they should stick with the one over-the-shoulder bag.

The skies over Europe are busy today and we have a one-hour delay on the flight. I'm filling up the time by compiling my TOP MOMENTS IN RADIO just in case anyone ever decides to run it as a feature. There are so many to choose from. Truly great programmes like *The News Quiz*, *From Our Own Correspondent*, the documentary on Radio 2 about Eva Cassidy that made me cry and buy all her records the next day. Then there were Chris Evans's early shows at GLR. But aside from the shows there are a thousand little moments. Just bits that have stayed in my memory.

There was an interview that Robert Elms did on GLR with Stephen Fry – after his breakdown. There wasn't one single moment that made it special – it was the whole thing. Robert did it well. There was this great, funny, sharp-witted man opening his heart and explaining why he felt he let himself down, so much so that he ran away. As simple as that – he just ran away. He talked very eloquently about his shortcomings and how depressed he'd got, and about thinking how to end it all. And Robert just let him talk – few interruptions, no digging and prodding. It was just deeply moving. As plain and simple as that.

But then there's that Brian Johnston and Jonathon Agnew exchange in the cricket commentary box – you know the one where Aggers says Ian Botham couldn't get his leg over? Brian Johnston just loses it completely and splutters through his laughter as it gets progressively worse – ending up only being able to say, 'For goodness sake, Aggers, stop it ...' I defy anyone to listen to that and not start spluttering too.

And there are much smaller moments, like when Nicky Campbell asked Will Carling if he had slept with the Princess of Wales. There was a monumental pause before Will said, 'I can't believe you've asked me that.' Neither could I but I'm very glad Nicky did. And there was a delightful moment on the same Campbell show when Nicky brought in a caller to join the debate.

'Eileen, Enlighten us!' he cried.

'I'm not in Lightenus ... I'm in Croydon,' she replied.

The muzak at Beirut International Airport's luggage reclaim hall is playing 'The Winner Takes It All' – which is perhaps appropriate for this country torn apart by civil war and regularly invaded by other surrounding countries eager to help/take advantage of the fact that they were having a civil war. The only problem as a Western tourist now is working out who the winner is. Things have changed a lot over the past few months here. On 24 May the Israeli troops and their accomplices withdrew from the Occupied Zone in the south of the country and although there is no signed and sealed peace agreement yet there is more peace than there has been for years. It is a momentous time here.

Gareth and I have perhaps foolishly forgotten to tell each other what we look like so I have no idea who I'm searching for among the sea of faces in the arrivals hall. Thankfully Gareth uses his journalistic nous to spot that I am about the only person getting off the flight without a small child, a slightly older husband with badly dyed hair or a Trundling Bag.

'Welcome to Beirut,' he says. 'Flight delayed then – they usually are. Car park's this way – prepare yourself for a bit of Lebanese driving ...'

There are many ways that you can tell where you are in the world – temperature, time changes, language and – if you are my mother – specific flora and fauna. Driving will do it too. The civilised but fast pace of Belgian motorways and Austrian autobahns is replaced by something truly spectacular in Beirut.

Perhaps if your life has been dominated by war and you have watched militia groups pound your city to near destruction then the junctions of everyday life have less importance to you. Or maybe Beirut's drivers are just crap. Just getting out of the car park with Gareth is an adrenalin rush. The reverse gear in this city seems to be used more widely and frequently than in any other city I have visited. One taxi parked across a central reservation in the car park simply reverses past us, swings round, reverses again and goes out of the entrance.

It gets worse. Missed your turning? Just reverse back down the road till you get to it. Stuck in traffic? Get the whole road to reverse so you can get out. Parked your car badly? Reverse over the pavement and drive down the other side of the road. All these features are on display in the fifteen minutes it takes to get from the airport to the centre of the city. It's a good ice-breaker if nothing else – allowing me and Gareth to marvel alongside each other at two near misses and a bloke doing a wheely on a motorbike all through one of the underpasses.

It becomes immediately clear that Gareth is not a man given to extraneous conversation – his comment on the bloke doing a wheely who whizzed past us at about 80 miles an hour was something along the lines of 'Barking, aren't they?' I'd say that Gareth is somewhere in his mid thirties with brown hair, some of which is standing up on the top of his head, and a slightly dishevelled appearance not unlike some of the more studious types at the British Library. He seems very proud of his adopted city and insists on a quick drive round before taking me back to my hotel.

The parliament buildings are lit up, perched on a hill looking back down over the city. Gareth says they are part of the rebuilding work that is being carried out everywhere. There are cranes all along the night skyline and throughout the Downtown district, which Gareth says is now prime real estate. I can't quite get my bearings yet as to which part of the city we have driven through – but even in the darkness you can see the bullet holes and the rubble of hundreds of buildings. Gareth weaves his slightly battered car through tiny streets to get to the hotel, which is a monster of rebuilding – huge and white and surrounded by a tooting mass of cars trying to get to the enormous polished revolving brass doors.

The Phoenicia Intercontinental has only been open for about a month and therefore is delightfully keen to get people's custom. Should I return to Beirut in a few years' time it will be well out of my price bracket but for the moment the marketing drive is on and the rooms are cheap for the five stars the hotel has acquired. It's a gleaming testament to Beirut's rebuilding process although its most enigmatic feature has gone – Gareth tells me it used to have a round swimming pool with glass walls so that the drinkers in the bar below could watch endless legs kicking about while sipping a Martini. I hope no one was foolish enough to think, 'Can't be bothered to get out to have a pee.'

The hotel stands on the corner of the Corniche – the long road that sweeps down the side of the Mediterranean – and I can see hundreds of people promenading along the wide pavement.

I've been good and waited a whole 17 minutes before getting in my obsessional question, but I do manage to slip it in just before getting out of the car. I ask Gareth what the range of radio is like in Beirut. He says quite a few pop stations, most broadcasting in French, a wide selection in Arabic and the biggest is the government-run Radio Lebanon.

'Is it any good?'

He grimaces. 'Well – it can be interesting ... only a few programmes are broadcast in English though – but it's got too many staff for a start ... that's a government thing, they can't go round sacking people even though most departments and state-owned industries have masses of extra people – most of the staff of Radio Lebanon probably live in Paris and never even go to the station any more. Middle East Airlines has the same problem. They have 4,500 employees and only nine planes. Which means 500 people to work on every plane.' I was looking forward to some pretty amazing service from the drinks trolley on the way out of Beirut.

If you put your aerial high enough and the signals were strong enough, then I bet you could hear every single perspective of the Middle East troubles coming at you in the ether here. Palestinians demanding land from Israel, Israel calling the shots in America, Jewish settlers standing firm, Hezbollah's call to arms, Syria's sympathy. They would all meet in the middle as what?

Intransigence FM perhaps. Each station would view the others as propaganda while being on the moral high ground themselves. There is nothing new about that. What better way to call people to arms? What better way to spread the word? Right from the early days when radio had surged forward as the people's medium, its basic power of spreading information was an immediate hit. The BBC was one of the first organisations to really take to propaganda broadcasting. It sent out programmes to the Arab world deliberately made to tell them how fantastic we were as a colonial power. It did this to counteract Italian broadcasts which were doing exactly the same for Italy's colonial stance. Both countries knocked each other over the airwaves in a fight that eventually neither side won.

The Second World War took propaganda broadcasts to new heights – the Allies sold their cause around the world through radio as well as using it in a subversive way to create havoc behind enemy lines. In James Woods' terribly thorough *History of International Broadcasting* he says that by the end of the war Britain was putting out 850 programme hours every week, in 46 different languages. This was more than the combined output of America and the USSR. Tiny country, big gob. Some things haven't changed.

Sadly the power of radio has been abused more and more as history is made. The part it played in the genocide in Rwanda was huge, to the extent that the UN recognised after the event that if the 'hate radio' broadcasts had been jammed then the course of history could have been changed. 'Hate radio' does exactly what it says on the tin. One of the stations monitored in the late 1990s in both Rwanda and Burundi called itself Voice of the Patriot. It was aimed at Hutu rebels and sent out a constant message that if the Hutus didn't kill the Tutsi soldiers first, then they would be massacred themselves. 'You know the cunning of these people. They come to kill us' – that kind of mild-mannered stuff poured out to thousands of people in remote villages every day.

At the time of the genocide Radio Télévision Libre des Milles Collines went even further. 'Exterminate the cockroaches,' it said. It called the fight against the Tutsis 'the final war'. In terms of their set-up the stations were only transmitters being moved around the countryside, so although both were shut down you don't have to be Marconi to realise that they could just as quickly go up again.

One good thing came of the hate radios in Rwanda though – a Swiss charity set up a station called Radio Agatashya in the huge and swollen refugee camps to act as a kind of damp tea towel on the chip-pan fire of incitement. It realised that if the radio was such a powerful part of these people's lives, it should maximise the potential for getting across messages of peace and reconciliation. I think it's still broadcasting a mix of news and information in the camps and beyond – and it's been responsible for reuniting families torn apart by the civil war.

It's still filling me with trepidation that tomorrow my love affair with radio is going to take me to a war zone. It's fear of the unknown that's troubling me – I have no idea how to picture the camp or the reality of the former Occupied Zone. Just to give me something to think about while drifting off tonight I ask Gareth what the radio station at the UN camp is like. He laughs for the first time.

'It's a hut, Fi – a very small, very hot white hut – in the middle of a very hot, complicated place ...'

4 And then he puked up over the minister

Beirut to Southern Lebanon

When I woke up this morning I opened my curtains to reveal what a glossy travel magazine would probably call a 'stimulating' view. I am at the back of the hotel (reflected in the price) and look out on to a massive rubbish dump and a towering building that is nothing more than a concrete skeleton now, such is the level of shelling that it obviously took. Great big holes – and I mean about twenty feet across – scar the sides. It defies gravity that it is still standing.

It used to be the Holiday Inn – which only just managed to open before the shelling started. Right up on the skyline of the building there's a semi circle of concrete jutting out from the top floor. Presumably this is where Beirut's finest cocktail lounge or restaurant would have provided its glamorous clients with a far-reaching view across the city and out to sea. There's now a tree growing where the piano would have been, its branches straggling out and dangling from 17 floors up. How did that little seed manage to grow on a bed of concrete and rubble?

Behind the Holiday Inn there are low-rise apartment blocks with washing hanging out on some of the verandas. For every lived-in apartment there is one next door showing no sign of life. Everywhere you look there seems to be a shattered shot-to-shit shell of a building next door to a newer gleaming one. On the gentle slope of the hill behind the hotel I can see beautiful old town houses with crumbling facades and high windows sitting next door to an office block showing off the talents of an architect who graduated in about 1998. It's as if you were going to fill your mantelpiece up with the kind of ornaments you usually find in the Design Museum, then bung in some bits and pieces your removal men broke and finish it off with a couple of old vases you've literally used for target practice.

I've arranged to meet Gareth early – before the heat of the day sets in.

Already it must be 25 degrees and it's only about eight in the morning. The cool marble of the hotel lobby is disconcerting – every time the revolving doors revolve there's a waft of hot air swept in with the sweating businessmen.

Gareth's is the little white car that pulls up among the glut of Mercs and limos outside the hotel. The Intercontinental had either a very astute or a rather dim designer as there is no discernible car park for the hotel – hence all the limos converge in a glut outside the front, creating an impression that a very high-class car boot sale is about to begin. I wonder what the collective noun is for a group of limos? A stretch perhaps? Or maybe a purr?

Gareth is in full tour-guide mode this morning; we are going to see the sights in between doing some necessary domesticity. So we set off round town – one pair of contact lenses to pick up for Gareth, one hat to buy for me (sun protection not Ascot type) , one drive round to capture the essence of the place and a Kiri Te Kanawa press conference to finish with.

This is, after all, Gareth's home town now – and there are chores to be done. It's rather nice to be in someone else's domestic routine. I have absolutely no hesitation in recommending that should you ever decide to come to Beirut you should take a Gareth Smyth tour. Up to the minute, delivered in a sometimes off-putting deadpan style and full of information that would make a travel journalist weep with envy.

We start off in Verdun which is the international glitzy shopping district with its predictable Charles Jourdan and Miss Selfridge.

'Beirut has an annual shopping festival in February when everything is half price – it's an attempt to get the Gulfies in with their money,' says Gareth.

'Do they come?'

'Oh yes – all the real estate people want to get them here in the hope that they'll turn up with huge amounts of green backed notes and simply hand them over.'

'How much would it cost you to get a flash place on the Corniche now?' I ask. Having grown up in the Eighties I find myself obsessed with house prices.

'God – about three-quarters of a million dollars.'

Verdun has a delicatessen called Goodies on one corner of a block. Gareth says that during the war it remained open, serving pâté de fois gras and caviar and all those things that you really can't get through a civil war without.

'There's a story that one day an armed robber walked in and attempted to hold them up and three very well manicured ladies waiting at the counter calmly got out their pistols and shot him dead right there and then ...'

I ask Gareth what the main business is in Beirut now.

'Banks really – big business banking, that kind of thing. One of the banks had a kind of PR drive on earlier this year where they bragged about the fact that you wouldn't have to queue at all – you could be in and out of the bank in minutes. People got really upset because they want to be seen to be spending time in the banks – means you've got a lot of money to sort out.'

Whatever I ask Gareth, he can answer. In quickfire succession we cover the upcoming elections, the areas of historical importance outside Beirut, where the football team lies on an international scale and who are all the blokes on the posters around the city.

Beirut's politicians like to see themselves a lot. The bigger the better, and not just on posters wrapped round the odd lamppost or on carefully monitored billboards by the side of the Earls Court Road but on the walls of any building they can find. Huge painted portraits of the parliamentary speaker Nabih Berri seem to be the most prominent. Unfortunately some of them are not standing the test of time and heat, and bits of them have fallen off, leaving him looking like an unfinished jigsaw. In all of them he is wearing a sombre dark suit and a look somewhere between stern and caring. I say that Berri looks like the kind of guy who is just about to announce the winner of the Rotary Club's annual raffle.

'That's about the size of it,' says Gareth wryly.

I thought last night while curling up in some more freshly pressed linen that it might be quite hard work hanging out with Gareth for a whole week. And more importantly it might be very hard work for him. There are only so many conversations I can have about Middle Eastern politics without starting to get lost in the maze of militias – and there are many. This is Gareth's specialist subject but because of his expertise it's a little like joining a MA in International Relations half way through the year. But today he seems quite happy to pootle along and after a few hours I feel I am getting the measure of his grimacing style.

He used to work in Britain – quite a while ago. Since leaving he has pursued what I would call a dangerous style of living. He has been taken off buses by Turkish guards, hidden away with the Afghans and entered various tricky parts of the world without the necessary paperwork. He would most like to go back to Iraq – to the north where the Kurds are. When he first came to Beirut he worked for a local paper – but things turned sour and now he is the *Financial Times*' bloke here.

All that doesn't really explain why we are going to end up today at a Kiri Te Kanawa press conference. I can't think that the *FT* would be that interested. Gareth says he'll be doing a piece on that for a different media outlet, maybe even the paper where things went pear-shaped. It all helps pay the rent.

We drive on through the city past the Palestinian camps which are no more than shanty towns really – huts and boards turned into homes. Many of the Palestinians came here expecting to have to live in tents for no more than a few weeks, maybe months – five decades on life is not good for them. Even if you are a fully qualified doctor you're not allowed to practise. The sanitation, says Gareth, is a lot like their fate – poor and with little hope of immediate rectification.

Beirut is not a big city – its main areas spanning no more than a few square miles but with suburbs spreading out along the coast and up into the mountains. It was divided into a Christian and a Muslim city by what was called the Green Line during the civil war. It separated East and West and, although this was never an official wall like Berlin it was a recognised distinction between two groups – and it still is.

Since the ceasefire in 1990 the city has been on a massive rebuilding spree but it doesn't stop people clinging on to life in these shattered buildings. In one I can see just a mattress and a plastic chair. That is home enough. We drive past a sign saying 'Hotel' with an arrow that ends in a pile of bricks. Gareth says he's taken that photograph for publications abroad quite a few times. He points to one building riddled with holes on the Christian side of the divide.

'The snipers used to fire from boxes built inside the building. If you look inside you can see where they built them for a bit of protection – some liked the lying down position, some liked to do it standing up ...'

I wonder if anyone made that into a car sticker.

We drive on past the river which is rather less than fragrant today and up to what looks like a concrete surface car park with some kind of iron plinth in the middle of it. This is BO 18 – a nightclub – or at least we are looking at the roof of BO 18. The club itself is underground, beneath the flat concrete that we're looking on to and the iron structure is a hydraulic system that opens up the roof of the club.

'This is the site of the Karantina massacre – one of the worst the city saw ... and that hydraulic system is so that the roof opens up like the lid of a coffin – they have ashtrays shaped like coffins too inside.'

I'm rather shocked by this – it seems a little sick. I ask Gareth if people here find it funny.

'Not really, but it's the kind of thing that Western journalists like to come out and write about.'

Point taken.

We end up in the Downtown area. This is where most of the rebuilding of Beirut is taking place; this is what all those Western journalists like me mean by the city 'coming on'. It's a mammoth building task being overseen and undertaken by Solidère – a stakeholding company that is turning the heart of the city into a shining new temple of business and residential buildings. We get out of the car to have a wander and to go and look at the plans in the information office.

On paper Solidère looks like a marvellous institution – there are the stakeholders, the promises to keep residential areas close to the financial districts to breathe life into them at all times, the park areas, the archaeological digs and the rebuilding of the *souk*. Gareth agrees that it looks like an exemplary piece of citizenship in action. In reality though some people are critical – the building is taking too long, there is a smell of money changing hands and because of the convoluted nature of property law, particularly inheritance law, there are families caught up in a nightmare of paperwork and tenure rights with the management of Solidère.

You can't see any of this on the plans though. The original facades of the older buildings with their high windows and porticos are staying. There are squares and pedestrianised areas in Downtown which I'm sure the occasional driver will manage to reverse into anyway. And there are the original churches and mosques sitting within hymn-singing and praying distance of each other. I'm particularly pleased to see that the Holiday Inn remains with its semi-circular bar or restaurant still in the plans. The trees are now down on the ground where they should be.

'We should get to the Kiri Te Kanawa press conference,' says Gareth. 'See how the press works over here.'

It's a funny feeling to be on someone else's patch in a normal working day. I have no pressure, no piece to file before a deadline, no insightful questions to ask Dame Kiri in order to get a good headline and no press officer to keep on the right side of – Gareth has all of these things, and me in tow.

Press conferences are the flesh on the bones of your average news room's daily agenda. Everything from government policy to the latest beauty treatment gets a press conference. Invariably there's a top table of People Who Are Going to Tell You Things and a rabble of journalists squeezing into the rest of the room. If you're lucky you'll get a cup of coffee and if it's something to do with the entertainment industry you might get a biscuit. If you are Dame Kiri Te Kanawa launching a concert at the Bieteddine Festival you get a little more ...

The presser is in the Palm Beach Sofitel, a hotel just at the start of the Corniche. It has a smart 1950s feel to it with uniformed bell boys delivering trays of late breakfasts to whoever it is sleeping in behind the solid wood bedroom doors. The press conference is up on the top floor, in a room looking out over the sea. Kiri is up on stage – looking every inch the star and flanked by Robin Stapleton, her conductor, and the Director of the Festival – a very glamorous lady with perfectly coiffured nails, hair, teeth and make-up. I'm beginning to realise that Lebanese ladies are never knowingly underdressed. The usual opening welcome is given with details of the festival and then it is thrown open to the floor.

'Why don't you sing the opera in Arabic?' asks the first reporter.

Kiri is very polite. 'You should sing opera in the language it was written – it helps the music, but I would like to sing something in Arabic – if I could one day.'

'Why do you like to come here?'

'It is a beautiful setting at the festival, in the open air with the stars out at night and it's exciting to be in a country that is rebuilding itself and still has such a thirst for culture,' says the Dame.

And so it continues for about twenty minutes with some pretty unremarkable questions and answers. Kiri and Robin are pros – mixing exactly the right kind of 'we are very happy to be in your country' comments without distorting their own views too much.

One guy asks a question that perhaps could have done with some subbing:

'This is a personal kind of question. I have been introduced to the music in the big outdoor concerts here but then I went to the opera in New York where there was a much more intimate feel and so I am thinking why is it that you are performing in such a large way with thousands of people and you are feeling that you are creating the same atmosphere as in an opera house and is it that you feel you can do that because people are not so close to you?'

Tricky one that.

Robin replies that they want to attract people who may not go to an opera house but might like the music and want to see it in a more informal way.

Kiri chips in: 'Some opera too is very long – I love Wagner but I have too much to do in life. I have golf to play, and tennis and countries to travel to and life to get on with – I love Wagner to listen to but it's too long to go and see.'

People laughed loudly at that, amazed to hear a great dame of opera slagging off one of its great names.

The questions have dried up a bit and there's a long pause before the PR girl to the right of the stage announces that this press call is finished. Then the members of the press did a very strange thing. They applauded.

Out of all the press conferences or launches I have attended I have never seen the press pack clap at the end of their Q&As. In fact you are more likely to lose a limb in the crush to get out of the room as quickly as possible. Occasionally you find that you are given a head start. Joan Collins held a launch once for a fitness video she had made. It was at the BAFTA headquarters in London which is frightfully smart and very impressive.

It was obviously very exciting to be offered the opportunity to meet Joan. For months my shifts in the news room had only involved covering house fires in Blackheath and trying to extract more angst for Virginia Bottomley from the Tomlinson report into the NHS in London. Joan kept us all waiting quite a while and then we were allowed only about five minutes with her, all being carefully timed by her press secretary or flunky or whoever she was. Now Joan may be a national institution but she can be very rude.

I asked her what I thought was a pretty mundane question – and it was meant to be flattering. It went something along the lines of 'Joan – it's quite late in life to be making a fitness video – do you ever think, blimey, I'll just stop all of this work and settle down and knit booties for my grandchildren?'

Joan interpreted this as me saying You Are Very Old. I really hadn't meant it that way at all. She went ape shit. Absolutely doolally. She said some very very rude things that bordered on the gynaecological and then asked me to leave. Which I did. On getting back to GLR I found that her lawyer had phoned up demanding that I didn't do a piece about how old she was. I would have been perfectly entitled to do this in legal terms – Joan's age was out there in the public domain and could therefore be reported on by anyone. The stupid thing was that nothing had been further from my mind before Joan turned her full shoulder-padded power on me – but now he came to mention it ...

Anyway, we thought better of it and made a nice little piece for the *Drivetime* programme featuring some excerpts of Joan exercising against a tree in her video. Obviously because you couldn't see that it was a tree she was pushing up against it all sounded rather odd – just the occasional grunt and puff and Joan telling you to hold on to it. Young-sounding grunts and puffs of course.

'So what do you think of the press pack here?' asks Gareth, over a sun-dried tomato and olive tapenade on toast now being handed round by the nice Kiri people.

'Mmm ... measured, would that be a good word for it?'

'Measured? ... Yes that probably sums it up. It's a small city, we all know each other – you can't afford to upset people, you'd never work again.'

Gareth knows everyone in the room and there's a lot of nodding and 'good to see you' going on. And a couple of the other journalists come over and mention something about a trip down south the day before that is causing a lot of mirth. I ask Gareth what that's about – he says we should go and meet his mate Khaled Yacoub Oweis and that he'll explain.

Khaled works for Reuters in Beirut – meeting him is an opportunity to kill two birds with one stone. Not a phrase that you should use that often in this city. I've always wanted to see inside a Reuters office – it conjures up images of men in flak jackets rushing in to file pieces of world importance before lunch. We get the result of all that rushing around back in London at the BBC where the copy they send flashes up along the top of our screens throughout the day and night. 'The wires', as they are known, go way back to that time before radio when information was sent all over the world by telegraph. Today's wires come through those bands of fibre-optic cables under oceans and via satellites circling the earth – but it's the same instant news that counts as the result. What I see on the top of my computer screen usually goes something like:

URGENT – REUTERS – MIDEAST – PALESTINIAN MURDERS – 1040

A story like that is about exactly what you would imagine it to be. And if it's Reuters you pay attention to it. Some of the other press agencies don't have the same reputation for accuracy, fairness and balanced reporting. In fact there are quite a few that you have to check against another source before reading out on air. But Reuters carries with it decades of reputation for news – and if it's something important and Reuters has put it on the wire service then you can go right ahead and put it on air.

Reuters offices are in the heart of the new Downtown area and several street cafes in the clean, newly renovated squares in between the buildings are beginning to fill up with people doing a bit of promenading. The office is a bit of a disappointment though – there are only three people in there. Khaled, his boss and a colleague who leaves as soon as we arrive. There are a few computers, a very tidy office for the boss and a big board on the wall covered in figures. On closer examination this lists how many people have been killed so far this year.

There are no whirring machines – or banks of TV screens or people shouting 'Filing copy now!' Khaled explains that they haven't been in the office very long. If I'd come a few weeks later I could certainly have expected more – and probably a few more figures on the board. We must get hundreds of pieces a day filed from this very building in the heart of Beirut. Somewhere at the bottom of the copy I read back in London there must be a code that identifies which Reuters journalist has written the piece. I'm ashamed to say that I never bother to look, but Khaled must be the author of most of them.

Usually engaged on stories of political struggles, Israeli forces and militia attacks, Khaled had taken a day's breather from the world of internecine wars and been on a press trip to the south organised by the Ministry for Tourism the day before. Gareth said it hadn't gone entirely according to plan. Khaled has a rare claim to fame. Yesterday he threw up on a minister.

'Oh it was terrible – we had three buses and they were all slightly smelling of diesel fumes and we went on and on through the south – every village in the Occupied Zone and then some that weren't and we got on and off and on and off and everyone was feeling ill. I was not the only person to be sick but I was the first – just by the minister – they said that if I sat at the front of the bus then that would make my car sickness better but I just couldn't help it – so I puked.'

This is causing Gareth to laugh more heartily than I thought he could.

'Actually on the minister or just near him?'

'None of it went on him but he was well aware that I was puking – I was very close to him.'

The Minister for Tourism, though, had gained some respect throughout the day simply because he stuck around whereas some of the other dignitaries had got a little too dignitary-like and had phoned their drivers and demanded to be picked up half way through the day – presumably when village number 364 emerged on the horizon.

'What was the point of the trip?'

'To show how the south could have potential for development,' said Khaled.

I think that may have backfired.

'Will you write that you were sick?'

'No, I can't.'

Gareth is chuckling away. 'You could if you were working for the *Sun* back in Britain – then you'd also have a diagram showing the direction of the vomit, other great puking moments in history, ten things that the vomit had in it, followed by a list of twenty other words beginning with V.'

And you can see it now on page five can't you? It would make a superb story back home. I don't think Gareth will ever be out of work. There is a terrible black humour that some journalists possess which I guess gets them through either the monotony of work sometimes, or the horrible nature of it. Like the Australian journalist who set himself the mighty task of getting the phrase 'never say die, like a kamikaze pilot' into one of his pieces without it being cut out by a more sensitive editor. He did.

I thought that in among the mirth this might be a good time to ask about the thing that had been slightly bothering me ever since I had planned this trip down to the south. Apart from the possibility of puking up I was still a little concerned with that 'is there any possibility that we might get shot?' thing.

Both Khaled and Gareth shake their heads.

'No, not now,' says Gareth. 'It might have been different before the Israeli withdrawal but it's really very safe in the south now. However, there are still landmines around.'

So I had it on good authority, from two of the best journalists in Beirut. I was going to have to sit on my feeble fears and stop being such a wuss. I left Khaled to his copy and Gareth to his piece on Dame Kiri and walked back along the dusty road to the hotel.

*

Now to say that the temperature had soared already would (a) be a cliché and (b) could never convey to you just how hot I was feeling as we bumped and jerked our way through the morning traffic of Beirut.

It's always tedious to read books where people complain about the heat because you are bound to be reading this in some festeringly cold environment where the idea of me being a little warm around the edges is positively appealing. I don't think there are many flaws in the human body – apart from not being able to pick spots on the small of your back – but my one teeny weeny criticism would be that it is absolutely impossible to remember what feeling cool is like when you are roasting and vice versa. I hope some scientist is working hard to put this right with the help of genomes and a lot of coloured pens. Suffice to say that I knew things were only going to get hotter – and it was simply a case of grinning and bearing it.

I also realised that I hadn't seen anything yet in terms of Lebanese driving skills. The rush hour was quite spectacular and as we fought through the mayhem of junctions with no traffic lights and six exits we eventually made it to the motorway, three lanes of easy cruising. The same luggage trundlers who show no care or concern for other airport users were in these cars. Several drivers were cruising along with their warning lights on for no apparent reason. Maybe they were warning other drivers that they were crapper at this than the rest. There is no fast, medium or slow lane and we passed several drivers who were sitting right in the middle of lanes.

'You see,' mutters Gareth, 'people don't really bother with driving lessons here – a lot of drivers think that you're meant to use the white lines as a guide to drive straight down the middle of the road ...'

That is quite a mind-boggling interpretation of one of the most basic international aspects of driving. How can you survive for more than a couple of days thinking that you have to drive down the middle of the white lines? How can you not notice that most other people don't? The ramifications for driving down a simple two-way street if someone else has the same idea are just terrifying.

The cars seem to come in two categories: the first are stuck together with bits of hope and string and have undertaken their own motoring industry mergers; it's not unusual to see a BMW with a Mercedes bumper and a Nissan bonnet. Category two is the top of the range jeep or limo. Gareth's is closer to category one.

'Does anyone bother with insurance?'

'Nope – about 80 per cent don't have it, so even if you do it's not going to be that useful.'

I had nothing to fear from stray bullets, I was going to die in a white line pile up. If the bad driving didn't get me I'd end up choking on diesel fumes in a government bus. This was making me feel so much better.

We were heading for Sour, a town on the coast where Gareth said we could stop for breakfast in the *souk*. He added that it was probably best not to get there too early because of all the animals being slaughtered by the butchers in the market. I just nodded my head to this and tried to angle the air vent a little further in my direction.

Gareth's considerable knowledge about all things Lebanese didn't stop at the suburbs of Beirut. There was little he didn't know about all the towns we passed through along the way. He talked about the motorcycle ban in one which was brought in because of too many drive-by shootings, the massacre of four judges in another, which militia strongmen had been born where, the Phoenician antecedents of another.

The countryside moved from grim and scrawny on the outskirts of Beirut to pale and pretty a few miles south. Pale because the heat had taken away much of the green vegetation and pretty because the Mediterranean was sparkling away to our right. The towns we passed through had seen better days but, like Beirut, the building work was everywhere – it was hard to tell what was coming up or going down.

We got to Sour with plenty of time to spare and parked up and wandered towards the *souk*. The old stone houses and patched-up buildings made Sour feel a little like an old French port that had seen better days. There were wonky signs to hotels that presumably struggled to attract the international beach set these days. It must have been about 35 degrees outside by now but the *souk*, built deliberately with its tiny passages to keep out the light, was a good deal cooler at about 34 degrees.

Spice stalls, rolls of material and butchers squeezed in next door to each other. Gareth knew a little cafe somewhere at the back where they served a mean *fuul* – a bean-based North African dish served like dahl, but with flat bread and fresh mint instead of the nan and the pickles that people take too much of and regret. It did look lovely but unfortunately I just couldn't. I was so bloody hot my internal organs felt like they were turning into a fry up. I had this horrible feeling that my kidneys had just devilled themselves. I had to sit there nursing a cold carbonated vegetable extract drink watching two big bowls of the stuff disappear into

Gareth Smyth Tours. Maybe that was the secret to his brainpower.

He had timed breakfast just right in terms of smell and views from the cafe. The massacre of the animals had taken place some time ago, judging by the little amounts of meat left on the massive carcasses hanging in the butchers' shops. I apologise to vegetarians for the following comment but it must be a much better way to shop for your meats – to be able to have a good look at the whole cow and then say to the butcher, 'Don't like the look of that rump today, could you just slice a bit off so I can have a look at the next layer down?' You do it in a box of Milk Tray don't you?

I still had no idea what to expect from the radio station, which Gareth said we should now be able to pick up on the car radio. I knew that it had been set up for the Irish troops among the peacekeeping force, by 2FM, the home station in Dublin which had paid for the studio and sent out the CDs. And that its main aim was to provide a bit of light relief and something tangible from home for the soldiers stationed out here.

The Irish Battalion are part of Unifil – a UN force which has the remit of monitoring and overseeing the Israeli withdrawal from Southern Lebanon. In fact it has a UN resolution passed in 1978, Number 425, which says that it can and will confirm Israeli withdrawal, restore international peace and security and assist the Lebanese government in extending its authority in the area. As you can tell from the 'Best Before' date of that resolution they have been quite busy over the past twenty years trying to fulfil the remit.

Gareth said he had been very impressed when he first went to meet the soldiers and the article he had written in the *Financial Times* was very moving – conjuring up the feelings of homesickness that you must get, even if you are the most hardened career soldier. Gareth said we'd probably be invited to take a trip out around some of the villages that were in the UN's area of patrol, which he promised would be an experience not easily forgotten.

I had a picture in my head of what the Occupied Zone would look like. That was formed from watching hundreds of pieces on television where someone with expert knowledge pointed behind him to the Golan Heights or the West Bank or East Jerusalem while telling me something tragic. To be honest it all looked pretty much the same. Most of those pieces begun with a sentence like 'The peace process hit another stumbling block today ...' and ended with something like 'Negotiations continue'.

Driving out of Sour we were only about twenty minutes away from Camp Shamrock and we started to climb up into the hills to get there. The UN base at Tibnin is one of many in the area. As well as the Irish battalion there is one from Fiji, from Ghana and from Nepal and we passed a quite steady stream of trucks and jeeps coming down the hill towards us – all white with the pale blue UN insignia flying above them.

We stopped at Qana, the scene of one of the worst atrocities in the south. In April 1996 Israel launched Operation Grapes of Wrath – a combination of land and air attacks aimed primarily at Hezbollah but with terrible consequences. As the pounding of the south intensified, civilians in the village of Qana sought refuge in the UN base there. Israel shelled the base and over a hundred local people were killed. A UN report into the attack reached the conclusion that the base had been deliberately targeted. Israel has always denied this.

Just outside where the base was there is now a monument built in memory of those who died. Long coffin-like structures stretch across a forecourt, each with a photograph of the victims. Some are children snapped in those happy-family photos that should be part of a life in an album that has many more pages to fill. Because of the recent withdrawal there is a tank parked outside the monument, an Israeli tank left abandoned in the haste to get back to the other side of the border and a family who arrived just after us are taking photographs of themselves in victorious poses on top of it.

'Tanks are everywhere now in the villages. They've been parked there as a kind of symbol that the Israelis have gone,' says Gareth.

We had passed a huge banner on the road earlier, strung across the front of a burnt-out army jeep. The banner said 'Thanks to Hezbollah!'

'Who would have put that banner up? The local villagers?' I ask Gareth.

'No, probably Hezbollah themselves. They are quite good at getting their point across.'

We get back in the car for the final climb to Camp Shamrock. The villages around Tibnin are a strange combination of hard-up people growing tobacco for what is not much of a living, and then huge socking great palaces and country mansions being built on the hilltops between them. Now, by huge I mean monstrous – enormous double staircases grandly going up towards three- or four-storey buildings with porticoes and turrets. These are the country houses of wealthy Lebanese. One that we could see in the distance appeared to have two driveways, four east wings and the kind of outbuildings that would class as a whole suburb in Milton Keynes. It seemed a strange part of the world to escape to at the weekends for a bit of peace and quiet. Gareth said that you'd regularly have heard mortars and gunfire coming from the same hills up until six weeks ago.

Camp Shamrock signposts itself with a simple white-painted board at a crossroads just past a strip of shops in Tibnin. We drive through the barrier and park up next to two white buildings.

'That's the radio station – that one on the left,' said Gareth.

And there it is – no more than 12 foot by 10, one padlock on the door and a stencil in red saying 2FM. As ever Gareth is right. It is a hut, and today it is a very hot hut.

We have arranged to meet Commandant Joseph McDonagh, the UN Battalion's Military Information Officer, and have been told to report to the DCO's office. I am not a regular at army camps and bases so I have little comparison to make between the stationing of the 87th Irish Battalion and any other military posting, but Camp Shamrock seems small. There are a couple of lines of white prefabs looking out over a valley with trucks and Armoured People Carriers doing some precision parking in various lots. A lot of men – and the occasional woman – are walking round in uniforms that would keep them nice and warm through an Irish winter. And there are lots of signposts using acronyms so beloved of armies and governments and local councils.

Commandant Joe McDonagh is a softly spoken Irish soldier with quite a bushy military moustache and a very welcoming manner.

'Hot today, isn't it?' he comments. I think he's just being kind to this sweaty crumpled thing that has turned up on his base.

'Oh we were like that too when we first got here – the jetlag and the heat – you think you'll never get used to it, but you do.'

He offers us coffee. I could have done with a Belgian water cannon.

We have a quick cup on the balcony of the officers' mess – just a glimpse inside reveals a nice rug, a couple of pictures of Irish beach scenes on the walls and the kind of nicely turned out furniture that your granny's house might have.

Commandant McDonagh is going to give me a briefing first about the current situation in the former Occupied Zone before we have a spot of lunch, visit the radio station and then head off round a bit of the territory to see what is what. Or what is shot.

Unlike the disappointment of Reuters offices, this briefing is everything you hope an army briefing will be. It takes place in the conference room – another white prefab – and involves the use of some technical display machinery, two huge maps and the Commandant has one of those long pointy sticks that he uses to show us what he is talking about. The acronyms are out in force. IDF (Israeli Defence Force), DFF (de facto force), SLA (South Lebanese Army). I hope he won't mind if I do a bit of precis-ing.

In the weeks leading up to the Israeli withdrawal the UN had noticed that the SLA – part of the de facto force, i.e. the invading forces in the Occupied Zone had become increasingly nervous. The UN had recorded far more gunfire and attacks than had previously been happening. For example in their reports of shots being fired in the UN area they had recorded 306 in March, 359 in April and a massive 521 in May. Hezbollah, the self-styled militia trying to get rid of the de facto forces, had been stealing a march on them. But then the extraordinary started happening – members of the SLA began to surrender to whoever they first came across, be it the Lebanese army or indeed Hezbollah. And on 22 May, realising that things were going a bit pear-shaped, the Israeli forces began to withdraw.

Now, overseeing a withdrawal of an army the size and force of Israel, with an accompanying SLA force too, is no mean feat. The Commandant said they were expecting many casualties. Think about it, in an area where some of the Muslim villages had been torn to smithereens and pasted with mortars, where many people had been killed, where a mass grave had been found – the knowledge that the enemy is on the move and is retreating would make many people shout and holler and perhaps try to vent years of frustration. But as the Israelis left their positions and compounds, local people walked calmly down the roads to witness the troops leaving. Men and women, not carrying arms but watching an enemy force simply turn tail and leave their positions.

'No one had anticipated that the situation and transition would be so bloodless,' says the Commandant.

He points to a dot on the map – a village called Tiri.

'Tiri had had a population of thousands – but that had fallen to 72, only the old people had stayed. It had been surrounded by SLA positions – but since 22 May the villagers have started to return. The local population is now very positive, the forthcoming elections are now being focused on by Hezbollah – the water pipes are being put in, the schools will open in September.'

He said he'd take us there after lunch and that concluded the briefing.

When a commandant tells you the timetable of events for your day, you don't tend to argue. Next on the list is the visit to the radio station so we plod slowly up the hill to the next white hut. This is radio in the wilderness. The door is shut and the Commandant says they have probably just left a CD on to play while the DJs have their lunch so he runs back down the hill to go and find the man in charge.

Gareth and I go and sit in the shade and the breeze on a bench in the Garden of Remembrance. This is the where the memorials are to the men who have lost their lives in Southern Lebanon during their postings as UN peacekeepers. One soldier was only 21. It's a tiny garden really – no more than 20 feet across – and if you sit on the bench you have your back to the camp and are looking out over the vast valley which counts as the UN patrol area. It could be a very beautiful view – I can see why the rich Lebanese want to build their weekend mansions here. Gareth says the hills are breathtaking when it's not so hot and dry and the rain brings all the vegetation back to life. They're sweeping hills not jagged mountains – a little like the west coast of Scotland up around Ullapool. Good for weekend mansions, but even better for vantage points in a guerrilla war.

A burly smiling man arrives and introduces himself as Signals Platoon Sergeant Paul Todd – the man in charge of running 2FM's most regional studio. He has a cheeky look in his eyes and the same sandblasted Celtic skin that the rest of the battalion are sporting. Few nationalities can have a less suitable skin type for a posting in the roasty toasty heat of the Lebanon. As we are all dripping with sweat – obviously I could at this point pretend that I was simply perspiring slightly but I wasn't, I was drenched – I suggest that we stay under the shade of the trees in the garden to chat amicably about how he got to be a DJ in the middle of a war zone. This is the army after all – no time for idle chit chat.

'Well, how did it all start you mean? There used to be a radio station out here called Radio Scorpion and that was the Dutch station. When the Dutch troops pulled out there was nothing left here for Unifil Troops so 2FM back in Ireland agreed to sponsor the radio station. They sent out all the discs, the equipment and the desks and that's how it started really – that was back with the 72nd Battalion … back in the old Camp

Shamrock. But when this place was built for the 78th battalion it all moved up here and this is what we have now.'

'And it's all in that hut over there?' I ask.

'Oh yes – that is our station. It's a hut ... you're right, just a hut. It's got a dividing wall inside with a door into the studio and it's got carpets on the walls to try and keep the sound in. It used to have egg boxes on the roof to try to make it soundproof.'

With a big smile on his face Paul explains that things have got a lot more technical now and they have foam on the walls instead of the egg boxes.

'We've actually done a bit of a revamp with the 87th Battalion because Gerry Ryan – a big famous DJ with 2FM back home – was coming out to do a radio show. Yes we've revamped it a bit – it's looking pretty good now.'

I ask Paul if he is the main DJ, Camp Shamrock's equivalent of Gerry Ryan.

'No, not really I do about two hours a week, maybe more maybe less ... In all we do about three hours a day as an opt out from the 2FM service, maybe between six and eight every evening someone does a show. Johnny Murray – another bloke from signals – he does a radio show. You've a fellow Paul as well and then there's the girls Martina and Joanne – they all come up and do some stuff. We might do something between one and three at lunchtime too – just playing some music.'

Given the larger job that everyone is doing here it's not like you can have a fixed list of shows. Paul says sometimes he might phone someone up and say he can't make it that night and would they mind doing a couple of hours.

'But it's just messing,' he says. 'It's a good laugh. Earlier on we were slagging off a few people ... we have a phone in there, and I was just phoning up Transport and I put them live on air and ask them some stupid questions – and they don't know that they're live on air – anything to have a bit of fun.'

Looking out over the harsh scrub of the hills I can see his point. Although there is no gunfire or shelling for the moment, the picture is pretty bleak. There can't be too many ways you can let off steam and have some fun in a camp in the middle of Southern Lebanon. The dangers of the job that they are doing lie in the names on the headstones only a couple of feet away from us.

I say that it can't be easy knowing that what is being broadcast to all your mates in the next-door camp is also going out to the local villagers and the Israeli and Hezbollah fighters you are trying to keep the peace between.

'Sure, we'd never say anything bad about religion or politics on air but you do get fellas cursing from time to time – but if they do say something rude we tell them that they're on air – it usually results in them just hanging up the phone.'

Well, it works for Steve Penk and Chris Moyles.

'And can you play whatever you like – in terms of you own music?' I ask Paul.

'Well, we get stuff sent out from Dublin all the time – about 60 CDs last time round – most fellas doing the show have their own type of music, though, and they'll like playing a particular thing. I'm a David Gray fan myself – avid David Gray fan, I've got *White Ladder* here with me ...'

White Ladder is David Gray's latest album and it's a peach. I bought it back in London where Gray's soft and slightly gritty ballads made me think of rainy days and dark nights in windswept Ireland. Maybe it makes Paul think the same things.

Camp Shamrock is the only camp out here to have its own station – although there are other UN forces in the region, but it seems to work in a pretty caring sharing kind of a way.

'It's not just an Irish battalion thing – other companies will phone up and ask if they can come up and have a go every once in a while. They love it because if B company come in they'll start slagging off C company and then C company will come in and have a go back ... It's just a bit of fun.'

Paul can't seem to say that enough – that it's just a bit of fun. I ask him if it's true that quite a few of the local people around Tibnin listen to it and that there's a woman in one of the villages who speaks English now with a heavy Cork accent. This is a story taken from Gareth's enormous range of Lebanese anecdotes.

Paul laughs. 'I don't know how many people listen to it – we have no way of knowing really. As for Irish accents, we haven't heard too many of them. Most of the output is dedications, stuff for people on the camp and other camps. It's just a way to let go a little bit...'

By this time we have all stopped sweating like that woman in the Sure ads. Incidentally, why did she always want to keep a tick section on her back dry but not her underarms? Didn't you find that a little odd?

Paul offers to show me round his hut which is now unlocked. Inside it is as small as it looks from the outside. It's one room divided by a partition – behind the partition is the studio part of the station and what little room there is left is basically enough for a couple of people to stand up in.

Joanne Douglas is on air at the moment, a blonde girl in uniform who is standing up at the desk putting a CD in the stack. The hut is indeed carpeted to maximum effect – a nice beige all wool twist I'd say. As well as sound insulation it is heat insulation too – which today is rather unnecessary. The station's studio is no more than a mixing desk with a dozen faders on it, a CD stack beside it and floor-to-ceiling shelves full of discs. Natalie Imbruglia is playing out. Joanne is a softly spoken girl who admits that she was very nervous the first time she played Miss DJ.

'It's worse, you know, because it's all your friends who're listening ... the first time I did it I was so nervous I wouldn't talk – I just couldn't – I just played the CDs one after the other.'

I don't know if I was expecting anything different – did I think that these men and women would be smooth-talking presenters hiding behind a uniform? I don't think I did. I think I imagined the station to be a little bigger – and perhaps housed in a building more likely to withstand gunfire and shelling, but Paul and Joanne are exactly the kind of people I thought would be manning the decks. This has to be one of the only stations left in the world where ratings and focus groups and management count for absolutely nothing. I suppose this is the closest thing you'll get these days to radio at its purest form. It is quite simply a way to amplify and carry sounds being made by people who want other people to hear it. No agenda, nothing to sell, no ambitions to be realised. Just good tunes and some banter in a wilderness. Nothing more complicated than that.

I ask Joanne what's been on the airwaves of Camp Shamrock's 2FM today.

'Well we came on air about nine this morning and finished about twelve. This morning we got about 15 to 20 calls – they all want requests. They phone up from the different posts across there,' she points out to the valley and the hills outside the camp, 'and some from the other camps too.'

The Lighthouse Family record that is now on is coming to an end. Although it's her show, Paul suggests that I might like to do the next link. I can hardly say no – but God, I wish I had done. Bear in mind that I am the only supposedly professional broadcaster in Camp Shamrock today. I think I said something appallingly obvious like:

'This is Fi Glover from BBC Radio, thanking everyone here for their warm hospitality today – and it certainly has been warm, hasn't it?'

I said this in a cheesy, patronising and stupidly bouncy voice. What a stunning observation that must have seemed to the men and women who have been patrolling this sunbaked region on many tours of duty. Paul looked at me as if to say 'and that's it, is it?'

We stay to listen to a couple more songs being played out. There isn't an awful lot to do while this is happening. There's a note on the wall, or rather the carpet, that catches my eye. It lists the rules and regulations of the station. Point 3 goes like this:

'Under no circumstances will DJs broadcast music that might cause offence to members of UNIFIL or the local communities of Southern Lebanon. DJs will not use offensive language or engage in 'slagging matches' on air or discredit IRISHBATT in any way.'

Given what Paul had said earlier about the mickey-taking that goes on I think that is one rule the army is not enforcing very strongly.

Point 4 says that: 'If for any reason a DJ is unable to report for a show as scheduled he/she will arrange a replacement and inform the Station Manager who will make the key available to the replacement DJ.'

'Unable to report for a show' back home would mean the usual excuses of food poisoning, i.e. a hangover or the more outlandish 'my flatmate has locked me in'. Here it would be emergency calls to duty and patrols following mortar bombardments. After that it must be great to go and sit in a hut and play some tunes and have a bit of a laugh and just escape for a couple of hours from the heat and politics and the mayhem of the region.

It struck me that this is radio inside out. For me – in my travels – radio has been about getting into a new place, about finding my feet in a foreign environment. It's been a way of taking a part of someone else's culture and gatecrashing their lifestyle. But here it's about bringing a little piece of regular life to your irregularities. When the station isn't on air and pumping out Paul's David Gray collection it broadcasts 2FM's output from Dublin. It's a soundtrack from home – with its travel updates and news and GAA scores. So if you're sitting in a post on one of the far off hills, scanning the distance for trouble, you can tune in to a little piece of normality and wind up your mates.

'What else can you do to switch off on the camp?' I ask Paul as we walk back down the hill, having left Joanne to her links and album tracks.

'Well, we have a band here – they do some covers and stuff.'

'What are they called?'

'H5,' he says cheerily.

'It sounds a little like a haemorrhoid cream – what does it stand for?'

Paul gives me one of his cheeky looks. 'It's the code in the army we use for going deaf.'

If Paul ever leaves the army then he should think very seriously about pursuing a career in professional broadcasting. I'd listen.

As we drive out of the camp, Commandant McDonagh points across to the hills and to the two wart-like bumps on the horizon. Those were the SLA positions, now lying empty but probably surrounded by minefields. A position isn't just a point on the map; these are stalwart concrete bunkers built to withstand mortar attacks and with highly complex systems of communications – some of them are a couple of floors deep. It's quite possible that given their proximity to Camp Shamrock the South Lebanese Army could have spent their days listening into Paul and the other soldiers on 2FM. I wonder if they ever did. Now there is no one from the SLA left to ask.

We drive past one house that is so badly riddled with bullet holes that it looks like it's got negative pebble dashing.

'It's called The Target House,' says the Commandant. 'It got shot from both sides.'

I'm quite tempted to ask the Commandant if we can put 2FM on the radio but manage to stop myself just in time as obviously he needs the radio for a slightly more important form of contact – the VHF talkback service keeping him in touch with the base.

Gareth asks him if they have to be careful about getting the balance right between work and play on the camp.

The Commandant pauses for a few moments. 'Yes – it's a very careful balance. People have to have time away from work. You have to out here but then we are here to work. You can't afford to be careless.'

'What difference does the radio station make?' says Gareth.

'A good one. For a start we can hear the news from back home every day and the music and the sports. It's good to have something constant out here,' he says, looking around.

We turn off the main road to bump into Tiri. It takes some powers of the imagination to try to envisage how it would have been before the occupation. This makes Beirut's collapsed buildings look positively upright. Whole houses have been pasted by shelling and are just mounds of bricks with the odd curtain or bedstead sticking out. Second floors have fallen into first floors and it's impossible to work out how many floors some of the houses ever had. There's rubble and rubbish everywhere – cars and walls and anything that could be used as a target. A couple of children are playing in front of a house that is still just about standing.

'That's incredible – to see children back here,' says Gareth. He has visited Tiri a few times and described it as a ghost town before. All the families had moved away, leaving only the old people who refused to go. Commandant McDonagh says that the place was completely surrounded by SLA forces to the point at which one taxi was allowed to visit the village once a week to bring them supplies. He says it wasn't exactly the most competitive means of shopping.

'The old people here were so weak and frail that when they had bodies to bury we had to come and dig the graves for them.'

The Commandant explains that if someone from the village had died elsewhere, probably in exile, their family would still want their body to be buried back in the family plots. So it would be left to the old and infirm villagers who had stayed to try to give this final dignity to their former neighbours or family. In the winter the ground would be so hard that digging graves would be beyond the strength of even healthy youngsters – it was an impossible task for the elderly left here, so the boys from Camp Shamrock would do it for them. All this only two hours away from a Kiri Te Kanawa concert.

There's a battered old Merc struggling up the street towards us and an old man and a younger guy get out and come over to the UN jeep.

'This is the Mukhtar,' says the Commandant. A Mukhtar is a local mayor-type figure – or probably more akin to a village elder.

There's a lot of hand shaking and smiles between all the men and I offer my hand to the Mukhtar too. He looks surprised. Gareth whispers that as a woman I'm not supposed to shake hands with men. The Mukhtar touches my hand lightly and gives me a grin. He says something to the Commandant who, with a bit of nodding and repeating, tells me and Gareth that they have asked us for tea. We leave the jeep and walk up to a large house which does still have a roof and all four walls, but only just. We're ushered on to the balcony to sit on plastic chairs. A couple of children are playing downstairs and come up and giggle at us.

The younger guy is called Nagi. The Commandant explains that he is one of the local Hezbollah leaders. I'd say he's in his late thirties, dressed in smart jeans and checked shirt and has a mobile phone dangling from his belt. He says that his English isn't good. In fact it's very impressive. He has an intense look about him – and the most extraordinary brown and gold flecked eyes. He tells us that he's been away for a long time – he left the village in 1985 to take his family to Beirut.

'When did you come back?' I ask him.

He gives me a very direct look and says very slowly 'May – twenty-three.' He repeats it even slower, 'May – twenty – three.'

There is a reason why this is an important date – it means that he came back at the first available opportunity, less than 24 hours after the Israeli withdrawal on the 22nd. One of the first people he saw when he came back to Tiri was the Commandant.

'I saw you then – on May twenty-three – we came back on bikes, on May twenty-two we were over there,' he points to the hills in the distance, 'and on May twenty-three we come back.'

So that was nearly fifteen years away from home. I try to ask him if he had visited or come back to stay at all during that time. He looks puzzled at this, and tries to answer in faltering English. The Commandant picks up and answers for him. He's met Nagi before, when they had an interpreter with them, so he knows his story anyway. He says that Nagi may have been around in the area – fighting in the hills – but that he wouldn't have been able to spend time in Tiri because of the way it had been surrounded. Nagi is nodding at all of this. He says that the Mukhtar hadn't ever seen his grandchildren until after 23 May when they came back to the village.

He talks to the Commandant. 'We need water here – can you get that?'

The Commandant gets out his mobile phone right away and sorts it out – the UN troops can bring water in on lorries for the villagers until the pipes can be laid and reconnected. They talk about mines too – about how the village is probably surrounded by them. Although the Israeli forces must hand over maps of the minefields they have laid, that doesn't mean that it is an easy problem to solve. There could be thousands of them in the fields around and as no crops have been sown for years the true extent of the problem is hard to quantify. People have already found out the hard way.

'It's not just the mines,' says the Commandant. 'Cluster bombs were dropped too. You know what cluster bombs are – they're dropped from the air but designed to go off when trodden on in the ground. You can't provide a map of them.'

The tea is served in tiny glasses with mounds of sugar piled into them. The children who I'd say are between five and seven years old are still giggling at us – the girl, in perfect English, asks me how old I am.

'I'm thirty,' I say. She looks puzzled so I draw it in figures on the table. She giggles some more. I don't think she was puzzled by not understanding what I was saying – I think it's because I look about 43 today in my crumpled sweaty state. Not exactly a shining example of an easy-going life lived in the West. I ask Nagi if she is his daughter – he says no, his family are still in Beirut and he will wait a while before bringing them back here. His children have never been to the village – it will be strange for them to come.

He tells us that he has been studying computers while in Beirut so that he can set up Hezbollah.com. I made that last detail up. But what a strange combination of lives he must have led over the past twenty years – a fighter in exile, learning computer skills in a city only two hours away from a home that he couldn't come back to, a home that his children know nothing about.

Nagi is obviously a highly intelligent man – the Commandant says that he has now swapped fighting for a role in Hezbollah politics. I can't help wondering if he has ever killed anyone – or how many people he has killed. He still has the scars of his previous profession – he was hit in the shoulder by a device called a Flechette. Although this may sound like the kind of name you'd give to a pair of American tan tights, it's a particularly nasty tool of war – a nail bomb that explodes with sharp pins and is designed specifically to hurt foot soldiers. Nagi shows Gareth a scar where one of those pins went right through his shoulder.

It's a bit of a conversation stopper. We sit in silence for a while.

The Commandant asks about one of the boys that he knew from the village before – a guy called Jimmy whom he knew when he was 14 or 15. He says that Jimmy spent so much time with the Irish Battalion that he really did speak English with a very strong Cork accent. Nagi tells him that Jimmy married a Russian girl and that he's living in one of the other villages. His accent must be very interesting now.

Time is ticking on for us and after one last mini cup of tea we say goodbye. I wish Nagi good luck – he wishes me the same. I remember not to shake his hand. He strikes me as a man who is going to go far. I wonder if the next time I see him will be on television as a spokesman for Hezbollah. Unfortunately the piece may still end with some TV journalist saying 'negotiations continue', because even though we've just spent a peaceful hour sipping tea on his balcony, that is no guarantee that peace has truly arrived.

Back behind the fences of Camp Shamrock Gareth and I have one last thing that we want to see before we head off to visit the Israeli border. It's an explanation of the various munitions found in the area over the years. Commandant John Phelan is a man who knows his weaponry and in another of the huts on the camp he talks us through the various bits of war that have been found in the battalion's area.

There are all kinds of bullets and mortars, ranging from one the size of a large marrow to one that stands about two feet tall. There's a Katyusha which sounds like a production from the Russian Ballet but is one of the more powerful and prolific missiles you can launch on land. There's also a box of pins that are the contents of a Flechette. If you imagine a tack about an inch long that you'd use to hang pictures on you'd not be far wrong. Light enough to fly though the air and sharp enough to go through someone's shoulder – or worse.

The most horrifying though is the 'disguised rock bomb'. This is a piece of plastic or polystyrene that has been moulded into the shape of a rock and painted to the same light colour as the rocks that lie all over the land here. Inside it would be packed with an explosive device covered with nuts and bolts so that when the detonator went off, maximum damage would be done to personnel in the area. It's dangerously realistic. You would never be able to tell, even if you were standing next to it, that it was a bomb and not a rock. It must have been designed by a very clever, very artistic person. The world of musical set design would welcome a talent like that. What a shame whoever it was chose to go into weapons of war instead.

Gareth and I have to go if we are to take in the Israeli border before heading back to Beirut. I also want to listen to a bit more of 2FM along the way. The Commandant says he has something for us and rushes off into the office while we walk slowly up the hill to where we left the car. It's still hot – although the frying-pan sensation in my kidneys is starting to go. Maybe I am getting used to it. Gareth is poring over a map trying to work out the best way to get a glimpse of Israel and the Commandant comes back with a glossy brochure for me and a shamrock pin as a little memento of my day out in Tibnin.

The brochure shows where the other Irish battalions are stationed under the auspices of the UN. Cambodia. El Salvador, Yugoslavia, Afghanistan, Pakistan – all over. This is just a little dot on the big map. It also says that Ireland is the sixth largest contributor of troops to the UN peacekeeping mission. I can't help thinking that for such a small country that is a big chunk to give.

Gareth had suggested we take a different route back to Beirut and visit the Fatima gate on the Israeli border along the way. He says that even though the peace is still fragile people are visiting it like a tourist spot – they're chucking the odd stone at the Israeli border control and buying celebratory key fobs with one of the Hezbollah leaders on it.

2FM's afternoon DJ is indulging in some soft sounds as the barrier at the camp gates goes down behind us and the Commandant waves us goodbye. Tears for Fears is fading into Robert Palmer's 'Addicted to Love' as we head out on the road to Shaqra. If you closed your eyes and heard only that mix you could be tuning into any station anywhere in the world. It's a pretty slick segue too. Slicker than Gareth's map which says Shaqra is to the left of the camp. According to the road sign it's back the way we came. We stop at a UN checkpoint and ask one of the Irish soldiers:

'We're listening to your station,' says Gareth while the soldier looks at our map.

'And so you are,' he replies in an Irish lilt as if it's the most natural thing in the world for two pale-skinned civvies to be driving along, getting lost and listening to a bit of 2FM in the afternoon. He takes one look at our map and suggests that we might like to have a look at his. It is completely different to ours but obviously more correct so we take his advice and head right, right again in front of the UN base and left somewhere along that road.

2FM zooms in and out a bit but keeps going, even though we are now a few miles away from the camp. It's not Paul on air now but one of the other DJs.

'It'll be Pixie and Dixie on after five … and just a reminder that H5 are playing in C company tomorrow night. We'd like to see as many of you as possible – or as many of you as are let out. Now we're going to take it down a little bit – with Foreigner:'

I've been waiting for a girl like you
To come into my life.

We stop for a few minutes trying to work out if this is Shaqra, with the help of some deft arm – waving from a helpful resident. Just outside the village is another Israeli tank, this one with a massive cardboard cutout of the Ayatollah on top. It is a rare photo opportunity – so we take a couple of snaps of each other standing in front of it. By the time we get back in the car Gerry Rafferty is on the turntable. We're leaving the range of 2FM still in 90-degree heat with craters from mortar attacks appearing every so often by the side of the road and collapsed houses all along the way and there is that breezy saxophone opener and Gerry crackling out:

> *Winding your way down on Baker Street*
> *Hisssss ... dead on your feet*
> *Well another crazy day ... whrrrrrrr*
> *Drink the night away*
> *And forget about everything...*

Whenever I hear that song I always used to picture some guy driving down Baker Street in a soft top on a sunny London day, past the hotel that plays on the Sherlock Holmes connection and into the traffic jam that invariably lives outside Selfridges. And now I'll always have a completely different personal video to go with the song – one that involves a cardboard Ayatollah on top of a tank. It'll be hard to explain to anyone else.

The smooth tunes continue until we dip down behind the first small mountainous range that had loomed on the horizon from Camp Shamrock. Gentle smooth tunes to loll away an afternoon with. The kind of tunes that you get on an easy-listening station, punctuated by a velvet-tongued host who'd let you know just how many more 'great songs in a row' were coming up. The kind of songs that you would find you knew all the words to. And here we were in this harsh bullet-ridden no man's land, where you couldn't even go for a walk at the end of a long day on patrol – just in case the landmines get you or the rock you brush against is a carefully disguised bomb.

How much would some decent tunes help you through the day here? Enormously I imagine. That's what I mean about radio being like an air freshener – and I mean one of the decent ones, not the Spring Fresh

Glacial Chemical Scent ones. It can perk your mood up just by being there. When you hear the opening bars of Van Morrison's 'Bright Side of the Road' or Stevie Wonder's 'Superstition', or The Verve's 'Bittersweet Symphony' – doesn't it lift you just a bit? Don't you reach for the dial and yank it and crank it? I wonder if David Gray sounds any different here. I'll never know. The radio is now just a sea of white noise. Gareth switches it off.

My tour guide and I have got to that slightly easier stage of not having to talk to each other all the time, so we drive in rarely punctuated silence towards the Israeli border. I can see what Gareth means about the countryside being beautiful. The closer you get to the border, the lusher it becomes. The wire fence lets you know when you have arrived. Just the other side in Israel are well-tended orchards and farms. We pass the spot where a driver for a BBC crew was killed only weeks earlier by shellfire from the other side. It makes me realise that after all my worrying I haven't been scared at all today.

Gareth is, again, right about the Fatima gate – there really is a man with a table who is selling key fobs of people who are big in Hezbollah. The border tower itself on the gate looks empty although there may well have been an Israeli guard inside. A few families have come to sightsee. The huge wire fence looks pointless with no one behind it. There's a burnt-out car parked up on our side. I've probably seen this as a background to a hundred pieces from TV journalists – I had an image of shots being fired and kids running scared stapled to my mind.

'Where are you off to next – after this?' asks Gareth.

God, I hadn't thought about my next step at all for the last few days. Where on earth was I going?

I'd drawn out a bit of a map round the States on my monogrammed hotel stationery at the Phoenicia which included New York, Las Vegas and Chicago. I suppose I could try to get an audience with Howard Stern in New York. But I wasn't sure that meeting him was going to prove that much about the personal joys of local radio.

Vegas was a must, in order to meet the man with the paranormal phone in show, Art Bell. Chicago was a personal luxury, to meet up with a couple I'd got friendly with years ago when I first went to the Windy City. But then there was a DJ in Australia, John Laws, who was in a lot of bother over being on the payroll of one of the major banks – he's been paid more than three million Australian dollars to say nice things about them on air. That sounded like a good story – although getting from

Beirut to Australia might not be that easy.

And there was a station in Monte Carlo called Riviera Radio that seemed to have a lot of ex-regional telly presenters working on it – but it might be a bit too similar to BDR. I'd thought about popping in to Vatican Radio as well, to give myself a bit of a spiritual high. And don't for one moment think I hadn't considered the possibility of getting to know Peninsula Radio, broadcasting in the hotel of the same name in Hong Kong. I spared Gareth my entire thought process and went for the most logical option.

'America, I think – the land of free speech and doughnuts.'

'Any particular part?' Gareth said.

I muttered something about starting in New York and seeing what happened.

I asked Gareth what he'd be working on next. It was the Bieteddine Festival for him with Kiri and Robin and a lot of culture under the stars. Which is why the next day we went shopping.

5 Why isn't there any radio porn?

Beirut to New York

I went shopping with Gareth and Khaled on the pretext of finding something for me to take home. Gareth said it would give me an opportunity to witness a pastime that is adored by the Lebanese, and to see a bit more of Beirut. So having eaten at the Le Chef underneath Gareth's apartment, where I managed to consume an artichoke while Gareth ate his body weight in chicken, followed by pudding and custard, we headed off to the other side of the stinky river for some serious shopping.

I was trying to find a Lebanese football shirt. It's not something that I usually have high on my retail list but it was a present for someone back in London who I hoped would like me more as a result, i.e. it was for a bloke I rather fancied.

There were two problems with trying to find this item of testosterone-driven nylon love. The first one was that the Lebanese football team don't play in sponsored shirts like England or Scotland do – Khaled said they probably played in whatever T-shirt they turned up in. The second problem was that both Gareth and Khaled had decided they wanted to buy some shoes. We tried three sports shops for the football shirt and were met with very blank gazes. One kind shopkeeper said that he could get one printed for me, but when he asked me if I would like to write down on a piece of paper what it was that I wanted printed I realised that I might as well get that done at home in the back streets of Dalston. To be honest I wasn't that fussed because I did have that Hezbollah key fob up my sleeve which I felt may turn out to be a coveted souvenir – obviously only for someone not directly involved in the death and tragedy of the Middle East.

Lebanon's shopping district is very well thought out. Instead of the range of high-street stores that you might get elsewhere in the world they have themed streets. The theme of the street we were now in was

Blokes' Things. Besides the sports shops, every other shop was a men's wear outlet or a men's shoe shop. Gareth and Khaled had brought themselves to the right place. And so it was that we spent two hours trying to buy them a pair of shoes.

Two hours may not sound like a long time, but when you realise that you are only having to walk ten paces in between shops – and that all of them have the same stock anyway, it is quite a long time.

Gareth and Khaled both turned from intelligent, witty and decisive journalists whose enormous brains had grasped the intricate historical melting pot of Middle East politics into the worst kind of indecisive, hesitant laydee shoppers I have ever tried to spend money with.

Gareth couldn't decide on the colour and Khaled was very worried about the size. Gareth was looking for something smart but casual, Khaled was looking towards a more sandalesque style of shoe. Could Gareth get away with a dark blue suede, or was a cream leatherette going to be a practical choice? Was it wise for Khaled to expose his toes and was it possible than one foot was much larger than the other? At one point I found myself kneeling on the floor in front of a man I had known for less than a week, pressing my thumb into his big toe to check that there was enough room for him to wear both summer and winter weight socks.

I felt that this was a bonding moment. Last week Gareth had been nothing but a grammatically correct and slightly intimidating presence on my email. Now we were saying things like 'Oh no, they're a bit "Morris Dancer at The Weekend"' and 'Mmmm – the colour's good but they say "I like experimental jazz" to me', while Khaled was persuading yet another shopkeeper to get fourteen different sizes out in order to accommodate his different-sized feet.

I could see why Gareth had come to love this city for its mesmerising combination of hostility and hospitality. He rather suited Beirut. If this had been the previous century Gareth would have been labelled as the brave but slightly eccentric Englishman who sought out new territories, settled into them and wrote books that would end up on a dusty shelf at the British Library . As it was he was doing this anyway with his pieces about far-flying radio stations in the pink pages of the *Financial Times*.

The three of us ended up back at the Phoenicia, one pair of shoes richer, watching France play Italy on a sheet strung between two palm trees outside the cafe. The dump trucks on the huge rubbish pile in the distance were still clawing away well into the night as the glut of Mercs and limos poured out their well-dressed ladies and sweaty businessmen into the marble foyer of the hotel. Somewhere Kiri was doing her warm-up warbling for the Bieteddine festival – and I had no doubt that Gareth's new-look footwear was going to go down a storm.

Just two hours away those merry Irish boys might have been lining up another smooth track as the sun set over their troubled peacekeeping region while Nagi tried to plan a future for his family in a village that would only ever be complete in his own memory. Somewhere in Beirut his kids might be packing up their things to go and join him in a place they had never been able to visit before.

All I was doing was getting ready to nick the stationery and head off on a long journey with no such poignancy. I had decided that America would be my next stop, via a change of underwear and suitcase fluff in London. After that I'd be going on to New York – a city I'd never been to before and a place in which I had no idea where my radio dial would take me.

'Pleasure doing business with you,' said the understated Gareth as we exchanged our goodbyes.

The pleasure was all mine.

I had brought Simon Bates' autobiography as reading material for my first long flight. I'd humped it round Vienna, checked it on to four European flights, used it to prop up my computer (which is a bit wobbly) and almost thought about leaving it behind in Beirut. It's called *My Tune* and it is well worth the effort. As well as charting the radio star's rise to fame through New Zealand to Portland Place it contains his bon mots on how to cope in broadcasting. One of his mentors was a man called Bob White, whose dictum on working in radio was this:

'No bullshit, do it straight and if you don't know what the fuck you're talking about, speak loudly and with great conviction.'

Simes goes on to say that in 25 years in the business, 'almost everyone I know who's adopted it and refused to compromise has gone on to greater things'.

I'm going to have to have a think about that one – it didn't seem to apply to anyone I had met so far in my radio travels. Nevertheless Simon's anecdotes and life story have kept me occupied for part of the flight. The rest of my time over the Atlantic has been spent thinking about new titles that I could write and sell at airports and make myself a fortune. These so far include:

1. *The Diary of a Bulimic Bridget Jones* who counts the calories in and counts them back out again.
2. *Men are from Bracknell, Women are from Slough* – a self-help book pointing out really handy hints like never trust a man who wears his trousers too high or a woman who wears hers too low.
3. *Captain Corelli's Electronic Yamaha* – an updated nineties version of a truly romantic tale set in the bars and nightclubs of Mykonos.
4. *The Famished Road* – a guide to the service stations of the M1.

I am flying American Airlines into New York and they have thanked me about 14 times for flying with them because they know that I have a choice and they appreciate my custom and are looking forward to welcoming me on board again in the near future. They have warned me about the overhead luggage shifting in flight; they have kept me well fed; put movies on for my enjoyment; and they have also suggested that I might like to take away with me their in-flight magazine, which is even kinder of them because it is quite priceless.

It includes a piece by Laurence Fishburne on his idea of a perfect weekend in London. It is strange how other people see your home city, isn't it? I might send him a piece about my vision of New York after I'm done just to see how well it fits. His idea of London is to live in Belgravia because there are lots of embassies there and this means you get a diverse range of people there. That's very true – there are both Philippino and Chinese maids working there. On the subject of restaurants, The Ivy is apparently where everyone goes for dinner or lunch. And the same 'everybodys' are going to a restaurant called San Lorenzo too.

The last time Laurence went there he had a typical London experience. Goldie Hawn was in. 'There was a band in the middle of the restaurant – guys playing guitars and fiddles, the next thing you knew Goldie was doing some interpretative dance performance in the middle of the restaurant and everyone was clapping.' Laurence says they weren't clapping because it was Goldie Hawn, they were clapping because 'a woman had decided it was time to dance'. How I would love to have seen that.

I guess that an international star like Mr Fishburne, with his *Apocalypse Now* and *Boyz 'n the Hood* credits, might see a very different kind of city to the one most people enjoy. A decade and a half on I have yet to see 'interpretative dancing' high on the list of London pastimes.

Incidentally Laurence, it's Hampstead Heath, not Hempstead – although that kind of pronunciation may give a clue as to the kind of people you hang out with in town.

The city of New York is being a little cheeky today and instead of the sun glittering off the Manhattan skyline like it does in his movies, I can hardly see Manhattan through a thick band of gloopy fog that has descended on the city Frank named twice. It's a dank day and the clouds are gathering above JFK – making cab drivers like Jean very happy. I know that my cab driver is called Jean because his photo ID is on the seat back in front of me. The fact that he looks nothing like the picture may be the result of age – either that or he is driving someone else's cab.

We drone past the trucks on the freeway and past the timber houses with four padlocks on every door – one inside the porch, one outside, then one on the grill and the half grill. Nearly every block has a car lot on the corner with a selection of motors that even Frank and Roy wouldn't sell on the car lot in Albert Square. The advertising slogans above the lots get straight to the point. I guess there's not an awful lot of point in trying to convince you that you are buying a runaway American dream – one old Nissan has $700 scrawled in white paint on the windscreen and underneath it simply says: 'it runs'.

1010 is on the radio – Jean says it's good for the travel. It takes its name from the fact that it gets to be good at travel every ten minutes. It does car crashes with a little too much detail.

'There's one flipped over on the freeway heading out of town to La Guardia – flipped right over the carriageway – two occupants still trapped inside, it's not looking good for them. I can't tell whether those are fatalities yet but it's sure backing up the traffic. 1010 travel over in Queens – there's an overturned tractor trailer – big delays and traffic piling back to the freeway junctions ... keep it ten ten we'll be back after these ...'

And in kicks an ad for people with depression who might want to participate in a survey about why they are sad. I can't help thinking that there may be a link between the ads and the reports.

I ask Jean what else he listens to. Music stuff, he says, for when he gets a bit edgy in the cab – he likes the oldies stations the best. Enough to choose from, I ask? He nods. What about Howard Stern? Jean catches my eye in the rearview mirror.

'He doesn't like me – I don't like him,' Jean states emphatically. 'He makes jokes about immigrants and niggers – he calls them niggers – and I don't like it. It's college boy stuff. It's not for me.'

Jean is right that he has a lot of other stuff to choose from. American radio is very big indeed. It has more than 12,000 of the world's 35,000 stations. Radio reaches 99 per cent of the population here. There are nearly a billion radio sets in this country. I could go on, but to be honest when figures get over the billion mark I lose consciousness a bit.

During my week back in London I have fleshed out my American plans a bit. I know that I want to try to meet Art Bell in Las Vegas – his is the paranormal, alien encounter show that broadcasts here overnight. I'm going to try to meet up with a man called Fitz in Palm Springs whom I met briefly in London. He told me that he is 'keeping the flame of Frank Sinatra burning in the valley' there. I'm hoping to get across to Montserrat where the radio station kept the nation safe through the volcanic eruptions of 1997 and then, if I have time, I'd like to squeeze in a visit to Steve and Johnnie. They are a married couple who do a talk show for six hours a night in Chicago. We've met before and they have a big place in my heart. New York is the only blind spot I have really – but the plan is to turn up here, tune in my radio and seek out whoever sounds most interesting.

Howard Stern would be the obvious choice because he is very very big. He earns more than any other radio star in the world and has a reputation that precedes him. The only problem is that he doesn't really fit my brief to take local radio by the horns and see what it's saying about life in a strange place. The other problem with both him and American radio in general seems to be that local stations, in terms of choice and content, are being slowly strangled by syndication. Following a lot of deregulation, several big companies have been chomping their way through stations across the country. They sell shows to hundreds of small radio stations from the west to the east so you can hear Howard Stern from one side of the country to the other. The stations simply pay for it and put their own ads in the empty bits. So I could hear Howard Stern if I pitched up in Mississippi – but he wouldn't be able to tell me a lot about that place.

There is still public service broadcasting in the States in the form of National Public Radio. You can't find this on one frequency like you would do in Britain with any of the BBC stations. Instead it is more of a radio shop from which stations can take programmes – there are over 400 who choose to do so, many of them are campus stations or are owned by non-profit-making organisations. There is also Public Radio International which is relatively new. It was born in 1983 and it operates on a similar principle. There are some community stations, run by groups and foundations, and religious ones, who also don't seek to make a profit. But the key word in the enormity that is American radio is definitely profit.

Michael C Keith's encyclopaedic book simply called *The Radio Station* lists all of the above things and a host of other nuggets of information for the radio anorak – I am proud to include myself in this description. There seem to be no lengths to which stations won't go in order to promote themselves and make a bigger profit. One station decided it would be a good idea to drop hundreds of turkeys into a car park where waiting listeners had gathered, presumably before Thanksgiving, to try to get a free bird in time for dinner. These were live birds – not frozen ones.

Unfortunately no one at the radio station had bothered to find out about the flying habits of these poor birds. They are not very adept at flying above 30 feet. Keith says 'consequently several cars were damaged and witnesses traumatised as the turkeys plunged to the ground'. You can't help feeling a little more sorry for the turkeys than the witnesses. But with that kind of imagination, or foolhardiness, involved in commercial radio in this country I am looking forward to my stay here enormously. With or without the giblets.

Jean has managed to swerve round enough traffic to get us downtown in half an hour. As we honk our way through the packed pavements of the city, New York's occupants look like they are all auditioning for a B*Witched video – everyone is moving too fast. The buildings are so high that even if there was any sunshine we would be in permanent shadow. The city seems to have laid on some special steam coming out of the manholes in the street – which is reassuringly familiar. And by the time we get to the block my hotel is on, there is a strong smell of cinnamon – it is Danish-pastry time of day.

The Ambassador hotel that I'm staying in on West 43rd Street must have catered for the least illustrious of foreign embassy visitors if, in fact it ever took in diplomatic baggage. It's definitely not patronised by the kind of embassy people that Laurence Fishburne hangs out with in Belgravia. I am currently developing a new kind of hotel category to add to the confusion over stars and rosettes and crowns that abound across the world. My method has only two categories – Realistically Named and Unrealistically Named.

The Ambassador is in the latter. So are nearly all the hotels on the Shepherds Bush Road in West London. They have names like West

London Towers and Chesterfield Lodge – or The London Heights. Were you to read those names in a guidebook or brochure abroad they might conjure up images of smart leather sofa-ed foyers and chrome accessorised bedrooms. They probably wouldn't make you imagine a No Vacancies, No DSS sign hanging on the door and a couple of kettles and milk cartons squashing up against the net curtains on the first floor.

Other English hotels fare better. The Ritz comes into the Realistically Named category, as does every Travelodge – but be very careful of anything with Airport in its title in Istanbul. Although you may be able to see the planes from your bedroom, it is only when they have reached 30,000 feet.

The Ambassador has a tiny reception area – the largest thing in it is one of those leaflet stalls that suggests your trip to New York will not be complete without visiting – you guessed it – a *musical!* There's a lovely girl from Ireland manning the front desk who is amazed that I've come all this way to listen to the radio.

'Well – you'll know all about Howard Stern won't you? And there are endless music stations here but I don't know what you'll find that is typically New York.'

'What do you listen to?'

'I don't really, don't have the time – but they list them all in the *New York Times*. Here, you can have this one if you want. Someone left it when they were checking out.'

She gives me a crumpled newspaper and the USA's most frequented sign off in a slightly Irish American lilt.

'Have a nice day.'

'You too.'

Up in Room 106 it's easy to find Howard as his signal seems to be bigger than everyone else's on the dial – or maybe that is just what he tells people. He is in the middle of delivering a rant about the station he works for because he doesn't like the ads that he has to read out. Then he's rude about his guests coming up for the morning – two of The Backstreet Boys. His lady sidekick suggests that they should have come wearing their diapers today so that they could be the Back Side Boys as this is the nickname that Howard has affectionately given them. And then there is the man who has the largest rubber-band ball in the world. Did this guy phone up the show and say, 'Would you like to slaughter me on air for fifteen minutes next week sometime and take the piss out of my life/intellect/personality?' The conversation goes something like this:

'How do you stretch the rubber bands over the ball when it gets really big?' says Howard.

There follows a detailed explanation.

'Where do you get your enormous rubber bands?'

Apparently from the Internet.

'I'm going to sell my bowel movements on email,' says Howard.

Interesting.

There is a lady who phones in to say that she would do anything to meet The Backstreet Boys.

'Would you tongue kiss Gary-the-Retard?' says Howard menacingly.

I think that Gary is one of Howard's producers – he does sound like he is retarded. I truly hope he is just pretending. Howard says she can come in and meet them only if she wears an adult diaper and then pees into it while in the studio as well as kissing Gary the retard. She agrees. He says she has to get there by the end of the show.

Apart from two of The Backstreet Boys, his big guest this morning is Kyra Sedgewick who is the wife of Kevin Bacon but also an actress in her own right. She sounds like a nice kind of lady for about the first ten minutes. Her and Howard do the kind of idle chit chat that you might overhear at some PR drinks party. But then Howard gets into his stride . Has she had a Brazilian bikini wax? Does that mean she has to lie naked on a table with her legs spread open? Is it done by a woman? Does she have to get on all fours? Kyra is quite happy to play along with this. In fact she seems to be rather enjoying it.

In the eventuality that on getting to New York I would decide that Howard was the guy to meet I had sent him a note while back in Britain, asking him about the possibility of meeting him. It went something like this:

Dear Mr Stern

I am a very polite British girl who is writing a book. Please could you be in it. I am very nice and would be very grateful if you could take the time to talk to me about your achievements in radio and the contribution that you have made to the inter-national audience.

Yours
fi

Unsurprisingly, although this letter would make my mother proud because I have used the correct form and punctuation, I now realise that it is never going to work with Howard. What I should have sent was this:

> Howard – Hi Big Boy. I'm a tiny bird from the UK who thinks you sound really huge, so can I come and sit in your studio and work myself into a lather for a book I'm writing about your genius. Which is obviously enormous too.
>
> I'm quite happy to talk about my fantasies and it's fine by me if you talk about my breasts. They are huge.
>
> love
> fifi glover

Obviously there are several lies included in this letter but it's not like he'd notice. Howard had not replied and listening to Kyra I could understand why. I would have had very little desire to talk about what position my leg waxing takes place in. Howard has managed to tear himself away from thinking about her ingrowing hairs and has moved on to infidelity.

Has she been unfaithful? Would she be tempted by a woman? Kyra knows exactly what she is doing by saying, 'I have kissed women on the set.' So we have ten minutes of extraordinarily explicit conversation about lesbianism and did Julianna Margulies seem to enjoy it and was it a full French kiss?

I suppose I shouldn't be so shocked. The world's media is full of pornography. Why should radio escape? It's probably quite an anomaly that you can get TV porn channels, Internet sites, chat lines and mags full of the stuff but that somehow the world's airwaves have escaped. Judging by the amount of people who enjoy all of those things it isn't surprising that there is a market for the spoken pornographic innuendo. Were someone to set up a pirate dirty-talking station I'm sure that it would be more successful than the techno-bashing baselines that seep into your dial on a Saturday night.

Kyra is more than happy to talk about how she looks this morning and why her breasts are being pulled in by her halter top and the fact that from the side Howard can see her breasts and they look like 'two puppy dogs fighting under a rug'. Kevin must be real proud of her this morning.

Lesbianism and Howard's desire to talk about it – in detail – is one of the most popular aspects of his show. I have heard that Howard's unique Lesbian Dial A Date gets a lot of listeners. During this segment of his show Howard encourages the ladies to make on-air assignations with each other. I imagine that they do more than talk about their love of countryside walks and great sense of humour.

For this and a lot of other shock jocking, Howard earns $25 million a year. He has been fined enormous amounts by the Federal Communications Commission: half a million dollars for discussing the merits of shaving and waxing pubic hair. He seems even more obsessed about hair removal than I am. But it gets so much worse. In Denver, the city closest to Columbine, his show was suspended for the following question aired a couple of days after the school massacre that happened in the town. According to one newspaper cutting this is what Howard said:

'There were some really good-looking girls running out with their hands over their heads. Did those kids try to have sex with any of the good-looking girls? They didn't even do that? At least if you're going to kill yourself and kill all the kids, why wouldn't you have some sex?'

Back on air today Sarah is the girl who says that she will kiss Gary-the-Retard (with the essential Stern word of the day – tongue). She is 19 and she is now in the studio.

'Are you wearing your diaper?'

'Yes.'

'Now that you're meeting Gary, would you still kiss him?'

'Yeah sure – I'd do anything to meet The Backstreet Boys.'

'You look a little young – how old are you?'

'Nineteen.'

'Yeah – but that's a young nineteen, isn't it?'

Howard seems to be having some strange moral attack.

'I'm going to let you off … You look way too young to kiss Gary. He is 40. I had no idea you were this young. We thought she was older. I don't think this is right … You don't even have to go in the diaper … Just wear it.'

Aaah – isn't that nice of him?

Meanwhile The Backstreet Boys have brought Howard a tube of KY Jelly in honour of him calling them The Back Side Boys. Howard has

118

done a piss-taking song, 'Let's tongue kiss tonight, Back Side Boys are back tonight'. Oh chortle away if you must.

The only things that I learn during the resulting interview are:

1. They have made more than a hundred million dollars.
2. They are suing their original manager because he is taking too much money from them.
3. They aren't particularly bright.
4. They haven't had sex with either Britney Spears or Christina Aguilera.
5. Howard has just said, 'Do you check their IDs before you bang them?'
6. I've really got to retune – this is a bad first impression of New York.

In Michael Keith's radio book he includes a prophetic comment from a man called Jay Williams Jr, whose exact position in the firmament of radio professionals I can only guess at, because underneath a picture of him it simply says 'Figure 1.24'. Anyway he says 'The concept of broadcasting is dead. Broadcasting, as with all media, must become interactive in order to survive. The listener must be allowed to "talkback" and communicate with the station.'

Now I do take his point because I don't want to see this beloved medium crushed under the wheels of the Internet chat room and the interactive website, but when I read that I couldn't help feeling that out of all media, radio is the only one that has always allowed its customers to talkback. And it's done it with the simplest of programmes – the phone-in. So perhaps this format would be a better place to start my journey round the States. I'd like to find a show where, unlike Howard Sterns, the phrase 'girl on girl action' just means one woman talking to another.

The newspaper the lovely receptionist had given me came up trumps – one of only two programmes they recommended in their tiny, tiny column inch about radio was a psychological phone-in hosted by Dr Joy Browne. It was over on the AM dial and within two minutes had filled the room with a warm but Waspish voice that belonged to the eponymous Joy:

'0800 544 7070 … This is Dr Joy Browne – you're on the air. What's your question today, Bob?'

'Oh, Dr Browne, I just want to say that I love the show – I think you're value system is awesome.'

'Well, in that case Bob, we have got to get you out more ...'

Dr Joy was very nice to Bob – in a strict but ever so slightly cheeky way – and she seemed to be adored by her listeners. Bob had a problem about how to stay being nice to his ex-wife, but judging by his adoration of Joy I think that he was enjoying talking to her more than he was enjoying having his problem talked about. The next caller had a bad relationship she didn't know how to end and while dozing through some of my jetlag Dr Joy's rich and dulcet tones seemed to be very appealing. I called the number at the end of the show and left a message with her assistant.

The American Museum of TV and Radio is a King Kong of a building just off Avenue of the Americas and right next door to Deutsche Bank, which is throwing out the kind of preppie men that make me think of the word 'sorority' – and not that many things do. There's a constant stream of clean-shaven young men wearing blue shirts and suit trousers and the kind of glasses that are sold to you in the opticians as being 'unobtrusively stylish'. I often wonder why people who design glasses spend quite so much time trying to design ones that look like they aren't really there – it must be quite demoralising work. Some of them have Barbour style jackets on and they seem to be emerging in packs. Probably all part of the same fund management team. I wonder if they are the kind of people Jean the cab driver thought listened to Howard Stern while at college – maybe it's a rites of passage thing to do. I've arrived half an hour too early – the museum doesn't open until midday. Honestly, these media types.

There were a thousand and one things that I could have done in order to get acquainted with this legendary city. I could have gone up the Empire State Building, down to Greenwich Village, shopped on Fifth Avenue or eaten an entire cow. But I felt that I needed to be a bit more prepared about Dr Joy's radio counterparts before meeting her.

The museum isn't really a museum and you get told this as soon as you revolve through the doors – you get told it about four times by a variety of well-dressed and well-spoken attendants. It is more of an archive and you have to book what you want to watch on the fourth floor by sitting down at a computer console. Then you can go and watch it at a viewing console on the fifth. My kind of museum. No standing around while your thighs start aching, no crowds of schoolchildren filling out questionnaires and it has a back catalogue of episodes of *The Simpsons* if you get bored with listening to radio excerpts.

I have chosen a selection of broadcasts from Dr Laura Schlessinger who is the number one rated problem phone-in host on American radio. Settling down into my booth I realise that I am the only one listening to radio – everyone else has some piece of TV history playing out on their screens.

On first hearing Dr Laura Schlessinger the immediate reaction is that she is really rather stroppy. I join her while she is telling one poor love:

'If you want to lead a gutless life then you're on the road.'

She calls her listeners 'dear' quite a lot in a way that suggests she means the Bambi variety that is about to be run over by a juggernaut on a bleak wintry road in the Highlands.

Dr Laura is huge, though. She has built her phone-in show up from a tiny local one to the most sought-after female voice on American radio. Her style is no-nonsense help and she is from the right-wing fraternity of high moral values and low tolerance. Her often troubled life has put her in the public eye for many things other than her actual show. She didn't start life as a psychologist and was broadcasting on air before she got her qualifications. She got some stick for that. She then converted to Orthodox Judaism and got some more stick for that, and then just at the height of her powers an old colleague published some naked pictures of her and a lot of her image went down the pan. More recently she called gays 'deviants', which led to demonstrations outside her studio.

In the excerpt resting in the vaults of the museum she is trying to help a girl who has phoned in with a family trauma. Her boyfriend is black, she is white and her mother is going to disown her if she marries him. Dr S is not impressed and says she should just do what she wants to do.

The girl keeps saying she wants to go her own way but she feels pulled in different directions and she wants to keep her family happy but she is in love with this guy. Dr Laura spares no punches.

'Moral progress is not made when the "buts" are so frequently entertained with such passion.'

That in my book is a bit of a conversation killer.

Of her own life she says it had its fair share of hardship and troubled family times: 'If life had been a slide on ice I would have been a marshmallow.'

She gets more and more angry with this poor girl and ends up almost cutting her off with a dismissive 'stick to your guns'. I wonder if the girl thought it was worth phoning up.

Dr Laura sounds like a tough piece of work – like the kid at school who goes round pinching everyone but then expects them to come to her party and bring her a present. But that hasn't stopped her amassing a fortune of millions courtesy of the radio show, the spin-off books and the speaking tours she does.

I have never called a radio phone-in show – not a problem one anyway. I have called Invicta FM in Canterbury to request a Waterboys song. They put it on right away which suggested I may have been the only caller that hour – it was very late though. But a problem phone-in, no. And I'm not sure that I ever will. Maybe that is a British thing – a slight reticence about talking to strangers – a slight embarrassment that things aren't perfect. Or maybe it's just me.

It would be fantastic if you could line up all the people phoning Dr Joy or Dr Laura today and sit them down in a room and ask them how they have the guts to do it. But that is the beauty of the medium they choose to unload themselves on – the anonymity and the absence of a direct audience. Whoever this girl is who believes that Dr Laura can sort her life out, she probably doesn't even know that her painful choices are being kept for posterity in a huge building off Sixth Avenue. I hope things work out for her.

Most of the other museum-goers seem to be watching or listening to something far more amusing and the guy in the next-door cubicle keeps bursting into peals of laughter. I give up with Dr S and return to the desk to ask if I can watch a *Simpsons* show from the archive instead.

The slightly stroppy man on the desk peers through some nearly invisible glasses at me.

'You'll have to go back upstairs and make another selection – have you finished with the ones we brought up for you?'

This is deliberately designed to make me feel guilty for wasting their time. For a museum dedicated to the entertainment industry, the employees really are thoroughly unentertaining. A bit like health food shops really – why do the people who work in them always look so ill?

I spent a lovely morning sitting in the Listening Rooms of the museum with a pair of headphones on – just mulling through the documentaries they have filed there. There was a superb series on black voices in radio with some fantastic women talking about the early years in stations in Detroit and Chicago where the managers just assumed that you were only good for secretarial work if you were a lady. One lady called Martha Jean 'the Queen' Steinberg said her motto was 'to think like a man, act like a lady and work like a dog'. Another lady laughed before saying that 'some of the old boys have a bit more melanin in their skins and look like me now'.

I listened to a bit of Studs Terkel – a man who has spent his life making radio programmes in the States, mainly social histories using the spoken word as an encyclopaedic way to chart the passages of time. I caught one interview with a girl called Andrina who was an Appalachian storyteller – she spoke movingly about the way American society had changed but her past and heritage stayed, simply through the stories of nature and community passed down from generation to generation. The chairs didn't squeak like the British Library and no one had tutted at me yet, but I thought the same thing – that I shouldn't stay too long in the carefully catalogued world of radio when it was all out there on my dial.

I had to get back to see if my appointment with Dr Joy was going to become a reality. She still seemed like the perfect choice – I could do with a female soundtrack to my stay in New York. Her assistant Deborah had left a message for me back at the Ambassador. She said it'd be fine for me to come and see Dr Joy but could I do it next week as she was busy recording a TV show over the next few days? As I had no fixed agenda at all – and a month to spend in this vast country – I said that it wouldn't be a problem. Deborah was terribly nice and efficient and said that Dr Joy was thrilled that I wanted to meet her. It was like putting a fantastic party invitation in your very empty diary – even if you were going to spend three weeks with no prospect of socialising at all, you knew that there was something nice and confirmed coming up. What was I going to wear?

It wasn't exactly a chore to have to sit in a variety of cafes and bars for a few days in New York with a map of the States and a timetable of flights, working out how to spend a couple of weeks. In fact it was bliss. Every state had a name that sounded like it needed a visit. Every airline seemed to have at least one flight a day to all those places. It was only the hotels that might fall between the two stools of Unrealistically and Realistically named.

I was tempted to go to Dallas, not only for the Southfork tour and lunch at the Cattleman's Club but also because that Michael Keith man had mentioned there was a station there which had, in yet another bizarre promotional venture, asked listeners to send them $20. They did, mailing nearly a quarter of a million dollars to the radio station. Keith says it left the managers with 'the interesting problem of what to do with the money'. It is an interesting question – and sadly one which he never answers. I couldn't really justify a whole week's trip just to answer that question personally.

I ruminated away about whether to head for the Deep South, maybe join two million other Brits in Florida or head straight up to Chicago to see my old friends Steve and Johnnie. The fact that it looked like it was going to rain for a week in New York had absolutely no bearing on my decision to fly down to Las Vegas in search of Art Bell.

One thing that did have a bearing on turning this plan into a reality was a piece on one of the local news channels one night. I gave up trying to work out where the big channels like NBC and ABC had got to, my TV only seemed to have things called Channel 1 and Channel 42 with nothing in between. I quite liked the people who did the news on Channel 42; I certainly felt I knew them well. Most of their programme time was dedicated to them introducing each other.

'Susy is at the crime scene now. It's over to you, Susy.'

'Thank you, Bill … This is Susy in Central Park, back to you, Bill.'

'Thank you, Susy.'

This was invariably followed by a weather bulletin of staggeringly detailed proportions and then Bill told me to stay tuned for some shock news about Art Bell. This was in their Entertainment News which was coming up after the break. When it did arrive it was a bit of a shock – Bill said that, following 'family difficulties', Art had announced that day that he was going to go off air for good. I felt it was an extraordinary coincidence, in fact it was something that only a man who specialises in the paranormal could think was just a coincidence. It was a sign. I had to get to Vegas quickly.

Incidentally after delivering that shocker, Bill and his co-presenter did that really annoying thing every local TV show seems to do. They shuffled their papers and started chatting to each other and laughing away with great big, natural smiles on their faces as the cameras panned back and the music rumbled to its climax. Why, after having delivered half an hour of annoyingly dull news, delivered in the same over-serious voice, do they have to do some kind of personal cabaret with each other? Why can't we, the viewer, be allowed in on their funny jokes and bonhomie?

*

Do you know why the carpets in Vegas casinos are so horrible? And they *are* truly horrible – great swirly patterns of garish hues that Allied wouldn't be able to get rid of on a Bank Holiday. I do. I read a book years ago called *101 Things You Never Knew About Vegas* – it was written by a former security guard at the Mirage, I think. Sadly it's the kind of book that your friends like to nick under the pretence of 'borrowing' because it's a one-off, not available in print in this country, easier to read and far more entertaining to quote from than Salman Rushdie. It answers questions like: 'Why are the carpets so bad?' Apparently this is so that when you walk into a casino you think 'Yuk, what a horrible carpet' and your attention is drawn upwards to the slot machines.

Other questions include: 'Why are there no seats in the foyers of hotels?' This is so that you are drawn to sit at the slot machines which invariably surround the concierge desk. 'Why are the lights so dim in the casinos?' So that you don't realise what time of day it is. Same reason for clocks – and no windows, no distractions. 'Why should ladies never wear red dresses in casinos?' Because the infrared cameras can see straight through them. Having read this before coming to Vegas is a little like meeting a celebrity whose love life has been well documented in the tabloids – you feel you know all their secrets already.

It's been a very long day and by the time I get to Vegas, it's 9.30 in the evening. I checked out of the Ambassador in New York at about 8am. That's because I had chosen the take-all-day flight from New York via Cincinnati and Phoenix – once again the length of time was reflected in the price and the extra bonus was that it afforded me the opportunity of buying some simply fabulous fridge magnets in Cincinnati featuring the Kentucky Derby. The choice was that or Celine Dion ones for some reason. Perhaps she passed through for another sold-out air-punching contest which lived long in the memory of the Cincinnatians.

These hop-across-a-continent flights are disconcerting for Europeans. If you take a flight of four hours, followed by one of three hours followed by a short one-hour hop, then you would expect to have passed through airport lounges selling the fridge magnets of at least three different religions; you would probably have sat in one cafe at Istanbul Airport, contemplating the fall of the Ottoman Empire – or how many germs are on your glass; and then had to change clothes in the last stopover airport toilet, probably Bahrain by this stage, because of a severe climate change. But of course this is all America and you can fly for a whole day and not have to fill in a single visa application, be met with the same universal American set of fridge magnets in every airport and get out at the other end to be met by exactly the same 'have a nice day' greeting.

Las Vegas, I have always thought, is a 'she' town. She sits in the middle of the Nevada desert like a fun-loving lady of the night advertising her services – skirts a little short, tops a little low and jewellery so gaudy it would make Pat Butcher look dowdy. I don't know what defines a city's sex really other than a certain feel and glow. I reckon that London is a 'he' town; I should imagine that most of the big Spanish towns are masculine too, rather testosterone driven and on a hot day positively randy. Bangkok is a pretty hermaphrodite and Paris is the ultimate lady town – tastefully dressed but wearing raunchy underwear underneath.

The enormity of the mountains surrounding Las Vegas makes you lose your sense of proportion and at first glance from the air she looks like a miniature town with just a few hotels dominating the skyline. But it's an optical illusion – a bit like seeing jumbo jets in the sky – they are so big that they look like they aren't moving even when they are doing 700 miles an hour. Vegas's hotels are so huge that they make the town look tiny. We touched down just as someone was switching all the lights on in the city – which must be a very large and prestigious job. The number of people visiting this city not only demands an enormous amount of electricity but has obviously presented a particular problem to the man in charge of lost luggage.

This is Armageddon for the Trundling Black Cases. Above every luggage carousel in the huge cavernous baggage reclaim area there is a Trundling Black Case suspended over the conveyor belt complete with a sign saying 'Most Luggage Looks the Same – is it your bag you have collected?' Aha. My theory is correct. God knows how many people have turned up here and rushed through reclaim picking up the first black case that looks like theirs – only to find back in the hotel that the frilly marabou nightie is not what they expected to wear to the Salesman of the South conference the next day. I was the smug one who swanned through safe in the knowledge that the bright blue canvas over-the-shoulder sack could only belong to me.

The Mobsters who first commissioned the city as an out of California gambling paradise would have been well pleased by the dedication that subsequent generations have shown to keeping the point of the city going. Make money and build more places to make money in. When the casinos start looking a little less than brand new, simply knock them down and build something even bigger. Repeat the prescription as and when you feel like it – and if symptoms persist then see a loan shark.

My appointed hotel is the MGM Grand. It is grand and it is run by MGM. The lobby is a cavernous marble affair and there are about a hundred of us waiting to check in. Is there anywhere to sit down though? No, there's a marble thing with a fountain in the centre that I guess allows about a dozen people to squeeze their buttocks on to – but nothing else. The lady standing behind me in the check-in queue is proudly telling her companion that this is Elton John's favourite hotel in Vegas. As a guy not known for his downbeat style I guess that he would like the MGM a lot, not least for its swirling carpets. Just to get to my room I have to pass over three different equally horrendous designs and of course you have to walk through a bit of the casino in order to get to the lifts. I am wearing red pants under my jeans today – heaven knows how exciting that is for the security guards watching my progress on the CCTV.

6 We have the technology to take you to hell

Las Vegas

Art Bell's show is on air. I get to it just at the top of the hour where he is setting out his audio stall for the evening. There is a great big rock tune playing in the background as Art delivers his nocturnal wake-up call to the listeners ... he has the kind of intonation that preachers adopt to stir up the passions of their flock – he goes up in the middle of sentences – only to end on a more hushed tone. Very much like Michael Buerk actually.

Tonight his guest is Kathleen Keating. She is an author – Art is introducing her to the audience:

'... and I warn you that what you're about to hear really may scare the hell out of you ... Kathleen Keating has a book called *The Final Warning* and I guess you'll find out what that is in a moment. You may not have caught her the first time round. She has got a lot of other works under way – an action thriller *Cat's Cradle* ... but *The Final Warning* actually is your survival guide to the new millennium. I wonder if survival is a keyword – could be.'

Kathleen says hello and Art asks if she's heard some of the alien encounters that they have been talking about in the past hour of the programme.

'Just before we get to that book, in my last hour I opened up the phone lines for people who had had alien encounters and I know that you heard the one lady who had the encounter with the dark black being that was so big it could barely fit into her son's room ... with the red glowing eyes. I hate red glowing eyes more than anything else I can think of – I get the shakes when I hear about that ...'

'You're not the only one,' says Kathleen. 'I take that very seriously.'

I'm sad to have missed that hour – it sounded rather peachy.

Art Bell is a radio phenomenon. His show is either the third or fourth most popular talk show in the whole USA, depending on which paper

128

you read, and given that it goes out from 10 'til 3 over the midnight hour then that is quite a feat. It's not dedicated to religion or space travel, or aliens landing, or the power of mind over matter but all of those topics will regularly crop up. I had a look through his previous guest list before coming – let me give you a selection. On 12 February Sylvia Browne was on to talk about her book *Adventures of a Psychic: The Fascinating Inspiring True Life Story of One of America's Most Successful Clairvoyants*. She was closely followed by one Lia Danks who had a book out called *Building Your Ark* and on 9 July 1999 Richard Belzer was on the show to talk about his book *UFO's, JFK and Elvis: Conspiracies You Don't Have to Be Crazy to Believe*. Art's listeners got a three-in-one lucky bonus that night.

This is where free speech gets very free indeed. Art has turned himself into a radio legend – his show has grown by word of mouth and is taken across the States. It's so popular that it's frequently repeated as soon as it's finished in the early hours of the morning and there's a webcam on line so that you can check to see what he is up to every 30 seconds or so. Art didn't seem to move much. Having seen what he looks like – 50-ish, greying hair, jeans and a T-shirt – I can't play What Does He Look Like? with his voice. I don't know if the webcam adds much to his show apart from assuaging a curiosity about his hair colour. We have webcams in the studios at Five Live now – and I find them disconcerting. Part of the joy of radio is not having to think about how you look or what you wear and whether you're grimacing at a particularly boring guest on the phone – part of the joy of listening to radio is not having to be distracted by all those things too.

I often sit on my hands during radio programmes – I don't know why, it's partly because I'm always dying for a pee – do I want people to see that? I always sit cross-legged and bare footed – will that look odd? There are some presenters who will get caught out when they have tantrums and throw things at the glass behind which poor producers are only trying to help. By poor, I do mean skint. And there are the guests who might not want to be filmed as well as heard. When I interviewed Armistead Maupin about his *The Night Listener* – a lovely book about the power of radio which made me love Mr Maupin even more – he was in a studio in Broadcasting House while I was in one at Television Centre. We were talking about the face that you put in your imagination on to a voice you hear on the dial. He said he thought I was a voluptuous strawberry blonde. My love for him went off the scale. Sadly, had he been able to study the webcam, he would have seen that I am a short bird with dark problem hair.

But it's interesting how different voices stimulate different pictures: for a deep and rounded voice I imagine a thick-set, dark-haired man. I don't think I ever imagine men to be blond. Scottish accents always make people thin, Irish accents a little more rotund. For the ladies high-pitched clipped tones are blonde bobbed women, and Charlotte Green is Lauren Bacall. I never imagine people to be ugly, even if I hate their programmes.

So Kathleen, Art's guest, I imagine to be petite, with short dark hair. I reckon she is wearing a complicated patterned jumper and probably has little, piercing eyes. A Delia Smith of conspiracy theorists.

Although Art's subject list is on the para side of normal his style is not to take the mickey. I haven't the faintest idea whether he believes in all the out-of-this-world and out-of-my-body experiences that half his guests have had, but he has made a name for himself by putting them on air and letting a lot of Americans take a break from building their alien-proof bunker in the garden or polishing their guns and call up for a chat.

You can presumably drive from one side of America to the other and never miss an Art Bell show due to the number of stations he is syndicated to, but he doesn't actually work out of any of them. Not for him the hot seat change over at 9.59 every night. Art broadcasts from his own bunker in the town of Parumph about 60 miles away from Vegas in the heart of the desert. I have heard that he is a little on the paranoid side and that he does have a tendency to believe that the government is after him – for what I don't know. Some people regard him as the best talk show host in the business.

I'm wandering round my enormous bedroom at the MGM Grand, wondering which things are coming home with me. It's very nicely done up, considering the explosion of jangling colours outside. All cream and calm. Kathleen has got well and truly into her stride now and her and Art are talking about the forces from 'the other side':

'Sure,' says Kathleen, 'the Internet's a big playground for the demonic forces. They use it quite extensively. I know as a fact that they've targeted television this year in order to get into your homes. And if you've noticed, a lot of people have written to me saying "Boy, people are getting more irritable lately" ...'

Art agrees. Kathleen carries on.

'They don't know what it is. Well, one of the visionaries with whom

I've been working said it's because the uh – the dark side – is coming to you through your television set.'

Now let's have a think about that one. I share the sentiments of Kathleen's public that everyone is getting more irritable lately. I am definitely more uptight than I was when I was 12. What are the causes of this? Is it because I am 30 and not yet married? Is it because the binman will never take my third sack of rubbish on a Wednesday? Perhaps it's because no matter how hard I try exfoliating I still get ingrowing hairs in my bikini line. Or is it television? If I were to agree with Kathleen then at least I could blame all life's anxieties on Carol Vorderman. Goodness, I feel better already.

Art and Kathleen move on to morality and sex on TV and it goes a bit Richard and Judy for a while. I eye up the TV in my room. Very big. Too big for my bag. There is a gap beneath it though in the huge wooden cabinet. A gap where the minibar should have been. This topic was also covered in the nicked Vegas book – no minibar because they don't want you to stay in your room too long. There's no slot machine or gaming table in there. At the time of writing this is the largest hotel in the world. The MGM has 5,000 rooms, 170,000 square feet of casino, 14 restaurants, a 1,700 seat theatre, two huge swimming pools, a health spa, a monorail and a rather annoying habit of overusing the adjective 'grand' in order to remind you of where you are. Even though I have only been in the hotel for half an hour I have already been told to 'Have a grand stay' followed by 'Have a grand night.'

I'd quite like it if someone just said 'Have a grand' and left it at that.

The wind-up radio has wound down while I'm in the palatial bathroom trying to arrange my deodorant, toothbrush and one bottle of moisturiser into some kind of display. When I do the requisite 40 winds it crackles back just as Kathleen is explaining that she knows who the antichrist is – but she's not telling. Read the book she says. Obviously Kathleen is no stranger to the art of publicity and making book sales. Art presses her on the true identity of the antichrist. All she will say is that his initials are A.C.

Who can that be? I'm racking my brains to think of A.C.s. Arthur C. Clarke, Alan Clark? No. Adam Curtley – that nice man from the BBC Business Unit? Surely not. A C. Who could that be?

Bloody Hell. It's Alan Coren. That's it. The genial team captain who I've sat next to on *Call My Bluff* – he's been sending out signals through the TV, he's been making the world more irritable with his bluffs, all those made up words may be code for the end of the world. Oh my God. I'm scaring myself. I'm sitting here in a huge hotel in the pleasure dome of the world, thinking terrible things about a very nice man in a blazer.

There's a knock at the door. It's the bellboy with room service. I've ordered this because I'm hooked on the show now and can't tear myself away, even for an all-you-can eat buffet with 32 choices of lite lo-cal salad dressing. Burger in gob and phone in hand I call the number for Art's show. I'm sure if I only got to talk to him he'd agree to meet me. It rings and it rings and it rings – and eventually a pre-recorded operator lady tells me that my number is not responding and could I try again later? I give it a couple of seconds and I dial again. Same thing.

Art is now putting callers on the line. Several say that they are sad he is going – he mutters something about his family needing him right now. The next one wants to talk to Kathleen.

This is Andy from Largo in Florida.

'Hi, good to talk to you. Kathleen, I, um, was privileged to talk to you the last time you were on. You do very good work, and I, I think the work is very important.'

Kathleen thanks him.

'My question tonight though is ... earlier tonight you mentioned that hell is geographically located in the centre of the earth ...'

'Uh huh.'

'In the past ten years I've seen certain people that claim that some division of the government basically has directions to where this place is at. And actually one of the entrances is from a deep cave system.'

'Uh huh.'

'I don't know if you've ever heard of anything about this but ...'

'Yes ...'

'Oh you have?' says Art.

'It's scary,' cries Andy.

Too bloody right it is. Kathleen is on my side now.

'Well, it is, but considering some of our politicians, does it surprise you that they know the way to hell?'

Art laughs loudly.

Andy is in his stride now.

'Yeah really. Furthermore if that's the case that would blow the lid off a lot of things! I mean we can keep a cap on the UFOs but hell itself being the centre of the earth ... it's the year 2000 you'd think by now somebody would have gone down there ...'

Kathleen says maybe they have – but they just haven't come back.

'Well, true,' says Andy, 'but do we have the technology to go down there? If we did, why we would ... who knows ...'

Kathleen is certain about this one.

'Well, I mean if they've got the space craft in Area 51, then I think we have the technology to get there ...'

The burger's gone cold by now and the phone's still ringing out. First Alan Coren may be the devil and now someone's saying that you can book a trip to hell. Who is Andy? How can he sit in sunny Florida thinking such thoughts? Shouldn't he concentrate on ridding the world of Disneyland first? Do people really believe that somewhere in the bowels of the earth there is a place where the fire burns eternal? Does Art believe all this? The radio's fading again and I'm not rushing to wind it up.

When the bellboy delivered my grand burger he had offered to draw the curtains in my room for me – I had rejected this kind offer. Now as the radio finally crackles out there is nothing but the gentle hum of the air con unit. Outside the Strip is still blazing away with its thousands of neon signs and moving billboards. There is a strange green glow coming from above the window outside. If I was Kathleen I might believe this was because an alien had just landed on the roof.

In fact it's because the MGM Grand is actually green – from the plane I could clearly see its massive initials lit up on the roof. This is very effective for the rather inebriated guest walking down the Strip who simply has to follow the green lights in the distance – but even when you're tucked up into your enormous American-sized bed, it's like someone has put one of those green-tinged bulbs in your light fitting. Tonight though I'm quite glad of it. We used to have little coloured nightlights in our bedrooms when we were tiny and afraid of the dark. I thought I'd grown out of that years ago. Tonight I'm not so sure. How kind of Vegas to leave the lights on overnight.

The green glow has gone by the morning and as the alarm goes off I get woken up in time to hear a weather person telling me it is going to be a 'real, bright sunshiny day'. I had tuned the bedside radio into the same station that Art was on last night, so this is the morning show for the same lot who were pondering the geographical location of hell only eight hours ago. A loud jingle tells me it is AM 840 KXNT – the Talk Station.

Then it's a bloke's voice and he sounds rather angry:

'I've got a solution for the homeless in this town – *broil their dogs!*'

There is a huge pause. 'Yup that's what I said ... put Fido on a stick – that'd sort them out ... if they can afford the dogs they can afford to eat – no one should be begging in this town.'

Oh my.

'There is no excuse for anyone to be homeless here. I've had to do jobs that I thought were beneath me – I went to college – I didn't expect to have life handed to me on a plate – get a job as a janitor, clean out toilets – just do something – don't beg on our streets – we don't need you here ... Hi, who's this on line 1?'

'Hi Paul. It's Margaret here and I agree with you ... do you know what? I keep seeing this blonde girl begging around the Strip, she's tanned and she's got long blonde hair – I've seen her on and off for a while now and do you know what she does? She begs and then she gets into a nice brand new white car at the end of the day ... I've seen her do it ... She's not poor, she doesn't need the money, she's taking people for a ride ... She's not even in the shelter ...'

DJ Paul Lyle joins in again. 'So where should the homeless go?' This is a question for him and not, it seems for Margaret. 'I know a place for them. Prisoner cemeteries. You can call us if you want to – tell us what should be done with those beggars.'

Mmmm and a good morning to you too. Gradually it becomes clear that they are talking about the main story in town – something to do with the local homeless shelter. Either it's going to close or it's just been given some more money to stay open. Either way it's annoying a lot of the valley's residents. I hadn't really thought of Vegas as having a homeless problem but I guess it's obvious that if so many people come here in search of their dreams the temptation is to just spend one more buck ... And then just the one more and before you know it there's no more money left in the pot. What do you do then?'

According to these callers you live off the state.

On line 2 there's a bloke who actually has proof that all homeless people are a bunch of wasters – getting up to 900 bucks a month in benefits.

'You can live off that,' says Paul.

'I'll put 'em on a chain gang if I have to ... You've got lots of telemarketing, fast food jobs ... jobs where you hand out stuff on a street corner ... There's no *excuse* ... If you took away the *damn* shelter, there wouldn't be any ... most of them are homeless by choice ... *They are bums.'*

Paul is trailing for calls again. 'Where are all the liberals? Where are all my homeless sympathisers?' he cries in a mock tearful voice.

Joy is on the line now. She is not a liberal but she has an opinion on them:

'The liberals in this country over the last forty years have created a dependent society. I remember back in Jersey where I come from. We had to work real hard to get on in life ...' And there follows a long ramble about the ethics of society. She has seen someone begging and then depositing cheques.

Paul and she agree. 'It's a disgrace.'

This is an odd way to wake up – the milk of human kindness seems to be running in semi-skimmed form this morning.

The seven o'clock news comes sponsored by some shop or mall called The Boulevard. And there's an ad for something called the 'Right Wing Romance Club' which seems to be a dating service. Its name may be a bit of a giveaway as to the politics of the listeners.

Paul changes tack after the news to berate one of their non-listeners. It seems that someone has a similar number to the stations and, whenever there is a competition on or a particularly popular phone-in, he ends up answering quite a lot of calls from people like Margaret and Joy. In an act of vengeance, whoever this man is has started to tell people that he is the radio station and that they have won an enormous prize. I think that's really rather clever. Paul doesn't.

'Don't give people false information on the phone – it's a federal crime.'

Then Paul starts on the court action of the day. There's a local girl in court who killed a car full of people when she drove after taking ecstasy.

'I think this girl should be charged with murder. She needs to go to jail for a million years. Any human being caught by the police with alcohol or drugs in their body above the legal limit – *no* trial, because there is no defence. If the physical evidence shows that you were intoxicated – *life in prison. No parole.* That will end drunk driving. No more Mr Nice Guy.'

At this point I really have to get up.

Today's mission is to try to find another way of contacting Art Bell. I can't spend all my time in Vegas lying on a hotel bed eating burgers – although I imagine Elvis did quite a lot of that. Perhaps if he too had eaten all the salad garnish that comes with a grand burger and which is still curling on the plate this morning he wouldn't have ended up dying in such an embarrassing position. There is obviously no listing for him – Art, not Elvis – in the phone book, but then if you were worried about the Feds spying on you then you simply wouldn't make it that easy. So I send him a fax which this time is completely over the top in a begging kind of way that Paul Lyle would hate. And I send an email off to the tourist office in Parumph in the hope that it might be the kind of close-knit town where everyone knows each other and marries their cousins and the word will get to Art that there's a little British girl who has come all this way to meet him.

So I could now go and start my day the Vegas way with a few spins on the roulette wheel and 19 hash browns in one of the hotel's many eateries. The term eateries hasn't really caught on in Europe yet, but America is very keen on it. Perhaps the term restaurant is a little confusing, with its close semantic connection to restroom and all that goes on in there. A drinkary cannot be many years away. Neither gambling nor eating fat appeals, though, so I might as well start with a gentle stroll down the Strip.

There is a uniform out there on the street. It is leisurewear. White T-shirts stretched over paunches and white socks and trainers to match, with denim shorts riding up in between. This is where the Upper East Side means part of your thigh. Some of the ladies have bottoms so big and fleshy that they look like netted bags of Brussels sprouts from behind. It's a fiercely hot morning and the word that comes to mind is 'chafing'. The pace on the Strip is understandably quite slow. I have gone for the pale pastel linen dress today with that scooped, drawstring neckline so fashionable a few years back. People are staring at me as if I have come straight from the set of a costume drama.

About a block down from the MGM Grand is a car-hire place alongside the tourist office. It had crossed my mind that, given the lack of immediate response from Mr Bell, I might have to drive out to Parumph and find the bunker and present myself like a groupie at the back door at three in the morning. So I should at least investigate how I am going to get 60 miles into the desert in a country that doesn't like trains or buses that much.

Only one problem – I have a fear and loathing of driving on the other side of the road. I've only had to do it three times and all of those were for *The Travel Show*. Simon Calder and I used to do these pieces together for the show where we would go to the same place and I would enjoy the expensive option and he would do the budget version. So in the South of France he was busy catching trains and buses and I was meant to drive down the Corniche in a hire car. The only time that I have ever heard Simon Calder swear was when we had to do a sequence in Juan les Pins which involved me pulling out of a parking space. On TV three weeks later you could quite clearly see him saying 'fuck' as I swung the hire car out into the middle of the road, glancing the parked car in front and then swerved either side of the white line, trying to remember which side seemed least familiar.

In San Francisco I also managed to drive all the way over the Golden Gate Bridge with the handbrake on because I was so nervous – the car nearly blew up. And once when I was driving myself to an appointed rendezvous with the crew in Italy I had to pretend that I had overslept by an hour. In fact I get so scared at junctions that I have to follow what the car in front is doing – there's a fifty–fifty chance with this method that you will end up going vaguely in the direction you want to. That day chance was not a fine thing and I ended up on a motorway going east while the crew were waiting about 60 kilometres west.

It's odd that you don't have to take any kind of test to make sure that you can drive a car that is the mirror image of what you're used to in a country that has completely different road signs and possibly a different language. But if you want to marry someone you have fallen in love with, chances are some bloke from Immigration will come round and rifle through your pants drawer and ask you if you know your mother-in-law's maiden name before you can.

There was nothing else for it though – and this was confirmed by the lady in the tourist office when I asked if there were any buses that went out to Parumph. I might as well have asked her if she could sell me a return ticket to hell for tomorrow. Feeling full of the adventurous spirit of someone who's only been awake for two hours I said, 'I'll take a hire car then' with as much gusto as I could muster. I signed up for the full insurance – and seven forms later was the proud part-time owner of something that looked a bit like a Ford and had no gear stick.

The tourist lady said did I want to collect it from the car park at the back and drive it back to my hotel? To which I said no – I didn't know when I'd be needing it so could I just leave it there. There was some raising of the eyebrows at this point. She was very happy when she had finished serving me and simply had the 14 Japanese women who wanted to rent a minibus to deal with.

It's still only about eight in the morning and, having failed to avail myself of breakfast at the MGM, I settle myself into the Starbucks next door to think things through – like if the steering wheel is on the left then you should always try and be near the kerb. No, that's not right is it? The thing to do is to draw a diagram. So I'm merrily constructing roundabouts on the napkin with arrows pointing all over the place and using sugar sachets as the cars when a voice pipes up behind me:

'Is anyone sit'n' here?'

'No help yourself ... sorry I've spread myself out a bit, haven't I?' I say, moving the napkin carefully because I'm halfway through a Mirror Signal Manoeuvre.

'Oh ... you're from England?' she continues. 'She' is woman somewhere in the hinterland of her forties with very permed, dyed-blonde hair and a considerable amount of make-up for this time of the morning, the ubiquitous denim shorts and a T-shirt from Disneyland that has been the victim of some washing machine errors.

'Yup, that's right – from London.'

She settles on to my table, plonks down two Danish pastries and a carafe-sized coffee cup. I carry on with the 1.8 GL Sugar Sachet driving lesson. Two seconds later:

'You here all by ya'self?'

'Yup. Yes I am.'

'So am I – where ya staying?'

'Up the road – at the MGM Grand. What about you?'

'Oooooh the MGM Grand – bet that's nice ... I'm a bit further up out of town – one of those apartments on the way to malls ... They don't do breakfast though ... I'm Joelene, by the way.'

'I'm Fi – nice to meet you.'

Joelene was ridiculously happy for this time of the morning and seemed incredibly keen to chat. Maybe she was lonely. So I tell her why I'm here and what I'm hoping to do.

'Art Bell? You're going to meet Art Bell?'

'Well, not exactly – it's not proving to be that easy – but I am thinking of going out to Parumph to try to meet him – so I'm trying to work out my junctions and roundabouts before I get in the car – I'm pretty shit at driving on the other side of the road ...'

It turns out that Joelene's husband – not in Vegas with her – is an enormous fan of Art Bell's and although Joelene doesn't listen to the show she has clocked the fact that he is a bit of a radio legend. Her husband likes 'all that weird alien stuff'. She seems like a nice lady – bit on the voluble side and either slightly hard of hearing or just not all that interested in what I'm saying, because she starts her sentences when I'm only about two-thirds of the way through mine.

'You don't want to go drivin' out into the desert all by yourself you know – there is nothing and I mean nothing out there ...'

'Well, I guess at least it won't matter if I'm on the wrong side of the—'

'No – I've heard about people who have broken down with no water and no nothing and it gets real cold in the middle of the night, no you be careful out there.'

Easier said than done. I thought Joelene might be exaggerating a little – after all Parumph is only 60 kilometres away. I try to steer the conversation off the desert scare stories.

'So your husband didn't come here with you?'

'Na – it's not his thing really – and someone's gotta stay home and earn the money,' she laughs.

Joelene hasn't touched the pastries and seems in absolutely no hurry to drink her coffee either. By the end of about half an hour I have learnt that she has four kids, lives just outside Dallas and likes to come to Vegas every year to gamble. She has filthy fingernails I've just noticed. She only plays the slots and usually loses about 200 bucks every year – except last year when she got lucky and went home 300 dollars up.

She can't believe that I haven't done any gambling yet.

'But what else do you come to Vegas for? Well I guess you've come for the radio, but you've got to give it a go – you might win a million and then you could buy a radio station ...'

This is a good point.

I can't make out whether Joelene is just the chatty sort or if she is desperately seeking company, but whatever it is I rather like her. And this is everything I hoped my travels would be about – meeting new people, broadening my horizons – getting involved. As I had learnt in Vienna, going to a musical would be an awful lot more fun if you had someone to share your half-time ice cream with.

'Don't you get scared, travelling all by yourself?' asks Joelene.

'Not really – I quite like it actually. This is my first week in the States for this trip, so ask me in about a month's time – I may not like it quite as much ... Don't you mind coming on holiday by yourself?'

Joelene thinks long and hard about this one.

'Nope – I'm the friendly sort anyway so I always end up with someone.'

I wondered if occasionally that meant getting friendly with someone other than her husband. Emboldened with the confidence of striking up a friendship so easily and so early in the morning I say what I'm thinking.

'Do you fancy coming out to Parumph with me tomorrow? I could do with the company – and if we break down at least I wouldn't be by myself?'

I hadn't really thought this one through but I reckoned that it would solve a lot of driving fear problems for me and Joelene didn't look like she carried an axe around under her Disney T-shirt. After all, she had four kids – granted she may not have any pelvic floor muscles left, but that must make her a responsible member of society. And she was so darned happy it was bound to rub off on me. Art would be impressed at my ability to forge bonds with the natives.

Joelene looked delighted.

'Yeah, why not? Great idea – we can go in my car if you like. Then you wouldn't have to use that diagram ...'

Fantastic. What a result.

I'm not sure if I can get the money back on my hire car but that can wait – I'm not going to get another offer like this one, no matter how long I hang around in a Starbucks.

So we plan to meet at the junction outside the MGM the next day and head out to Parumph to try to locate Mr Bell. Isn't the world a lovely place when you just give it a bit of a chance?

I spent the rest of the day wandering through an endless series of shopping malls and casinos, putting a few dollars here and there into slot machines and winning nothing at all. Back in my room there was no reply to the fax from Art, but there was a nice message from Fitz in Palm Springs on my email saying that he was happy to 'hang with me' if I wanted to come to Palm Springs after I'd done my time in Vegas.

Fitz was the morning host on a jazz station there – he was the one who was keeping the flame of Frank Sinatra alive in the valley. Those were his words not mine. I'd met him very briefly in London when he'd appeared on my show there. He was smoother than a freshly shaved armpit and a far more appealing prospect. I only use that daft analogy there because I have a problem with the phrase 'as smooth as a baby's bottom'. From what I can make out most babies' bottoms have nappy rash and all sorts going on and smooth just isn't the right word for them.

While fannying around in my room I had flicked through the radio channels on the TV and happened upon a very comforting station called Sunny 105.6 – or Sunny 106.5, whose name derived from the happy sounds it played and the upbeat delivery of its DJs. There was a relentless medley of sunshiny tunes from the likes of Ricky Martin and The Backstreet Boys. It made a welcome change from dog broiling chat. And it had an ad that made me laugh out loud. It was advertising Vitamin World – a huge superstore on the outside of Vegas which sold vitamins. The man with the blancmange voice told me that I could go on a tour while I was there.

'Haven't you ever wanted to know how they get all those vitamins into those little pills?' he asked me. 'And how they get them to stay there?'

At first I thought – don't be daft. I've got better things to do with my time than think about that. But then it started to bug me as the day wore on. It's actually a terribly good point. How do they get B12, B6 and your RDA of Vitamin C to stay in a little pill for years on end? This was another thing I was going to have to investigate before leaving Las Vegas.

Joelene is about half an hour late and I'm beginning to think that she isn't coming. She's probably got carried away on a slot somewhere on a winning streak and is now, as I'm sweltering on a corner in the middle of a highway, jetting back to Dallas in the front of the plane with champagne corks a-popping.

Just as I'm thinking my plan has failed an old charabanc of a vehicle slows down and starts hooting. She came after all. I'd say that her car is about ten years old and may not have seen a carwash in all that time. There's an overflowing ashtray and a rather strong smell inside and as the windows are all down I guess that air con was an optional extra that remained optional.

Still – it is being driven by someone else and all I have to do is pay for some petrol and buy Joelene a drink when we get back. She was delighted with this offer, especially because her husband would go crazy knowing that she met Art Bell and he didn't. It takes all kinds of things to keep a marriage sweet.

It doesn't take long to lose Vegas behind us – the low-rise condos get tattier and tattier as the big hotels of the Strip fade into the rearview mirror. Joelene seems a little less chatty than this morning. Perhaps she is one of those careful drivers who doesn't like to be distracted. She can certainly put her foot down and quite a few other motorists are beeped out of the way as we zoom out of town in Thelma and Louise style. Joelene was right about the desert. There is nothing out there. And within ten minutes it's just us and a lot of rocky scrub and those big hills in the distance. I try and make a bit of polite conversation:

'So how old are your kids?'

Joelene seems to have to think about this one.

'Janie is the youngest – she's just 8, then there's the boys ... Darren is 10, Kenny is 12 and Darren is 16 ...'

'Sorry – two Darrens?'

'No, did I say that? Declan and Darren – Declan's my big man now. He's real tall – tall, tall, tall as his daddy ...'

Joelene seemed a little dreamy today.

'... And what about you?'

'No – no kids yet.'

Silence again.

I ask Joelene if she'd mind if we have the radio on and tell her about the hilarious vitamin world ad. She doesn't seem to find it funny at all.

'Don't think the radio works ... It hasn't got one of those thingy things ... you know,' and she points her fingers up in the air and starts waving them. This she finds extremely amusing.

'An aerial?'

'Yup,' she sniggers away. 'Haven't had one of those for ages ...'

Out of the corner of my eye I could see Joelene concentrating very hard on the road in front of her.

A huge truck – one of those ones that looks like a great big shiny toy – was looming up ahead of us. Joelene puts her foot to the floor and roars past it, pulling in way too quickly and getting a great big toot along the way.

'Aah – sod off,' is her response.

And then it dawned on me. Joelene was pissed. That was the smell and, having occasionally been in the same condition myself, I can recognise the sudden humour that can be found in things as daft as an aerial.

Now this was going to be tricky. What was the current state of modern etiquette concerning being in a car in the middle of the desert with a woman you didn't know who was pissed at the wheel? There were some big issues here – i.e. we could both die and there were some less important issues like offending Joelene. And to be honest getting to meet Art Bell was not even on the list.

'Errrr ... Joelene are you OK?'

'Yeah sure, Fi.'

'I mean are you OK to drive?'

'Yeah – why?'

'Well, would you like me to take over for a bit?'

'But you don't want to drive ...'

'Well, I think it's quite a straight road and I could cope.'

So I start pretending that I would love to drive – in fact I can barely contain myself at the prospect and there is nothing in the world I would rather do. Joelene doesn't seem to think that it is at all odd that this girl she barely knows now wants to drive her car, having previously insisted that she didn't.

So we pull over – some feat in itself and I take over. Why didn't I spot the warning signs? Looking back on it that would explain why she was so friendly yesterday – in that first flush of whisky or vodka or whatever she had woken up to. If I'd been back home would I have been so keen to hook up with a total stranger and drive off into the wilderness? In fairness, I could understand why Joelene had been keen on the idea too – she probably thought she was on some great adventure, meeting a girl who wanted to drive off into the desert in search of a reclusive radio star. I've got more excited about considerably more mundane things while a little bit under the influence. There was nothing for it but to head back to town. I couldn't exactly turn up in Parumph and leave her in the car while I searched out Art. And what if she had a nastier side to her when she'd got further down the bottle?

Joelene fell asleep about 30 seconds after I took over the driving and only woke up when we were approaching the same junction she picked me up at an hour or so ago.

'Are we here?'

'Well, I decided you were a bit tired so I thought maybe you didn't want to go to Parumph after all, so I thought I'd just go some other time and spare you the trip.'

This seems to be a perfectly reasonable explanation.

I drop Joelene off. Her apartments have seen better days – there are only two things in the forecourt: a Dodge van with Colorado plates and a mangy-looking dog panting in the shade.

'Nice meeting you, Fi, good luck,' says Joelene and she wanders off to her room.

She looks very forlorn.

'Will you be OK?'

'Yup – I'll be fine.'

Slam. Door shuts.

I parked the car at a very odd angle. I could hazard a guess that none of the other residents would notice anything different from previous parking attempts by Joelene herself and walked back into town.

Vegas was making my head hurt – in a different way to Joelene's – and I was going to have to do some thinking. This is how the thought process went:

Things I do want to do in Vegas:

1.   Meet interesting people at a radio station and gain some deeper knowledge about the city.
2.   Stare at as few carpets as possible.

Things I didn't want to do in Vegas:

1.   Lose all my money and end up in a homeless shelter with a dog whose prospects were worse than mine.
2.   Die in a car crash out in the middle of the desert.

So I phone Paul Lyle at AM 840 KXNT.

Six-thirty the next day and it's another American Breakfast Show experience. Paul is in full flow by the time I get to the station which is located in a building delightfully called the Marbella Plaza. It's painted very pink and is in the middle of Vegas's low-rise condo outskirts. Paul is nothing like I thought he was going to be. I imagined a rather jowly tubby Chris Moyles lookalike, probably in his mid thirties with a revved up jeep standing by outside. This is a cross between Bob Holness and that bloke with the gap between his teeth who always did vaguely funny upper-class sitcom and said 'Awwwwfully' a lot. Terry-Thomas, I think.

Paul is in his fifties with a slightly wizened look to him, a mousy moustache and today is dressed entirely in beige – from the blouson jacket right down to the slip-on shoes. He gives me a wave from behind the glass of the studio and his producer Steve says he'll come through and talk to me in the next break which is for the Finance News. For the moment he is mid rant:

144

'That Sandra Murphy – she is guilty as hell – just look at her – there is a woman who is going to jail for a long, long time … ' There is much glee in his voice.

Sandra Murphy is making the front pages of all of the papers here right now. She is standing trial for murder. Her case has been getting a lot of coverage because it's the kind of thing that you would imagine used to go on in Vegas all the time when it was a mobsters' paradise.

Ted Binion was a big fish in Vegas – he was big in casinos and had made a fortune. With that fortune went a life to match – drugs, girls, cars and intrigue. When he died of a suspected heroin overdose, his girlfriend Sandra Murphy was arrested and charged with killing him and stealing his valuables – which were very valuable indeed. A male accomplice is also in the dock. He was found trying to dig up part of the desert with a JCB not long after Ted passed away – it was said to be the place where he had built a vault full of gold.

According to this morning's *Las Vegas Sun* the jurors were told yesterday that Sandra had undergone quite a severe personality change in the 24 hours after her husband's death and had gone from 'grieving, hysterical girlfriend' to a 'foul-mouthed, materialistic heir'. She had started asking whether she was going to get the $900,000 house only one day after he died. So, things weren't looking good for the former topless dancer.

Still, she had yet to be found guilty and it surprised me that Paul could go on air and say that she was, before the jury had made its decision. The legal idea back in Britain is that you shouldn't say things like that because if a juror happens to be listening they might be swayed. But it seems that, like Vienna, you can say these things in America. I would also disagree with Paul's verdict that Sandra Murphy looks guilty – I'd say at this stage of the proceedings that tarty would be a fairer assessment.

'So what's Paul like then?' I ask Steve and Stuart the engineer, whose job it seems is to listen to three radio stations at the same time.

They look at each other nodding, 'He's cool.'

Steve is from England too – in fact he used to work at Radio One but came over here because he got fed up with 'BBC management'. I don't really want to go there so I ask him about the tone of the station. By this I mean the rather right-wing attitude it seems to have.

Steve knows exactly what I mean.

'It's not the same as Britain – here you are defined by your politics and if you're right wing then you're very right wing and if you're not then you won't be listening to us. I don't get involved in the politics here. I just leave that to them. I just work the show and pick the things that'll get people a bit wound up – makes better radio. '

I ask him if he ever feels that sometimes it goes a bit too far.

'Not really – what's too far?'

'Well, is there anything that you wouldn't say on air? I mean if it was racist or really homophobic or perhaps getting people too wound up about things?'

'Mmmm ... you should hear some of the things I get called just when I answer the phone.'

Steve is black, although I don't know how people would know that by talking to him on the phone. Maybe some of the listeners just take pot luck and launch into a diatribe on the off-chance that they have picked the right target.

At this point another bloke comes into the studio anteroom with a sheaf of papers in his hand. He's tall and blond and looks every inch the kind of young man who should work in the promotions department. He is, and his name is Pete.

He nods at me, and he and Steve chat about some competition coming up.

'... and then there's the Right Wing Romance ads ...' says Pete.

My ears prick up.

'Do you mind me asking what that is all about?'

Pete doesn't at all.

'Well, it's kind of a dating service run by the station – you know, you call and register and tell them your details and they match you up – mostly men at the moment so we need to get some more women in. Paul's done it, which is good. That might get more women to join.'

'Really,' I say, 'Paul's gone out on a date with one of the ladies?'

'Yup – don't think it went that far.'

Steve and Pete have a chortle at this.

'And the title – is it really called the Right Wing Romance Club?'

'Sure – we had to think of a name that people would remember and we're right wing and it's about romance ...'

'It's funny 'cos back in Britain that would mean that it's kind of going in search of the Aryan race ...'

Steve looks at me with a kind of 'don't push it' expression.

Steve cues the Finance News in and says that Paul now has about

seven or eight minutes to chat. The man himself comes through from
the studio and gives me a warm but bone-crunching handshake.

'So what's all this about then?'

'Well, I was listening to your show yesterday and thought it was very
... erm ... interesting ... and I'm just travelling around the world really
trying to key into places by listening to the local station so I thought I'd
come along and say hello and stuff ...'

Should I tell him he was second best to a bloke in a bunker in the
desert? Oh what the hell – he sounded like a man who could take it ...

'I actually came to Vegas to try to meet Art Bell but he doesn't seem
very keen ...'

'Pah! Art Bell – you'd be lucky – that guy is paranoid. He won't talk to
anyone right now ... No, you won't get him ... So what do you think of
our show?'

'Well, I think it's quite ... outspoken isn't it? I was listening to your
homeless phone-in yesterday, you know the Broil Their Dogs thing? And I
thought you can say a lot of things we can't back home so I'd quite like to
talk to you about that ... you don't seem to have any kind of restraints ...'

'Nope, free speech – that's what it's about – we give 'em what we
want out there – and if they want to sling the homeless out we'll talk
about it.'

'Who chooses the topics every day?'

'Steve and I go through some things before the show – and we just see
what happens.'

Paul is either dying for a pee or he just can't stand still and this entire
conversation has been carried out while he is pacing up and down.

'Do you ever get tourists and visitors phoning up?'

'Good question – no I guess we don't, but then Vegas is a whole
different town away from the Strip. You lot just come here for the fun
but we live and breathe it—'

Steve chips in, 'I haven't been to the Strip for months – you just don't
go there if you actually live here ...'

'What kind of an audience do you have?' I ask Paul.

This is Pete-in-Promotions' department and he reels off the statistics
before Paul can open his mouth.

'A hundred thousand out of a million potential listeners age 35 to 64,
over 60 per cent are males and half of them earn over 75,000 dollars a year.'

You would have thought that that would get some ladies into a
romantic mood.

'What do you think of Vegas so far then?' asks Paul.

Well, now, there's a thought.

'Mmmmm ... I'm finding it quite strange actually – I haven't won a penny yet and I had rather an odd day yesterday and I guess I'm not really doing what everyone else here comes to do, so I'm finding it a little disconcerting ...'

'Oh, go out and lose some money – you'll feel better for it,' he laughs.

Paul was not nearly as bad in the flesh as he sounded on air – in fact he had a direct way of talking and seemed genuinely interested in why I was interested in him. I was starting to realise that American talk radio exists for a different reason to our tiny versions back home. Being more established in terms of decades, it holds less fear for the punters and with so much airtime to fill, any topic is worth throwing out into the ether.

In Britain the term 'talk radio' really means 'speech radio' where you'll get a blend of features, news and chat with the occasional phone-in show thrown into the schedules. Talk Sport is the only station which is dedicated to the phone lines every day. Here in the States every town has a station that is encouraging you to phone in. Most of these will have a mix of self-generated shows that, like Paul's, are actually presented by someone in a studio at the station – the rest of the schedules will be bought in syndicated programmes like Russ Limbaugh, Dr Laura and Art Bell.

And that is the key to right-wing radio. Russ and Dr Laura thrive on their right-of-centre politics and attitudes. Russ is a mouthpiece for Republican politics; Dr Laura is apparently so high up the moral high ground that she must need an oxygen tent most days. Paul's show is followed by Russ Limbaugh's, so all Stuart the engineer has to do at the end of his show is press a button and go for breakfast.

'And do you ever have a bit of a clash with the things that you talk about or the things you advertise? I mean, if there was a story in the news tomorrow about lots of kids being shot, would you then do a phone-in about gun control – even though presumably a lot of your advertisers don't support it?'

Pete looks at me as if I'm totally daft.

'Well, we're not for gun control at this station. There's nothing wrong with the law – it just needs to be upheld better.'

'It's in the constitution,' Pete goes on. 'It's our right. And it works – I mean, you are less likely to go and attack some guy if you know that he might have a gun on him and could shoot you.'

'Do you have one ... a gun I mean?' I ask.

'No,' he snorts.

'Well, would you like to have one?'

'No – but I like to know that if I think I need one I can get one.'

I am not the first person to be dumbfounded by the arguments over guns and those amendment thingies. These lovely burghers of the city of entertainment are doing exactly what their constitution tells them to do – they are speaking freely and airing their views, they are arming themselves up with AK47s (you have to wait a little bit of time to get one, says Pete, but get one you surely can). All this is just in case they have to defend themselves. Now they all find this reassuring and patriotic even, but I find it distinctly scary. What kind of a constitution is that?

Paul is just about to try to answer my question when Steve points at the clock and he disappears back into the studio to finish off the show.

'Do the audience like him, Steve?'

'Yeah – I think so – he's only been here a couple of months though.'

'Oh right – is he kind of on trial?'

'Oh no, he runs radio stations normally – he was just filling in as a bit of a favour. Today's his last day. He's off to run another talk show company – you know, selling programmes as syndicated shows? There's a lot of money in that.'

'Is he loaded then?'

'Yup – Paul's rich – this is a guy who gambles one to two million dollars a year.'

My jaw is on the floor.

'One to two million? Does he win?'

'Well, I guess that he must be up, year on year,' says Steve, very matter of factly.

It turns out that Paul lives in a Hugh Hefner style apartment in Vegas – complete with his own personal slot machine. He has lived in about twenty states and only recently came to Vegas. I can see now why Steve and Stuart had a slight awe in their voices when I asked them about him before.

The calls have stopped coming in now as Paul prepares to hand over to Russ Limbaugh. Given that it is his last day on air he doesn't seem too sad to be going. He trails the new guy who will start on Monday and says goodbye to his listeners.

Paul comes through and offers to drive me around town a bit after the show so we can carry on chatting.

'Don't you want to stay, though – you know, 'cos it's your last day?'

'Nah – they're all friends here, not like I'm going far.'

He shakes Steve's hand and says he'll keep in touch and we leave the Marbella building. No fanfare, no cake, no champagne.

We get into a huge, sleek, burgundy Lincoln Town car with Cartier etched into the doors ... and Paul does that smooth one-handed driving that you can do with an automatic. I ask him if he'll miss not being on air any more. Paul says he's not sad and he could go back to it if he wanted, but now it's the business side of radio that grabs him more – he's done more than his fair share in front of the microphone.

Mr Paul Lyle has interviewed seven presidents. He thinks that Carter was the best – 'Not at being a President, but at being a nice guy.' Nixon was the worst – 'Couldn't look me in the eyes.' And Ronald Reagan – 'Well, he was just acting a role – those were our cowboy years.'

He is single and says he has chosen to be that way.

'I decided a long time ago that family wasn't going to happen so I've made this my life.'

There is something of the Jimmy Saville about that.

'What about the Right Wing Romance line – did you really go out on a date? What was she like?'

'OK, I only did it so that I could say on air that I had – they need to get more women in so we thought that might work.'

We talk about why he ended up in Vegas.

'Same as everybody else – to make more money. I had to get out of Sacramento – too many people were hassling me there. You know, I'd become quite well known so I'd get recognised all the time and even if people didn't recognise my face as soon as I started talking in a restaurant or a bar they'd come up and want to chat ... and I needed a change, never stay in one place for long. I used to do all the big interviews for Public TV when the British stars came over – John Thaw, John Inman – all those guys – they were great – are they still big over in London?'

I'm ashamed to say that I have a momentary blank and I can't for the life of me remember whether John Inman is dead or alive, but I figure that now is not the time to make a series of phone calls and find out.

'Oh yuh, they're huge.'

We have the usual chat about why it is that old-school British comedy is still showing to the masses in the States.

There is no answer to this and Paul and I didn't find one either.

'So this is my first stop in the States really, Paul, and I hope you don't mind me saying but I'm a bit shell-shocked about all the things that you can say on air – you know, like saying people are guilty before the trial is over ... and the homeless phone-in. Didn't you get anyone standing up for them?'

'Well, in answer to the first question – if you're in the public eye then you're fair game and secondly, yeah, someone did phone but they wouldn't go on air – you just give 'em what they want here and no one takes it too seriously.'

'But if Sandra Murphy isn't guilty then could she sue you for saying that she was?'

'No – I don't think so – who would care anyway?'

Well, perhaps Sandra might.

'I bet you had fun with Monica and the President ...'

'Oh yeah, we had real fun with that ... But then this is a guy who is really powerful, he's got a sex drive – what's he meant to be doing with it? I don't care what the President does as long as he carries on being good at his job. What I don't get though is your Prince – I mean with *Camilla* though? He had *the* most beautiful lady in the world and now – I mean, what is he doing with *her*? ... We've had some fun with that one too ...'

I bet he has. By this time we are down on the Strip.

'Do you think I should try and find Art Bell – do you actually know him?'

'Yeah – I've met him – he came to an awards ceremony I was involved in last year – boy, what a drama that was ... He had to come in the back entrance and he made us put up this bullet-proof glass around the podium and he only spoke for about 30 seconds and then he disappeared. He's got a lot of problems, and they say he's got a lot of guns too – you should be careful of going out there and bugging him. If you want my opinion, then stay away from him – the more you hassle him, the less likely he is to talk to you. You do know what happened to his son, don't you?'

'Er, no.'

'He was kidnapped and attacked a while back – no one really knows the truth of it but it was something about some teacher at the kid's school who abused him. But I'd leave him alone right now if you know what's good for you.'

Paul gave me one of his business cards – and he is the President of Talk America – and purred off in the Lincoln.

Right. So far, travelling with my radio hasn't got me very far in this place of dreams. Should I carry on pursuing a man who was obviously having a lot of personal problems right now? Was it really that unwise to head out again into the desert? I was beginning to go right off Las Vegas. I had proved a little thing to myself in just listening to Art's show, and that was that it existed.

In a sea of right-wing chat and samey music stations there was a bloke who was doing something truly individual and who had done it his own way. Just that one conversation Kathleen had had about how to get to hell had been proof that radio serves all kinds of people. Maybe I should leave Art Bell alone. Or at least wait until he got back in touch with me. What was I going to learn about Vegas by hanging out with Paul? However palatable he was as a person, his style of broadcasting was a bit like watching kids on swings in the playground just egging each other on to go higher and higher. I had a stark choice to make. I either went to Vitamin World to find out how they keep the goodness in pills that look like bunny balls – or I tried to win some serious cash.

So I decided to go on *Wheel of Fortune*.

Yup, *Wheel of Fortune* is filmed in Las Vegas and there's a sign in the foyer of the green glowing MGM Grand saying that there is a choice of not one or two but three shows to join today. Yippee – I might get on TV ... and it's been some time since that happened. So I gaily hand over twenty bucks in return for a little ticket telling me to be in the studio at 2.45 prompt. A huge wave of release passes over me – I'm going to join the masses in the throw-good-money-after-bad camp.

There's not much of a queue at the door and very little frisking, which I associate with TV studios. I had fully expected some nice researcher to be standing at the door, asking all of us where we came from and how old we were and making sure that we were wearing something suitable in which to appear on television. Instead we are simply given a sticker with a number on it and told to find a seat in the studio.

As soon as I walk in I realise that I have made a terrible mistake – this is not the live TV version of the show or even the pre-recorded one. This is the MGM Grand's own personal little Wheel of Fortune hosted by a man called Mike – who is introduced as the star of TV's *Mike and Mandy*.

There's a tiny little stage and about 200 tourists flopping about drinking beer and comparing T-shirt slogans. This is not where *Wheel of Fortune* is filmed.

I don't know who Mike is or what has happened to Mandy but he gets the same applause as Roy Walker might get for *Catchphrase* – affectionate but not exactly a Robbie Williams-hold-onto-your-pants-type welcome. It's a little tricky trying to work out the calibre of a celebrity when you don't live in the country that they star in. I don't know whether he is considered cool, or if he's involved in a scandal or even if this is a good gig to get, but he gets a few whoops from the ladies in the audience so he must be doing OK.

The man on the door had slapped a sticker number 247 on to my linen dress and everyone else has a similar tag on their shirts by now. The doors are closed and Mike gets on with the show. Perhaps it is just a run of bad luck on my part, but everything I do in Vegas is going badly wrong.

We start off with an explanation of the rules – apparently when you go on the real *Wheel of Fortune* you have to take a test, not just in spinning but in general knowledge and only the cream get through.

'No really ...' Mike jokes, 'those people you see on TV – they really are the cream.'

The numbers of each contestant are picked out by computer so it doesn't matter how much the young ladies at the front stick out their chests, it is not going to matter to Mike.

'Here goes! ... Nuuuuuumber 61 ... Where is number 61 – come up and play! ... and ... nuuuuumber 24 ... 9 ... your lucky day! and the final one in this round is ... number 72! Hey – make way for number 72!'

The first of three contestants are up on stage, spinning that wheel, having the mickey taken out of them by Mike.

'So you're a pharmacist, are you? That's a mighty spin you have ... Take anything home from work ever?'

Some contestants are concentrating very hard indeed. I guess that $64,000 would concentrate your mind. A horrible conversion has taken place deep within me. Sod the carpets, sod the lily-livered liberal who cares about the homeless and has spent the last few days raging against free speech and drunk drivers – *just give me the cash.*

So when Mike gets to the second round and the computer picks the numbers, my buttocks are clenching in anticipation of getting up on stage and winning the cash.

'It's nuuuuuumber 74! Come up and play! ... Number ... 24 ... 1 and hang on to your seats ... Where is ... number 6!'

Oh bugger.

My number doesn't come up at all and within half an hour we've got down to the finalist who correctly guessed the missing blanks in the Empire State Building. Bit piss easy too ... and then, would you believe it? We get to the final and instead of just having to complete the blanks in the big screen to win, the lady just has to give three figures from the numbers on the wheel. It turns out that these will then have to match – in the correct order – three other figures picked by the computer. She doesn't have a chance of winning $64,000. That's impossible – the chances of that must be a million to one! Mike says that they have only got as far as two correct ones in their entire run. The poor woman up on stage looks about as disappointed as I am feeling . She picks her three numbers and – what a surprise – she doesn't even come close.

'What a swizz,' as my mother would say. Think about this for a moment. The MGM Grand has 5,000 rooms and even if you average it out at $100 a night (that is ridiculously on the low side because Elton must be paying at least 2,000 to light a candle in his wind in those suites at the top), then they are making half a million dollars a night. That's before the sandwiches that cost $12, the leg waxing that is 50 cents per hair and the gambling where people are just giving them cash hand over fist. Take that and add the total from 200 people paying $20 a go to buy tickets for the Wheel of Fortune show. So let's say that on average people are spending $150 per night – that is a grand total of 27 million dollars a year. So they could afford to give away $64,000 every day and still replace the carpets every year, which I highly recommend. What was going on with this city?

So I wandered out into the dusky half light of the huge casino and took a solitary $20 note up to the cashier's desk to buy a token for the roulette wheel. OK, Vegas, I'll play it your way. Here goes – my immediate future lies on Black no. 9. If I win I'll stay and make Art Bell talk to me – come hell or high water, a bulletproof vest, and a personal re-enactment of the Roswell incident. If I lose I'll go to Palm Springs.

Whirrrrrrrrr clunck clunck clunck.

Thank goodness for that.

7 Where do retired air stewardesses go?

Palm Springs

The Greyhound Bus Station on East 7th Street is the bit of Los Angeles that they left out of Beverly Hills 90210. It's seven in the morning on Palm Sunday and most of the people on the benches look like the world has given them up for Lent. There's a girl in a long tatty black leather coat and she's wandering around hawking bits and pieces – she shows me what's on special offer today – a comb, two nail files and a couple of worn down lipsticks. All are from someone else's purse and God knows how she came by them but she's incredibly polite and could teach those department store sprayers a thing or two –

'I ain't gonna hassle you, maaam – you wanna buy a nail file – all dis tings for one dollar, maaam.'

She comes out of our deal two dollars richer and pity the person sitting next to me on the bus if the sound of nails being filed annoys them as much as it does me – unless I'm doing it, obviously.

There's a slightly pervasive air of sick about the terminal and whole families, complete with bags and sacks and binliners are waiting very patiently for the buses to roll out. You can go anywhere from here – mostly for $19.50. I'm on the 7.50 to Palm Springs, just seven small stops away from where the American Dream retires and plays 'Who Wants to be a Millionaire – Oh Look I Already Am!' in between rounds of golf in the valley below the San Jacinto and San Bernadino Mountain Ranges. Our bus is packed – one whole family gets on in their pyjamas with duvets and pillows too. As we sit with the engine idling just by the sign saying 'Do Not Idle Engine', tempers are fraying slightly as there are more passengers than seats. The driver is being very patient.

'Good morning ladies and gents – my name is Romeo and I'll be your driver today. Now is anyone *not* going to Palm Springs today? If you are not then you are on the wrong bus. If you want to go to San Diego you

155

are on the right bus but you'll be changing at San Bernadino ... so ... anyone wanna get off?'

No one stirs. The old ladies in the front clutch their bags even tighter. They are upholding the International Convention of Bus and Coach Travel which states that old people must sit at the front, families in the middle and slightly younger and rowdier elements at the back. At least one person must get on pissed or have brought enough alcohol to end up that way and if you can have a mad person who simply starts talking to thin air after about half an hour, then every subclause has been upheld. After about five minutes of shuffling and luggage pulling, four sulky boys get off and head back inside the terminal. This seems to create enough space for everyone so Romeo ticks some boxes on a form, gives the throttle some welly especially for the anti-idling brigade and with a swoosh of the doors we're off.

Palm Springs is about a three-hour coach ride inland from Los Angeles in the warm flat heat of the Coachella Valley. It's a place defined by the people who live here – or have lived here. Bob Hope, Dinah Shore and Frank Sinatra are among the legends and all relished the sunny desert winters and the privacy that a place in the middle of nowhere, yet two and a half hours from LA, afforded them.

That's why Liberace went back to Palm Springs to see out his last days in his Casa there – toupee intact to the last – so as to avoid the public gaze of Los Angeles. After he died his body was taken back to Los Angeles where he was to be buried – except that his final wish for secrecy about how he died was not going to be upheld. His body was hauled back in a hearse through the desert on the orders of the Palm Springs coroner who insisted on the autopsy that led to the world knowing he died from AIDS.

On a happier note, Jennifer Aniston is said to be on her way too ... as are a whole generation of timeshare weekenders from LA who are pooling together their high disposable incomes to buy shared houses that they can flop in after their busy, busy weeks in the smog.

Like Vegas its reputation is of a pleasure place where life's little gripes can get worn away, especially in the autumn years of one's life. Unlike Vegas, the first white settler chose Palm Springs for a different reason than the money.

In 1884 John Guthrie McCallum moved his family there in search of a place that would restore the health of his son who had tuberculosis. He had met Bill Pablo, a guide and interpreter from the Agua Caliente tribe who told him about the powers of the mineral waters in the desert. McCallum packed up his family from their house in San Bernadino and set up home in an adobe hut in a tiny desert village at the foot of the San Jacinto mountains. Things went well and he wrote to his mates in San Francisco, told them all about his little oasis and within a year someone had built the first hotel in what became Palm Springs.

Robert Louis Stevenson was among the first tourists to stay in the hotel and to fall in love with desert. They have a saying for first timers here – once you get a little sand in your shoes the desert will be hard to resist. Either that or your feet will be really itchy.

The bus labours through the huge sprawling suburbs of Los Angeles, dropping off the ready-for-bed family in Claremont and picking up a gaggle of spring breakers who are also heading for Palm Springs. The suburbs of Los Angeles have spread this town into most of its neighbours, so it's one long conurbation of tidy houses interspersed by strips of low rent offices. Attorneys at law, weight loss centres, animal surgeries – all fill the spaces left in between the huge car lots.

The grannies at the front are in full swing now, sharing their bags of sweets and chatting away about the terrible traffic and displaying an encyclopaedic knowledge of illnesses affecting their friends and family. The spring breakers have nodded off and I'm just staring out of the window. Every so often on East Interstate 10 there's a huge billboard advertising some local radio station – all beginning with K. All commercial radio stations in this huge country begin with either a K or a W. The K means that the station is west of the Mississippi and the W means it is east. This is a rule upheld by the Federal Communications Commission – the government regulatory body.

These 'call letters' are more than a simple way to distinguish which side of the Mississippi you are on. They are the audio tattoo of a station – and they get said on air, a lot. Station marketeers believe that they have to carve these letters into the brains of the listeners and so it's not unusual to hear them said every time the DJ opens the microphone. Brent back in North California had this down to a T – everything sounded like it was sponsored by KZST – he brought us KZST weather, KZST travel ... even KZST time. At first I found this an annoying American habit, but by now it is washing over me and I hardly notice it. Most DJs seem to be able to blend in their call signs as if they were just another adjective that everyone would use – all the time.

As the 'burbs of Los Angeles fade away the distance between the tidy houses gets a little bigger and the length of time between Greyhound bus stops a little longer. Romeo gets a chance to put his foot down on the freeway. The little rows of shops and services pop up on the outskirts of every town we zoom through. Just outside San Bernadino there's a Hose Mart next to the Infertility Institute of South California. I hope they don't share equipment. The bus is emptying rapidly now, and it's just me and the grannies left by the time we get to Banning.

The landscape is getting more desert-like and the billboards are selling something new. Two grey-haired smoothies with beatific smiles on their faces are holding hands underneath the legend 'Sun Lakes Active Adult Community'. Then there's another one for 'Heritage Palms' and one for 'Paradise Springs', all with similar-looking happy older couples glowing with the health that living in an 'active' community has given them. Pity the poor old folk who just want to slob out when they retire – where are the 'Decidedly Inactive Communities of Sloth'?

In the distance the stretches of scrub and sand are punctuated only by fields of huge white wind turbines, gently rotating. As we are approaching this enormous demonstration of the power of wind, there's another fantastically helpful road sign for those who may not understand the basics of nature saying 'High Winds Ahead'.

One huge out-of-town shopping mall later and we are into the outskirts of Palm Springs. Nothing stands tall in this part of America because of that unfortunate little thing called the San Andreas Fault, where the tectonic plates of the earth aren't stacked properly, so there is little in Palm Springs that rises above four storeys. Most of the main street seems to be painted in pretty pinks with classy shops selling rattan furniture and knick-knack thingies that you think you need but probably don't. It's not exactly busy. There are a couple of ladies dressed identically in white shorts, ankle socks and gleaming trainers looking idly into the shop windows but apart from that the main street of Palm Springs is deserted. The bus lurches round a corner and with a final fart of the air brakes comes to rest at the terminal.

At some stage if you work in radio, or if you decide to go in search of people who do, you will come across the PR industry. It has a symbiotic relationship with any form of media that promises that oxygen of publicity. In return for the publicity, radio gets to fill its airtime and blag freebies and sometimes you get to go to parties where there might be more than just a few mini pizzas on offer. During my email chats with Fitz, the man I have come to see, he told me that I should get in touch with the Palm Springs 'people' who would be able to help me plan my trip here. These weren't Kathleen Keating type 'people' with red eyes and a desire to visit hell, they were PR people. Some would say there is little difference.

Fitz had been terribly helpful in his emails. I felt rather guilty already because all I wanted to do was come and hang around in Palm Springs with him and listen to his smooooooth jazz station. Fitz does the breakfast show at KJJZ – the valley's number-one rated jazz radio station – as well as doing a special show called Frank FM. This should be self-explanatory – it is dedicated to Frank Sinatra. All I wanted really from Palm Springs was to indulge in some smooth sounds and watch a music DJ do his thing. Fitz, though, seemed determined to make it special.

He had asked me where I was staying and as I had yet to do the budget for this part of the trip I had made vague noises about 'finding somewhere close' and 'sorting it out pretty soon'. He said he'd talk to Gary Sherwin about it. Not having the faintest idea who Gary Sherwin was but imagining him to be some hotel guru I had said 'Oh, OK that'll be good.'

Turned out several emails later that Gary was from the Palm Springs Visitors and Convention Bureau. Just the fact that he had 'Bureau' in his title was enough to make me very envious of him. It made him sound officially American in a way that watching too much *Quincy* and *Magnum* as a child can. Gary was more than a hotel guru – he had magic powers – he was the bloke who had the power to compel hotel managers throughout Palm Springs to let little British girls passing through stay in their finest rooms for *free*. Yup – totally and utterly complimentary, gratis, not-costing-a-penny type of free.

So getting off the Greyhound bus I thought I'll just pop in a cab – after all I wasn't exactly going to have to dig deep into the wallet during my sojourn in the valley.

Mr Cabbie said the ride would cost me $35. Even if you are reading this in the year 2020 and whoever presided over the American budget and economy after Bouffant Bill Clinton, you know that 35 bucks is a fair old whack for a cab ride. But thanks to that enormous bill I had learnt something very, very important about Palm Springs. A lot has changed since McCallum decorated his hut and although throughout the tourist world this whole area is known as Palm Springs, it is in fact a collective term for nine little cities that all sit back to back in the valley. The hotel I was placed in by Gary was about vertebra number 6 – otherwise known as Indian Wells. It was quite a long way from the high street of Palm Springs.

By this stage in my trip I have turned into an absolute and complete radio nutter – incapable of starting a conversation without sneaking in a reference to radio. I haven't been able to sit quietly in a hotel room without feeling the need to wind up the wind up thing and every cab I have taken has had to obey my addicted orders.

'Could you turn the radio up a little bit? and any chance that we could listen to a bit of KJJZ?' I ask, in a slightly too urgent tone.

The cabbie says he already has it on ... so he turns it up – Ruby Turner is in full flow.

'Listen to it all day – it goes a bit elevator style in the afternoon but it's good to drive to and I like the tunes.'

'Do you listen to Fitz in the morning?'

'Sure I do – he's cool, I like his tone. His music is OK – I don't know what happens to it during the rest of the day though ... Why, do you know him?'

'No not really – but I'm going to spend a couple of days with him – try and get to know this place a bit better.'

'Well, you picked the right guy. I saw him on TV last night. Some golf thing he was selling – he probably knows all the right people.'

'What would you suggest I do while I'm here?'

'D'ya play golf?'

'No.'

'Tennis?'

'No.'

'Well ...' There is quite a considerable pause here. 'You could see a concert or something – most people come for the golf though – they just stay in the hotels and chill I guess.'

'Are most of your visitors a bit – erm – old?' I ask.

He laughs. 'You're about the youngest ride I've had this year ... I grew up in the valley – there ain't nothing to do between about 10 and about 30.'

'So why did you stay here?'

'I didn't want to leave.'

Mmm. Fair enough. Teenage rebellion isn't all it's cracked up to be.

We trundled along the main route past endless manicured kerbs and the inevitable long lines of palm trees. Road after road of well-kept bungalows stretch up off the main drag. We pass Bob Hope Drive, just on the borders of Cathedral City and Rancho Mirage – another two of the nine little cities. The cabbie tells me that Bob is about the only person with a street named after him who is still alive here and only just. He is 97 and not a well man, but that doesn't stop him being trundled out in his wheelchair for various functions.

His last public appearance was at the appropriately named Bob Hope Golf Classic – a championship that attracts the big names of the fairways to the heat of the desert. Apparently Bob is not entirely 'with it' these days, and given his age you can't blame him for that. He started singing like a child when he was pushed on to the first tee; it's what he does now when he sees a crowd. Whoever it was who was teeing off – and the cabbie can't remember which golfing great it was – turned round and shooshed him before realising who it was.

'He was cringing with embarrassment,' says the cabbie. 'He almost missed the shot ...'

It can't have been nice for Bob either.

'Tell you the truth though, I wouldn't have recognised him if it wasn't for that little nose ... he's just a bag of bones now.'

You can see Bob's house from the road as we pass from whichever competing conurbation we are in now. It is a strange modern affair up on one of the hills. Like a turtle's shell, with a huge dark curved roof. It looks as if a strong gust of wind might send it frisbee-ing down the valley. The cabbie says that it is 75,000 feet of prime real estate but although the dining room seats 300 there is only one bedroom – Bob likes to entertain but he doesn't like people to stay over. I ask him if he's actually been inside. He says he hasn't but that everyone knows what it's like up there, because you are bound to know someone who knows someone who has at least been married to a pool cleaner or a delivery man who has been into the compound. I wonder if it's a case of Chinese whispers and perhaps the dining room only seats two and there are in fact 35 bedrooms. Maybe Bob is more fond of the slumber party than he likes to let on.

So we come to a halt at the Hyatt Grand Champions Resort. This falls well and truly into the category of Realistically Named Hotels. Definitely Grand, probably number one choice of many golf and tennis champions, and I have no reason to doubt that it is owned and run by the Hyatt Group.

I can't quite believe that I am here and, judging by the look on his face, neither can Robert who is the bloke manning the front desk.

'How was your journey here today, Miss Glover?' says Robert.

'Well, it was OK thank you.'

'Did you drive? Do you need someone to check your car in?'

'No thanks – I came by Greyhound bus.'

This causes a little raising of the eyebrow.

'Oh. Did that take long?' he asks.

'Nope – about three and a half hours – from LA ... It was quite interesting really...'

The eyebrow is still up a little bit. I don't think 'interesting' would be Robert's adjective of choice. I can't imagine many grand champions choose this method of transport. It seems to make the next statement from Robert a little harder for him to say.

'Well, we have been expecting you ... and we have upgraded you to one of our penthouse suites.'

'Oh, gosh – that's very good of you ...'

Now there are subtitles going on here and mine are currently displayed on the screen as:

Oh My God. Shit Shit Shit. Can't wait to tell someone ... Who can I phone? Penthouse, penthouse, penthouse – always wanted to stay in one of those ...

'It's on the fifth floor, you have to put this card into the slot in the lift to get access to it...'

'Right. OK, yup – got that.'

Oh oh oh my. I've always wanted to do that.

'Have a nice stay here.'

'Thank you.'

I love you.

You do indeed have to use a special key in the lift which immediately stops conversation among your elevator partners and once on the fifth floor there is a communal area with sofas, TVs and a complimentary bar where I guess you can hang out safe in the knowledge that you aren't going to be disturbed by someone who is just moderately well off. There are two young girls – I'd say about 14 or 15 – slobbed out on the sofa, wearing swimming costumes with damp towels wrapped round them. They're watching some sitcom type thing on the TV. One of them is delightfully picking lunch out of the braces on her teeth. I hope her father paid good money for those kind of manners. I expect when she grows up she may well go backpacking in search of cheap deals and Indian artefacts.

This is the kind of hotel where I really didn't need to bother bringing the wind up radio because there is a full stereo system just to the left of the inglenook fireplace and just opposite the writing desk, which is set against patio doors opening on to a sunny west-facing aspect of the golf course. I too could have been an estate agent. This fine property, of which we are privileged to be the sole agents also boasts a large double bedroom with Entertainment Console and en suite bathroom facility with integrated shower. In the dressing room the owners have thoughtfully installed a minibar and basin – there is a second toilet off this room. Much thought has also been given to its interior decor which creates the ambience of a light and airy country house. If you need to ask the price then you can't afford it.

Fitz is on the radio right now, I recognise his voice from our meeting in London and because he has just played Frank's 'Chicago'. He's reading an advert, a service that companies pay extra for:

'The new Purple Sage restaurant in downtown Palm Springs is an absolute must on your dining calendar this summer – the romantic candelit ambience, fine art and well-spaced tables provide an intimate setting for one of the hot dining spots in the valley and once you experience their cuisine you'll know why ... mention KJJZ for a locals discount.'

You can deduce a whole load of stuff about what Palm Springs is like just from that 30 seconds of copy. Well-spaced tables, eh? So restaurants here don't have to pack 120 covers in to make ends meet. And people here have a dining calendar? And there are two populations. Locals and tourists. And of course tourists aren't expected to listen to the radio. It's a club for people who pay their taxes in the valley. But because I've done something that the tourists aren't expected to do I could cheat now and rush down to the Purple Sage tonight and mention KJJZ for that local discount. If the cab bills carry on like today's then I might be glad of the savings.

I can't remember why Fitz came on the programme back in London – I suspect that it may have been a very smooth push from the Palm Springs PR people. He did do this fantastic turn though, in true DJ style, talking right up to the lyrics of a couple of songs we put on just so he could do that. I'm heartened to see that he employs this technique on a daily basis in his own studio.

'... as we keep the musical flame burning bright in the valley that Frank loved so much – his biggest hits here on smoooth KJJZ 102.'

In comes Frankie himself ... right on the beat that Fitz finishes speaking.

> *I get no kick from champagne.*
> *Mere alcohol doesn't move me at all*
> *So tell me why should it be true*
> *That I get a kick out of you.*

I wonder why Frank never sang about Palm Springs? Why only Chicago and New York? I guess that would be because no one ever wrote a song for him about this little playground. What are Fitz's listeners doing as he winds them down at the end of a long weekend with his Frank FM show? Are they watering the lawns? Popping down to the Purple Sage to sit at a well-spaced table? Still out on the golf course mastering their swings and putts?

The doorbell goes – yes of course the suite has a doorbell. There's a bellboy holding a tray with a little pastry tartlet cake thing on it – all dripping in cream and swirly chocolate with an exotic fruit garnish bit going on too.

'This is your complimentary welcome sweet, Miss Glover. Where would you like it?'

I'd like that to go straight to my thighs please.

'Oh anywhere,' grandly gesturing towards the many tables and desks and surfaces that you could place it on.

'Have a nice day, Miss Glover.'

Good Lord could it get any better – and what did these PR guys want in return?

The next day I realise that I'm feeling disorientated by the sheer similarity of wealth. Every street looked the same on the drive through the valley – and quite frankly the cabbie could have taken me on a wild goose chase, circling the same seven blocks and I would never have known. I need to get my bearings in this perfectly preened place. That means going up in something. Everywhere that has a tourist industry has something you can go up in to marvel at the view, take pictures and if you're lucky visit a gift shop. In Palm Springs it is the aerial tramway – another budget-busting taxi ride back to where I started yesterday. I'll take the bus.

Public transport doesn't seem to be part of daily life here and there is no one else waiting with me at the little bus stop on the main thoroughfare at the end of the Hyatt's long drive. There is so little to do if you're a teenager in this town: there isn't even any graffiti – not even a tiny, bored, angry 'Palm Springs Sucks'. Time ticks on and a stream of jeeps and Mercs and big shiny directors' cars zoom by.

The long wait gives me plenty of time to study *Palm Springs Life* – the free glossy magazine left in the suite alongside books called things like *Championship Fairways of the World, Loud Jumper Weekly, My Bunker* and *Third Wife Monthly*. If you have about a million and a half dollars to spend and you need a new place to live, then this is the mag for you ... most of the advertising is for property.

It would seem that the sought-after houses are the ones that look out over some aspect of a golf course. All come with pool and air conditioning to make sure that the desert heat doesn't get in the way. Most of the ads rely on the personal touch so you have Dave Welch and Claudia Close who both work for some 'realty' company. Their photograph looks like the kind of picture your mum and dad would have done for their thirtieth wedding anniversary. Ginny Becker is another one who has an airbrushed soft focus picture – she is selling a house in Thunderbird Heights in this issue – and she is a lady who is not adjectivally challenged.

The pad offers 'profound' elegance, a lot of gates for your 'ultimate' privacy and a 'custom etched double entry on sunset marble steps'. I am finding that a little tricky to visualise – just how active are these adult communities? Lots of rooms are being 'flanked' by things and 'you sense a feeling of unending spaciousness as you move through the space and step down into the sunken bar near the media room'. It's even got a 'secret bookshelf entry to a private office'. Not so secret now. Perhaps I couldn't have been an estate agent after all.

By far the best bit of the mag though is the diary section at the end – a full twelve glossy pages of Palm Springs society doing what I imagine it does best – partying. Many, many noses that have become completely unrecognisable later in life due to the surgeon's knife and hammer are featured on beaming faces. They've been dining and dancing in support of housing charities, education programmes, AIDS awareness, guide dogs for the valley, business achievement awards – if you can think of it then you can raise money for it and wear some pretty impressive frocks too. And get to meet not only Howard Keel but Leeza Gibbons too – so that is what she does in her spare time. She looks more than happy to no longer have Chris Quentin at her side. I wonder what the other members of the Business Women of the Year lunch would make of the new lap-dancing venture her ex-husband is busy setting up in London. No sign of Fitz, though – perhaps he MCs so much that *Palm Springs Life* no longer regards him as a photo opportunity worth having.

When the bus does arrive I am the only passenger on it. All the way to Palm Springs. And I was right, the scenery is all remarkably similar as we pootle past the same well-watered lawns and high walls. I only know that I have arrived in Palm Springs proper by the little flags waving on the main street declaring this to be the Heritage Area. It still seems to be a row of shops though. The bus driver advises me to get a cab to the tramway – I'll be in for a long wait if I want to take the bus out to it. Public transport is obviously not at the forefront of people's minds and routines here.

The tramway is enormous – this is not just a little cable car trip up a hill. I can hardly see the top of the mountain from where we are all waiting to get on. According to my overpriced guide book this thing passes through five weatherscapes, takes 20 minutes to go up and lets you out at a height of 8,516 feet. The herd of tourists who are just coming off the carriage all look a bit blue around the gills. The guy selling tickets warns me that it'll be freezing up there as there was snow last night. Oh I'll be fine, I reply.

Everyone is standing in a very nice and orderly queue until the carriage door opens and suddenly it's time to play 'Me first!'. One preppie guy and his long elegant wife shoves his kid through the legs of the rest of the herd to the front – the poor little thing must be all of four years old and looks back at him with that 'please do I have to?' look. His dad says: 'Go on, just push yourself through.' Presumably they hope that this attitude will get them to the penthouse suite of their own chosen careers ahead of the rest. Sadly I don't really have the knack and end up right in the middle of the carriage with a very fine view of several necks and loud golfing jumpers.

By the time we get up to the 8,516 feet bit I am very envious of everyone else's choice of knitwear – it is freezing at the top … and it's all gone a bit alpine. The dark wooden cafe looks as if it might any moment start hosting a fondue party for the school skiing trip from Littlehampton. Half the carriage head straight for the serve yourself buffet line which seems a little odd – surely you don't come all this way for a $10 hot dog, even if you do get to be first in the queue. You come for the view and what a peach it is.

The panorama stretches right across to the Little San Bernadino Mountains in the distance, which have gone all pinky purple in the afternoon light – and the valley is flat as a pancake down below. All the towns are teeny weeny now – spreading into each other with only the neat dots of bunkers on the golf courses marking out any boundaries between them. There's a background sound of cameras clicking as we all try to squeeze a whole desert landscape into one lens. The clouds cast huge shadows over the little cities – thousands of people clustered round the pools of the resort hotels will be tutting as their sunshine quota goes down just a tiny bit.

It was quite an appealing prospect to go and join them though. I could easily spend my week just flopping into a pool and flicking through glossy magazines. I might even have time to learn a bit of golf – something I had been saving, like Radio 4, for middle age. Looking down on the valley I could see why so many rich and famous playboys had taken up residence here – it is in fact its own gated complex. Nature has created a high wall of mountains to keep out the sprawl of the cities, and the underground water table is keeping it all green and lush. Just as thousands of residents down in those little cities are keeping out the riffraff from their private houses, so Palm Springs is keeping out the rest of California.

What did I want from the airwaves here? Something soothing and comforting – a radio mouthwash to take away the taste of Las Vegas. I wanted something that said glamour and glitz and fame and stars. I hoped that Fitz would oblige. And in a very selfish way I wanted to go to a party, get a bit tiddly and relax, make idle small talk over a few large glasses of wine and stop asking people what their favourite radio station was. Looking down on all those gated complexes, all those private charity functions, all that ultimate privacy – how was I going to gatecrash one of the valley's private functions? It was all going to rely very heavily on Fitz.

*

167

Diane is from Mississippi and has what she calls the advanced stage of Chronic Fatigue Syndrome. She is trying to help cure that with an oversized margarita while sitting at a bar stool in the Mexican restaurant at La Quinta Resort. This is pronounced La Queeta – a bit like Elton John's marvellously mixed up homage to Checkpoint Charlie – Nikita.

'The service here is sooo good, you know. I got woken up today even when I had that Do Not Disturb sign on my door – so I phoned the manager and yelled at him. I said "I've come here to get well. I have Chronic Fatigue – don't you realise I have to sleep?" And you know what? He upgraded me straight away ... came to move my luggage and everything. Now I've got the most lovely room right at the back – much nicer than before.'

I felt a bit guilty I hadn't had to endure years of tiredness to get my upgrade.

'Are you on the mend though now?' I ask.

'Oh yeah – my husband sent me here for a week to get away from the kids, they're what do it.'

'How old are they?'

'That's the problem. The youngest is 19 months – the oldest is 17 years.'

'Blimey – that's quite a gap,' I say, realising as soon as I have that I probably don't need to point this out to Diane.

'Yup – one in between as well – but the baby has just knackered me right out.'

I'm not surprised. Diane looks like she is well into her forties. Maybe she's married to a prime minister.

I tell her that I am waiting for four men to turn up who I haven't met before and that I'm not sure if I've come to the right place. The La Quinta resort seems to have a lot of different restaurants and I didn't write down exactly which one I was meant to be in to meet Fitz and 'the guys'. The guys are the PR men including Gary the Hotel Magician and they are taking me out to dinner. I have tried to insist that it really should be the other way round but even in our brief phone conversation I sense that people do what Gary tells them to do – and he tells them in the nicest possible way.

'Well, if they don't show up you can always have dinner with me ... I could do with the company, although I might talk a little too much after another one of these.' Diane glances at the rose-bowl-sized margarita she is halfway through. Oh God, I think, no, because I'll end up asking you to drive me out into the middle of the desert just because we have the same number of X and Y chromosomes.

She was a teacher, but can't face going back to the classroom, so now she wants to do an Internet start-up called Wall Street Kids because a friend of one of her kids used his birthday money to invest over the Internet and has made quite a bit of profit. Diane reckons that there are a lot of kids who would want to do the same. It's at this stage that I realise I have entered a completely different world of tourism with none of the Vegas brashness but all of the hoped-for wealth. Diane is quite happy to admit though that she lives vicariously through her husband these days and keeps putting off going back to any kind of work – 'what with the baby to look after too you know ... and we do so much travelling now as well ...'

I ask Diane if she ever listens to the radio when she travels.

'No, come to think of it, I never do – what are you listening to here?'

'It's a jazz station – I thought it'd be good to listen to some music – all the talk was getting me down a bit.'

We're halfway through discussing whether or not we would ever phone a radio programme (Diane says not one of those problem ones, unless they use a special machine to disguise her voice), when I get a tap on the shoulder and a smiley looking man in a brown leather jacket and slacks says:

'Hi, are you Fi? I'm Gary – we're sitting out on the balcony. Sorry I must have missed you when you walked past – we've been there a while.'

So it's goodbye Diane and Hello Boys.

These are my dinner dates – Gary is the teamleader, Mark is a commander of the force, JT does UK-based marketing and Fitz is the very smooth one with the slicked back hair. As with any profession there are good and bad PR people and I have told myself that these men are probably from the good side. If I hadn't told myself that then I wouldn't have turned up for dinner. Bad PR people can be quite hard work. They are the ones who write press releases that go:

BIO FERTILISERS – SUITABLE FOR ALL OCCASIONS!

This one came from the makers of Baby Bio – and seemed to be making something of a wild claim – how could it be suitable for all occasions? Even dinner parties or quiet evenings in with your boyfriend? Births, marriages and deaths? How could a bit of plant fertiliser help you with all those? There was another corker I got sent a few years ago – it went:

RAMER – THE SPONGE THAT LOVES WATER!

Well, you would kind of hope so wouldn't you?

Bearing in mind that the station I was working at had an audience of predominantly upmarket metropolitan thirty-somethings who like a bit of indie music along with some hopefully intelligent chat, it was hard to work out how they would care about how effective their sponges were or how many times they should water their bathroom ferns with a bit of fertiliser. Neither of these press releases made it to air.

Good PR people are those who give you something you want but make it easier to get. I wanted to get a little bit involved in Palm Springs and Gary and his chums were making it ridiculously easy ... so far. They were also drinking Diane-sized buckets of margaritas with extra shots of gold tequila in them. I can't drink spirits as they do to me what drinking bio fertilisers would do to most other people. But I thought it would be rude not to at least attempt a margarita in order to show my gratitude for the hospitality I was being shown.

They call Gary the PM down at the visitors and convention centre on account of his diplomatic skills and all-wielding power and influence. It was obvious that he was going to lead the conversation:

'So what do you think most people from the UK think of when they think of Palm Springs, Fi?'

'Well, I guess it's kind of a playground for the rich and famous playboys of Hollywood – they come out here, buy a fuck-off gated house, pop on a pair of little white golf socks and drive round the golf courses in buggies until they pop off ...' As an opening gambit I think I could have been a little more circumspect and I should definitely have left out the swear word. The boys looked a little shocked.

'What do you want to do while you're here, Fi?'

'Just hang around with Fitz really – I'm kind of hoping that this might be a bit more of a partying place than Vegas turned out to be.'

I tell them about the failure of meeting Art Bell and the ranting station I turned up at instead.

They all shake their heads when I tell them the subject of the phone-ins I listened to.

'Well, you won't get that here,' says Fitz. 'We don't have any shock jocks in Palm Springs.'

I ask them if they think things have gone a little too far in the free-speech department and Mark, the one who I think is probably Gary's number two, says no one really takes it that seriously any more.

'You know what you're going to hear if you put Howard Stern on – he used to be shocking but it's pretty predictable stuff now – it's just kids who find it funny.'

'But what about saying that the Columbine killers should have thought more about sex?'

Everyone shakes their head as if they're embarrassed that I've heard about this.

'We just don't take any notice of it any more,' Mark nods at Fitz. 'Howard Stern's just an act now, isn't he?'

'I don't think I know anyone who still listens to that garbage these days ... but he's tied into all this syndication and he can still sell the advertising space so all the little stations round the country just keep on taking it. They'd never know if they could do a more popular breakfast show themselves because they never try.'

'How's that going to change?'

'When Howard Stern goes to his own personal Columbine,' one of them quips.

I'm learning fast that Fitz is a bit of a marketing tool for the PR boys. They take him on trips for exactly the reason that I've made the trip out here – because he sells the Frank Sinatra connection so well and is the very image of what a smooth-talking jazz aficionado should be. We talk about him for a while because I get the feeling that he's not all that interested in talking about the giants of talk radio.

'So do you do a lot of other things here besides the radio shows?' I ask, hoping that Fitz will say that he goes to endless parties and would I like to come along.

'Oh sure, sure – I fix up concerts, MC a lot of stuff, I have a social soirée every week at the Ritz Carlton – that's like a weekly drinks party for the listeners of KJJZ – you should come along.'

And it was as simple as that. I had only been in Palm Springs for two days and here I was with a personal invitation to a party. And not just a party – a social soirée at a Realistically Named Hotel. I was on a lucky streak.

'You know, Fi, he never takes a day off,' says Mark.

'Well, playing golf at the weekends and hosting at the Ritz aren't exactly work are they?' Fitz quips back, before anyone else can.

Fitz is looking well on it too – I'd put him somewhere in his early forties – maybe a bit more if this was the cold light of day. He's got the kind of slicked-back black hair that you'd expect a guy who says 'smooooth jazz' for a living to have and if he suddenly got up on stage and burst into a Frankie number then his linen suit wouldn't look at all out of place.

Fitz is a little more than just a DJ. According to the *Desert Sun*, the local newspaper, 'he has more pals than the United Way'. Fitz has realised the power of the microphone in quite an impressive way in the desert – he is not only the voice of the mornings on KJJZ but is a concert promoter too. So he books the acts, gives the radio station the opportunity to make money selling ads and sponsorship and then plugs the concerts on the radio show too – neat, ha?

When Fitz started on air at KJJZ – and that was only three years ago – he also started up a listener appreciation society. When it reached 1,000 on the roll call – he rewarded everyone by putting on a concert by saxophonist Warren Hill at the Ritz Carlton hotel.

A stream of people come over to say 'Hi' or 'How ya doin' to either Fitz or Gary – they are obviously rather big fishes in this small starlit pond.

'So is Fitz a bit of a star then?'

I've posed this as a general question but am also hoping that it might illicit a long answer from someone so that I can eat my dinner. All these questions mean that the margarita-to-stomach-contents ratio is not looking good.

'Most people here know you by now, don't they?' says Mark. 'If they don't listen to your show they'll have seen that TV ad ...'

They all chuckle a bit. Fitz looks a bit put out. 'What ad?'

'He does one for a hotel here – and it's got him sinking a putt from about 20 feet,' says Mark. 'Just how many takes did you have to do to get that putt in the hole? Now that's what you should be asking him Fi.'

'Oh, ha ha ha,' says Fitz. 'Only about five ...'

I realised that evening that it was quite a long time since I'd had a full-blown conversation with anyone that wasn't just about radio. I'd turned into the Pete Sampras of chat. Big on serve but hard to sustain a rally with. These boys though seemed very happy to chat so we moved on through Gerry Adams to Tony Blair and gun control and the importance of having a constitution and all that stuff that you can do so easily in America. It is strange that, given the 'special relationship' we are supposed to have with these people, it's always easier to have a conversation about the differences between our two countries and not the similarities.

'There must be some dirt on Tony Blair,' says Mark. 'He can't really be that squeaky clean?'

'It depends what you mean by dirt really,' I reply. 'If you mean wine, women and song then no, I don't think he's done much wrong.'

'But the baby – is it his?' This seems like an entirely natural question to Mark.

I am shocked. 'Is that what people are asking over here? Good God, we haven't even gone down that path.'

Of course, that's exactly what we would have asked if it was Hillary announcing that a late in life ovary had popped – but Cherie? I felt almost protective of her. I had missed a great opportunity to start something, though. Who could I have picked as illicit dad – John Prescott, Jack Straw, Michael Portillo?

By the time the bill comes the boys are saying something about Celine Dion being pushed into a pond and I'm explaining my latest theory of hotel ratings. This has moved on now from Realistic Names. It is now the Chair Based Rating System. It is quite simple: the more chairs in your room the higher you are in the luxury category – the Hyatt's Penthouse suite has twelve. I'm not sure that Gary is going to adopt this as the new star rating system in his bureau's literature. But he is being kind and humouring me, although he looks a little shocked at my language which has slipped a notch for every margarita drunk. As we walk to the car he is still doing his gentle PR stuff.

'You know the valley is full of creativity, Fi – that's another thing people don't really know. Many people came to write and paint here, especially from the Hollywood crowd. You see the hotel entrance over there?'

He points to the reception of La Quinta Resort.

'Well, Frank Capra, you know, *It's a Wonderful Life* and all that – well, he liked coming to stay at the hotel so much that he wanted to give something back to the people who ran it. So he used to sit outside at a little table and welcome all the guests as they came in.'

'Did people know who he was?' I ask.

'Not immediately, but they did when he said "Hi – I'm Frank Capra, welcome to La Quinta."'

I bet this guy writes a mean press release.

Fitz's morning job is in another slightly out of town block grandly called the Palm Springs Business Centre and houses a few offices, a gym and two radio stations. KPLM is the country one and KJJZ is Fitz's smooth jazz.

I wonder if the PR boys know that he has to broadcast from a very small box every morning for three hours. His studio must be all of 8 foot by 4. It is smaller than the hut at Camp Shamrock – and I never thought I'd see a studio smaller than that. It's reminiscent of the Socatel Hotel in Charleroi, only because the air con has bust today so it's rather sauna-like inside. It's packed with CDs, signed photos, a huge banner for the station, Fitz, his desk of faders and a large man called Jeff who is about to read the news when I arrive. Jeff is squeezed into one corner of the box, which means that we have to leave the door open while he reads the news because there isn't actually room for the three of us.

It's a million miles away from 840 KXNT. This is how to slip gently into your day without the hassle of actually waking up disturbing you at all. It's a breakfast show for people who do not need to get their adrenalin pumping and their aggression out in the open. I should imagine that there are thousands of perky older couples waking up to Fitz of a morning. They are having a gentle swim in the architecturally designed pool, before wafting into the country-style kitchen for some breakfast, before pushing some secret button in a bookshelf and settling into the private study area for some serious financial portfolio studying.

Fitz's show is basically three hours of music from the smoother end of jazz – Phil Collins Big Band sounds are in there right alongside Ronnie Jordan. He introduces a track off Ronnie's latest album, pulls up the fader – waits until about 30 seconds of the music has gone by and says 'Hot Jazz' into the microphone – except he makes it sound more like 'Haaart Jazz'.

While Ronnie is heating up the speakers, Fitz answers his own phones and chats quite happily to whoever it is.

'Hi Dennis, what can I do for you?'

I can only hear one side of the conversation and from Fitz's response I have no idea what it is that Dennis wants. It's not until Fitz has said 'Mmm' and 'Uhu' and thanked him for calling and told him to keep listening that I find out. Dennis did a bit of work for Frank Sinatra at his house in Palm Springs and Frank gave him a Jack Daniels bottle, specially engraved with all the characters he had played in the movies. Dennis needs a bit of cash and, although he doesn't want to sell it, he thinks he might have to. Does Fitz think he can get $300,000 for it?

'Would he really get three hundred grand for it?' I ask.

'Well,' he says, 'it's got Frank's name on it – but then so do a lot of things round here, like his grave for instance.'

'Fitz, did you actually know Frank?'

'Well, kind of – I met him once when I was in a bar in New York with a friend of mine. I was only 24 and we saw him sitting over the other side so my friend goes up to him, you know, real polite and said, "Hi Mister Sinatra ... I'm in the business too and I'm with a guy tonight who would just love to meet you," and do you know what? Mr Sinatra just said, "Bring 'im over."

'So I go over and he's so kind and he says, "I'm going to be at Caesar's Palace in a few days' time – be my guest if you wanna come to the show." Well, I mean we're not going to say no, are we? So we go and we kind of think he'll have forgotten but then – can you believe it? – when we get there there's a bottle of champagne waiting for us. He was nothing but a gentleman ... hang on a minute.'

Ronnie has come to the end of his hot jazz. Fitz swings round to the CD stack and pulls out another CD. 'I'll just do this link.'

It's someone I have never heard of in the jazz world – I have to confess that isn't saying much. Whoever it is will be playing in Palm Springs this summer – Fitz plugs away and the red light's off within about ten seconds.

'Just think of how many people Mr Sinatra must've said hello to on a daily basis. I mean the guy was mobbed wherever he went ... but wow ... what a guy.' Fitz looks genuinely sad. 'I always try and end the show with a Sinatra song – for the locals ...' He pauses. 'And for his memory out there.'

It's gone very quiet in the box. I reckon old Frankie must have had some sixth sense about the kind of people who would keep his reputation well and truly alive after that final curtain came down. He was right about Fitz.

'He's buried here, isn't he?'

'Yup, in the cemetery on Ramon. I went to pay my respects on the anniversary of Mr Sinatra's death – took two bottles of Jack Daniels, drank one myself and put the other by the graveside. Some people had laid cigarettes and Martini bottles ... It was a sad, sad day when he died.'

But how fantastic that his fans keep his memory alive with miniature bottles of booze in the cemetery. Will Geri Halliwell inspire that kind of well-thought-out grave gift – maybe some lip gloss and a small poodle? I doubt it.

I ask Fitz why he came to Palm Springs after his bigger career life in syndicated radio.

'Oh, fed up of the city – got a good offer. I'd go crazy at this stage of my career if I just had to read one-liners. They're major market people here; it's got more of a cosmopolitan feel to it, they know I'm a syndicated broadcaster ... so you know, it works for everyone.'

'We get a lot of stars here – Barry Manilow phoned up the other morning to ask about a song he'd heard me play – I couldn't remember which one it was though, can you believe that? So he listens to the show. When Celine Dion played at the golf tournament she said that she had KJJZ on because her and Renee loved to listen to it ... Sidney Sheldon, he listens too ... It's like a great big city here but nooooo hassles.'

I vaguely remember that Celine had cropped up in the conversation at La Quinta – unfortunately I can't recall quite how. I don't have much time for her warbling myself but I'd still like to meet her.

'Is Celine Dion nice?' I ask Fitz. 'I've always thought it might be tricky to get close to her, you know with all her air punching going on.'

This was meant as a joke. Fitz didn't seem to get it at all.

'Sorry not with you there, Fi.'

'Never mind – what was it that you were all saying about her getting thrown in the pond last night?'

'Oh that – cuh! don't get me started. She was the big name for a recent golf tournament, she was so nice to everyone and she signed autographs and chatted and had her picture taken and you know she didn't have to do all that. And then at the end she jumps in the pond with the winner because that's what the big name always does – you know, it's like become a tradition and the local paper here – you've seen the *Desert Sun*?'

I nod.

'Right, well they start having a go at her and saying that she's jumping on the bandwagon. Wrote something really petty about her, something like "How would she feel if the golf winner got up on stage and started singing with her?"'

Fitz delivers this quote in perfect mock bolshy five-year-old tones.

'I called 'em on that – stupid people, don't they realise that the big names are good for us here? What some little paper editor thinks is bad enough but when they get to print it while her people are still here … pah …'

Obviously not everything about living in a small town is appealing. Because Fitz's show is largely music we have plenty of time to chat – it's the added advantage of jazz tracks coming in at 7 minutes.

Fitz left home at 17 in Washington and was married by 19. He could claim to have always worked in the media – he started out as a newspaper delivery manager – but always had a love of the tunes so he went to work for a 'prog rock' station back when an advertising salesman got $100 a week. I can't work out whether this is twenty years ago or two – depends how much commission work he was doing. He got to do some on air stuff at the weekends and fell in love with the glamour of it all.

'You know, when I was first working there I walked into a studio one day by mistake and there was this guy sitting there in full make-up – real tall guy in drag and smoking dope … do you know who it was?'

'No idea – could have been a lot of people I guess.'

Fitz laughs. 'Yeah could be a lot of them today – it was Roxy Music … what a great place to work, eh?'

He spent a few years in country and doing on-stage and backstage work for TV and radio and when he worked his way to New York, things really took off. He got nominated for a Billboard award, got syndicated and met Wendy – his now wife and 'partner for life'.

There's an even easier way of telling how long a music DJ has been in the business and that is by the volume level of his headphones. Fitz's were at Tommy Vance level, which shows he must have been wearing them on a daily basis for about twenty years. They are so loud that pretty soon he'll be deaf and able to buy a big house near one of those motorways that are now going quite cheap because of the noise.

We've run out of time for a Sinatra track today so Fitz just manages to squeeze in a thought to leave his listeners with at the end of the show.

'Don't let what you can't do get in the way of what you can do … I'll speak to you tomorrow – I'm Fitz and this is KJJZ – smooth jazz.'

And with that Fitz picks up his wad of papers on the desk, the red light goes off and he shuts the door to the studio behind him.

'Where's the next programme coming from?' I ask.

'Oh, from Denver, via satellite – it's syndicated.'

Fitz's show is the only one that comes live from the studios of KJJZ. He says that's the way most stations operate these days. And even though Fitz has done what I would call a full day's work already, he says he hasn't even started yet. There is business to attend to, but he says we can go and see Frank's house first. Yet again I find myself in a motor vehicle cruising the long streets of Palm Springs.

Frank's compound isn't as impressive as I'd have hoped – at least not from outside. But, you've guessed it, it's got high walls and huge gates to keep out nosey parkers like me.

'Have you been in?' I ask Fitz as we sit outside in his black jeep.

'Yup – and it's incredible – you can feel the parties they used to have in there ... See that roof there – that's the bit that Frank built on when JFK came to stay ...'

It looks like a suitably presidential roof. I'm half expecting him to say 'and you see that grassy knoll ...' but he doesn't.

I can't think of much to say really while looking at the wall – although once again I am impressed by Palm Springs' ability to live totally behind closed doors.

At most radio stations if you suggested having a social soirée it would be down the nearest pub and based on the following criteria – it has to be smoky, badly furnished, serving only the worst chemical lagers and have a very wide selection of crisps because everyone will get so pissed they'll have forgotten to eat.

KJJZ is not a typical radio station. Fitz at the Ritz is the weekly social soirée hosted by the eponymous DJ and the Ritz Carlton is one of the valley's most desirable hotels. It's the only hotel to look down over the valley and because of its unique height it doesn't have a golf course. Fitz says that is about to change because these days you just have to have a golf course to attract the right kind of business. He points to an area of what I perceive to be vertical scrubland which is going to be turned into a lush green bunkered paradise. Good luck to them.

It's only about 4 o'clock but they're already setting up a sound system in one of the hotel bars. It's got a huge terrace outside which overlooks the valley. A couple of people are splashing about in the pool below but other than that the staff to guest ratio is in double figures. And everyone **knows** Fitz.

One couple is already ensconced in prime position at a table by the dance floor.

'Fitz! Fitz! over here – come and say hello!'

Don and Elizabeth are Fitz's biggest fans. Don says they get there early every week to make sure that they get their seat and have the perfect vantage point for the evening's events. I'd say they are in their early sixties but everyone looks so ridiculously healthy in this town that they may well be in their early eighties but just enjoying the active lifestyle.

'Oh, we listen to him every morning and we go to all the concerts and this – this is the highlight of the week,' they coo. 'It's so nice to meet a man in the media business who is so genuine and down to earth – and you know we've met his wife and he is really kind to her too. In this age where all the big stars seem to marry and divorce every week – well, he strikes us as a real gentleman.'

Don and Elizabeth are relatively new to the valley. They came here on holiday the year before last and had such a good time that they went home, sold their house in Dallas, I think, and came back to Palm Springs permanently a couple of weeks later. Don did something in the airplane industry. Now they just hang out. Elizabeth says that the social soirée is great for them because they get to meet lots of like-minded people. I can't help thinking that of all of Palm Springs' advantages, a diverse cross-section of population is probably not one of them. But they've made a lot of friends on evenings like this – all fellow listeners of KJJZ.

Within about twenty minutes I can understand why they come early every week. The room is filling up and all the chairs around the sound system and the tiny dance floor are filled. Strong perfumes are blowing in with the desert breeze from the terrace. There's a lot of air kissing going on – 'Oh daaaarling – it's so luuuuvly to see you ... mwa mmmmmwa ...' Fitz has dashed off to do something important so I make my excuses to the pre-eminent members of his fan club and head out to the terrace.

There are two women standing by the door, eyeing up the tables which have filled up too. Everyone is top-to-toe glamoured up.

'I think that man might be going over there, Barbara ...' says one of the ladies.

'Shall we go and ask him? Otherwise we'll never get one ...'

Getting a table seems quite an imperative this evening. These ladies look like they have been to Fitz at the Ritz before. I introduce myself.

I can't believe my luck. God, how it's changed since Las Vegas.

Mary-Anne and Barbara are not only terribly friendly but they are air stewardesses with one of the big American airlines. They are everything that I imagine an off-duty air stewardess should be: immaculate make-up, matching accessories garnered from duty-free shops around the world and the kind of hair that is most definitely in a 'style'.

'I'm from London,' I say by means of a conversation opener because I'm boring myself if I ask them what radio stations they listen to. It's pretty obvious they listen to Fitz, otherwise they wouldn't be here.

'Isn't that funny?' says Mary-Anne. 'We're in London all the time. I'm not flying at the moment because I've got tendonitis in my arm but Barbara has done the London run for years...'

Mary-Anne's tendonitis is, like Diane's chronic fatigue, being aided if not cured by a Cosmopolitan. Both she and Barbara have made a special effort tonight. I presume that they don't dress up in little black cocktail outfits every night of the week, but I may be wrong. Mary-Anne's cleavage, which is very impressive for a mature lady, is attracting admiring glances from right down the other end of the terrace. It has the same gradient as the hill on which the Ritz Carlton is going to build its golf course. Quite happily the man sitting at a table by himself makes room for the ladies and they insist that I stay and have a drink with them.

Fitz comes over to make sure I'm OK. If he ever needed another job then New Hampshire society host should be high up on the list.

'Oh – it's fun, isn't it?' says Mary-Anne, casting her eye over the terrace. 'We never miss a Fitz at the Ritz – it's a great chance to catch up with everyone ... Are you new in town?'

I explain what I'm here for, which creates much interest among the people hovering around. One of them says it's a shame that the photographer from *Palm Springs Life* isn't here.

'Have you seen the photos from the dinner yet?' says Mary-Anne to a blonde lady who's just sat down. Mary-Anne explains that they have just done a special charity evening and that she is the organiser of the Dusty Wings Group.

'What's that?' I ask.

'Well, it's made up of air stewardesses – some of them retired – and we do a lot of charity work in the valley, dinners and things like that, and we all call ourselves the Dusty Wings.'

Only in Palm Springs could there be enough air stewardesses to make such an organisation worth founding. And what a top name. By the time the nice waiter comes along with a Chardonnay top up I have decided that I am in radio heaven. When I was up on the tramway looking down on the valley, the best I could have hoped for was that Fitz might take me to a drinks party with him where we could have a serious chat about the merits of syndication. And here I am, on the balcony of the Ritz, with two incredibly friendly members of a group called the Dusty Wings who might just tell me all the things I've ever wanted to know about life as an air stewardess.

Within about twenty minutes I'm reeling from the number of people Mary-Anne has introduced me to. They are all ladies of about the same age – to be polite I'll say over 40. Impeccably dressed in a variety of pale trouser suits or little black dresses, hair highlighted, make-up glistening, impossibly high-heeled shoes – they are all confusingly similar. There's Darleen, I think she is the former knitwear model – tonight sporting some leopard-skin trousers along with the knitwear. Connie is the one with very high cheekbones and a very low-cut top – she may be the one Mary-Anne is sharing her house with at the moment. Barbara is easier to remember just because she was introduced first. Actually I think I've got that the wrong way round – was it Connie who was the former model?

I know that I'm not going to forget Barbara's name because, like me, she is an outsider here and we have had a chat about New York where she lives. She is a Dusty Wings member and knows Mary-Anne through the airline. I am very heartened that she appears to be having the same memory problems as I am.

As Blonde no. 9 approaches the table Mary-Anne says to Barbara, 'Oh you must remember her – she was at our house the other day ...'

Barbara peers at her. 'Nope, don't recognise her at all.'

'Yes you do – she was round by the pool,' says Mary-Anne in a stage whisper.

'Oh, look at her ring – I remember the ring ...'

I can see why Barbara did. This new arrival is sporting the most enormous diamond ring – four rows of sparkling stones. It is quite breathtakingly big, like looking into a small torch.

'Hi, nice to see you again,' says Barbara once her pupils have dilated to normal size. 'I was just saying to Mary-Anne I only recognised you because of the ring ... hahhahhh.'

'Mmm – yes – people do that,' says Blonde no. 9, quite nonchalantly. 'You know Mary-Anne, I found some other diamonds I had the other day so I've been down to the jewellers to have them set in a necklace –

a bit like this one,' and she clutches at the one round her neck.

'Oh – that'll be fabulous ...'

She pulls up a chair to join us.

'Now – what do you have on your cheeks, girls?' she says to Mary-Anne, Connie and Barbara. There'd be no point in asking me because the answer would be 'thread veins'.

There then follows a ten-minute conversation about the latest bronzing powder. It is much more effective because it comes in little balls that you sweep a large brush over and then sweep across the cheekbones – so much better than the flat powders which can cake a bit and once you've got the little glittery bits on it's impossible to get them off, etc.

Now I can talk about make-up and shopping a lot but these ladies put new verve and gusto into it. And I don't for one minute intend to sound patronising either because I was gripped. And learning something new every minute. The noise on the balcony was growing and growing as more people tried to squeeze themselves through the crush next door. Every once in a while the faces round the table would change as people came and went. Mary-Anne and Barbara remained though, quite happy to wave people over rather than have to circulate.

They were both charming ladies. Mary-Anne said she was divorced and that was why she was sharing a house with one of her girlfriends right now. She wasn't flying because of her tendonitis, and she was having to take it easy. But my God, her life sounded fantastic. There were stories of barbecues they'd had at the weekend and plans for a pool party and a good bit of gossip about the other people on the terrace. Mary-Anne had just taken delivery of a green convertible – she wasn't sure about the colour. There was talk of her showing it to everyone later. She seemed like a divorcee having the time of her life.

I was too polite to ask how old she was but I reckon probably mid forties. Imagine what a divorced lady back in Britain would be doing on a Wednesday evening in Slough? What would your conversation be about? Crap maintenance payments, the pains of living alone, the lack of decent evenings out. If any of those ring even the slightest bell, then get on a plane to Palm Springs.

I bided my time before getting to the nub of it.

'Mary-Anne, can I ask you lots of things about being an air stewardess?'

'Well sure, Fi, of course you can ... Here, Barbara, Fi wants to talk about flying ...'

So I did. Yes, a lot of air stewards were gay but more so on the European carriers than American ones. And of course they had been propositioned by businessmen, especially the ones at the front of the plane.

They didn't know the specifics of where the contents of the loos went, but they were pretty sure that there wasn't a release button the captain could push over the Atlantic. The alarms would still go off in the toilets if you tried to smoke in the vacuum of the sink plug and, no, they hadn't ever had a passenger who had got pulled into the vacuum of the toilet.

I think both of them thought I was mad.

But I was on a steep learning curve of airplane trivia and had no intention of stopping there. I was saving my *pièce de resistance*, but in the meantime Mary-Anne was more than happy to expand on life in the skies.

'Did you know, Fi, in the old days we were expected to know all the names of all the passengers – even in the coach section? It was unreal ... every single name of every single person, can you imagine that now?'

'And do you prefer doing the business and first class?' I ask. 'Does everyone have to draw straws for the people in donkey class?'

She laughs at 'donkey class'. 'Have you heard this girl, Barbara – she calls it donkey class! Nope, I don't mind doing coach – I quite like it really ... Oh look over there! It's Sue! Oh Fi, you just have to meet Runaround Sue. Sue! Over here, darling! Come and meet Fi – she's from London!'

So along bounces this lady sporting a very daring combo of black and animal print and perches on the side of my chair like a little budgerigar.

'Now would you believe it, Fi – Sue is 76.'

It was quite a conversation opener. I was stunned actually – I thought maybe late fifties. Especially for the animal print.

'Oh – get away,' says Sue, not in the slightest bit bothered by this introduction.

'She's raised 11 children you know, Fi – and look at her!'

'Good God – congratulations.' It's the only thing I can think of saying apart from 'Do you want to sit down properly and I'll stand up for a bit?'

I felt that after all that childbirth I should at least offer her a chair.

'Pah, don't even think about it Fi – that's why we call her Runaround Sue, she just won't sit still,' says Mary-Anne.

'I'm fine, darlin' – but thanks,' says Sue. 'Now – who is here tonight?'

Mary-Anne runs through some of the names. 'Well, Connie is here, and Darleen was sitting there, but I think she may be having a dance – and Bob's out too and have you met my friend Barbara?'

Introductions are made – Barbara is looking a little the worse for wear after another Cosmopolitan.

Runaround Sue is still perching on my chair arm. She is a tiny woman and the mind boggles at how she managed to raise 11 children. She too is a member of the Dusty Wings group and for a time lived in London with her husband.

'I hated it. People were so boring – I never met anyone – my husband worked for a tiny company so he never brought anyone interesting home. And people were just so hard to get to know.' Sue makes a face likes a cat's bottom.

'They were all so snotty. I sat in a pub one day,' she says pub like it's 'parrrb', 'and I just thought I'll have a chat with the guy sitting next to me and you know what, Fi?'

Unfortunately I could guess.

'He thought I was a hooker! All I wanted to do was have a chat! No, I didn't like London at all.'

And with that she's off. 'Gotta dance, gotta dance, see you later – are we eating tonight Mary-Anne?'

'Don't know yet – I think so though – I'll ask around ...'

I thought about recommending the Purple Sage that Fitz had advertised with its special KJJZ discount but as they were all his listeners anyway they would already have it down in their dining calendar.

The terrace is now heaving. I think I can see Fitz over the other side of the room waving wildly at me, so I wave to him to come outside. I'm not losing my place at this table. I can also see Sue doing some pretty nifty moves on the dance floor with one of the gentlemen here this evening – quite a rare breed. This may well be the downside of life in Palm Springs as a lady.

Fitz is looking a bit shattered – while I've been out on the terrace he's done a competition draw, introduced the band, shaken hundreds of hands and circulated through the crowd like a whirling dervish of good manners.

'Everyone's having a pretty good time, aren't they?' It was a stupidly obvious thing for me to say.

'Well, that's what you do in Palm Springs,' replied smoooth Fitz.

'Do you think you'll stay here for good now – at KJJZ I mean, not at the Ritz Carlton?'

Fitz looks around the room. 'Got absolutely no reason to leave,' he says.

Mary-Anne is by now getting ready to go. I have just one last question for her – if I don't ask it now I never will.

'Is it true that you use the oxygen masks on planes to get rid of hangovers?'

She lets out a squeal. 'Oh Barbara – have you heard the things this girl comes out with? She thinks we all use oxygen masks on flights when we're hungover! Now I have never heard that one before in my life! Oh really – how funny!'

With that she was off. As she walked through the terrace I could hear her rounding up her Dusty Wings troupe:

'Darleen? Connie? Anyone up for a salad in town? I've got the new car here ...'

8 I just love your value system

New York

WOR, the home of Dr Joy's talk show, is housed in a huge skyscraper on Broadway. At eight in the morning me and about a thousand New Yorkers are racing down the street in some kind of a competition to see who can get wherever they are going first. I've stepped up my own pace now from my Palm Springs dawdle. This has been helped by ordering the kind of coffee that Gareth Hunt could only shake a handful of beans at (Americano – double shot – no cream with a bit of cold water on the top) along with a packet of regular fries for breakfast.

It was strange to come back to New York. It felt a bit like I was coming home. I recognised the route back into the city – I even thought I recognised the car lot with the 'it runs' $700 heap in it. The only thing I didn't recognise was the Ambassador because they were sold out and I'd had to book into the Comfort Inn a few blocks away. It seemed very comfortable and I was definitely in it.

By comparison to Palm Springs everyone had too many clothes on – but that would be the difference between the desert sun and the drizzle. I'd promised Fitz that I'd come back to visit him in Palm Springs again as we said our goodbyes outside the Ritz Carlton. I was pretty sure that I would – if I'm ever in the unhappy position of being on the receiving end of an affidavit then I'm first on the plane. I flew to New York the next day with a couple of flannels from the Hyatt Grand Champions that I didn't think they'd miss too much. I had my appointment with problems to keep.

So I'm charging past the huge bill boards for Elton John's *Aida*, past the queues already forming for something on ESPN – the Sports Channel and over the 41st Street junction to 1440 Broadway. Deborah, Dr Joy Browne's very helpful assistant, had said take the elevator to the 22nd floor and then walk down the corridor to the glass doors and just knock. Deborah sounded very much like the kind of efficient New York woman who could organise your life in one of those tiny filofaxes and still have time to colour-coordinate her trouser suits of a morning. Security is tight at this station and you can't just walk in like you might be able to in Palm Springs. So I follow her instructions to the letter and after tapping gently on the door a lady dressed in a blue trouser suit comes over to let me in.

'Hi, you must be Deborah ... I'm Fi Glover – I've come to talk to Dr Joy?'

Slight pause here

'I am Dr Joy Browne.'

Ahem. Right. Flying start.

Dr Joy Browne hosts the fourth most listened to talk show in the whole of the United States of America. I am very impressed by this. Although she broadcasts from New York she too has reached that zenith of broadcasting and is syndicated. She is only beaten in the rankings by Russ Limbaugh, Howard Stern and Dr Laura Schlessinger. She gets more than six million listeners and, as I had heard for myself, her callers seem to love her deeply.

Given that Dr Joy is an enormous feature in the radio world that I find myself in, she is remarkably normal. By this I mean that I am not asked to sit in an anteroom and wait for her. No one has asked to see the questions first and Deborah appears to be her only assistant. The walls in her office looking out over Broadway are covered with certificates. The thermo printing industry in New York must love her. There are several talk show host awards, some charity ones thanking her for her participation – I think I spotted a book one too and lots of those radio societies that have meetings about themselves, for themselves and give out prizes to themselves.

Dr Joy looks me up and down.

'And what is this outfit we are wearing today?'

It's a good point. I had noticed quite a few New Yorkers clocking me as I strode down Broadway. The uniform for young ladies in this city is obviously the trouser suit and the colour is black. If you want to be a little risqué then dark blue will do. I have on a pair of low-slung white trousers, a white kind of tunic thing over the top of them and some decidedly dodgy trainers which are beginning to require hanging outside the window of an evening. I've topped this all off with a diagonally slung rucksack which seemed a great idea at the time but I know that several pickpockets have come remarkably close to opening it and robbing me while my back was turned, that is, all the time. The effect of this ensemble is that I look like a Hare Krishna devotee. All I need is an orange sarong and I too can part the crowds in Oxford Street.

Dr Joy has a wry smile on her face. 'All you need is a bindi in the middle of your forehead and you could convert me at twenty paces.' She opens a drawer in her desk. 'Here ... I've only got a green felt pen, but go right ahead ...' and she starts laughing.

Dr Joy has a blondish hairstyle that may require a considerable amount of brush maintenance to keep it straight and sleek. Judging from the many photos of her around the walls in her office, the blonde element is quite a new thing. She has previously been warm brown, autumn chestnut and spicy auburn. I'd put her somewhere in her forties, probably the latter part. She has a very direct gaze that is really rather scary. I think she is very in control. It's an odd job to do, though – to listen to other people's problems all day – and perhaps staying very in control is the best way to go about handling that.

Dr Joy says she loves her job and I want to give her an award as soon as she starts speaking, one that says 'You are Great, You Really Get Radio.'

'On the show it's just the two of you – there's something mystical that happens ... a barrier is released. Maybe it's because people are anonymous yet it's public, so it's a very kind of intense experience, people forget that they are public ... I mean, I do ... my crew is notorious for saying that they can't get my attention, I'm so focused. Someone asked me once what I think about when I'm listening to the callers and I have no idea ... that's because it's all I have. Just the sound of their voice and I have to concentrate on them – I have no pictures in my head, no notes and quite often they'll say, "Oh and my children Samantha and Jo ... uh – no ..." and they'll suddenly forget that they are talking in public too and they'll let their anonymity drop. I need to be objective because if I get sucked into what their unhappiness is, I'm no use to them.'

Dr Joy is very interested in why I've decided to come and meet her – out of all the other hosts in New York I could have chosen. I tell her it's because she sounded to me like the quintessential New Yorker – and I wanted to meet a female host. I leave out the bit about wanting to listen to lots of people in misery because I feel that makes me sound warped and with my strange outfit she might call security right away. It seems that I have made the same mistake as a lot of other people about where Dr Joy is from.

'I was born in New Orleans, grew up in Colorado, went to college in Houston, then medical school in Boston and lived in San Francisco. That's the joke that everyone thinks I am the quintessential New Yorker but I'm not. The typical New Yorker is pretty smart, pretty impatient, sophisticated and maybe fairly verbal and maybe a little rude and it's kind of funny because I'm really none of the above. I am high energy though.'

The very fact that she has delivered this entire statement in under ten seconds may go some way to proving that.

Given that the whole world is made up of people with problems, it's quite strange that America is still the only real home of problem phone-ins – in Britain we haven't really got the bug yet. As the TV stations vie for the opportunity to mimic American confessionals, it is kind of odd that the cheaper, easier-to-set-up radio version is hardly touched. I ask Dr Joy why she thinks that Americans can't do without their daily dose of woes and spilling the beans.

'I think what happens is that, in spite of national stereotypes, we all have things we care about and I think the idea that there is some place you can actually get some help overcomes people's reticence. In theory a lot of radio works because you can't see – it's more that sense of urgency, the feeling that they can leave their shame behind that overcomes people's shyness.'

There's the standard thought process as well, about us Brits just not being so media trained – although I think that has changed hugely in the past five years. You seldom get stuttering voices on the phone in shows we do have – even first-time callers now seem to know the ropes. What we haven't yet fully grasped is a gender balance. At Five Live the majority of callers to every show are men. That's not just the sports-dominated programmes – that's the daily morning phone-in too. I don't know why that should be, because as a sex we can talk. For Dr Joy the challenge is completely the opposite.

'You know the really funny thing about my show is that it's half and half – men and women – so you have men sharing their innermost feelings, that's the interesting thing. In fact I get interviewed a lot by the Japanese because it's hard to imagine a society that is more reticent – they are absolutely fascinated by my show. But what is fascinating for me, is that they ask me how I got to be such a good talker and I say it should be how did I come to be such a good listener, because my kind of show can only work if you listen – I'll get in a cab and even Pakistani men who are notorious for having no emotions whatsoever will start babbling ...'

I'm intrigued by the power that this woman must have on air. I ask Dr Joy if she has ever had callers who she truly believes are about to unscrew the childproof cap and end it all if she can't help them.

'There was one guy when I started years ago when the whole talk thing was a new phenomenon and I talked to him for about forty minutes because I knew that if I didn't he would kill himself ...'

'Doesn't that scare you?' I ask.

Dr Joy shakes her head. 'At least I'm a clinical psychologist – actually the real stuff ...'

I sense this may be a dig at Dr Laura because she started doing on-air guidance way before she decided she wanted some qualifications to back that career up. Having not exactly been impressed by Dr Laura and her style, I am by no means averse to hearing a bit of bitching in her direction so I try to dig a little bit.

'What, as opposed to people who pick it up later in life?'

'Oh no,' says Dr Joy. 'I don't mind that. It's when people lie right from the word go – I mind people lying about something so important to me, which is my authenticity. I had a private practice for a while and had been broadcasting for a zillion years doing the TV show ... I'm on the board of the American Psychologists Association – get lots of awards and stuff from them ...'

'Yes, you have obviously been to a lot of dinners,' I say looking round the room.

'Yeah sure – these are only half of them, the rest are over at the TV studio ...'

'I'm feeling very small and unqualified myself now,' I joke.

Dr Joy laughs loudly and says, 'That is the entire reason they are here. I have a tough decision to make soon – either I have to stop over achieving or get a larger office – one or the other ...'

By now it's only three minutes away from the start of her show so she suggests we make a move down to the studio and chat along the way. As with all good broadcasters, it's essential to go for a pee first so I find myself dashing down a long corridor and continuing the conversation all the way into the ladies and into neighbouring cubicles. It's quite an odd place to chat about one of the big things in American radio – the right to free speech and the wrongs of abusing it.

Dr Joy agrees that a lot of people are pushing it at the moment. 'It sort of scares me a bit too – I find it as alarming. We are a country that believes so strongly in first amendment rights that I think we go overboard ... I think there has to be a level of responsibility that says "stop a bit".'

By this time we have both flushed and are washing our hands:

'I'll tell you one of my wake-up calls which was when I was working one Thanksgiving Eve and I was feeling vaguely solemn so I said to the audience, "You stuff the bird and I'll stuff your head and we'll all have Thanksgiving together ... unless it's frozen in which case just put it in the oven at 100 degrees and it'll be ready by Christmas." And I got so much mail saying "How could you say such a thing? You'll give people salmonella, don't you realise how dangerous that is? Don't you realise that some people will actually do that!"'

God it's those bloody turkeys again – creating mayhem wherever they go. It's odd that something so obviously jovial as that will get people going, yet there's a bloke on air at the moment just down the road who is, in my humble opinion, doing as much for sexual equality as Peter Stringfellow is for chastity.

We're pelting off to the studio now – down another corridor and through yet more doors that need security codes.

'I've never messed with it psychologically,' Dr Joy is sweeping along ahead of me now, 'but there is that temptation to do something goofy like that – perhaps some of my fellow political hosts have failed to take into account how much clout they really have, but part of my set-up is "do no harm". The problem is that other people who don't have my credentials are out there doing the same kind of show and if you're really trying to come on and be the most flamboyant or controversial or whatever, then you might end up doing harm. But I think you're right – a lot of stuff now is lowest common denominator and stirring the pot ... Hi John, how are you this morning.'

John is a man looking a little bit hassled, sitting in front of a phone and a computer screen with a Madonna-style microphone thing on his head.

'Hi Joy – go right through – we're all ready ...'

Joy's studio is huge and the kind that Fitz could only dream of in Palm Springs. We still have a couple of minutes to go while the last of the ads do their thing.

'Do you think American radio will change itself much – perhaps go back to a time that was a bit more conservative?'

'I don't know ... I'm firmly convinced that if I said to everyone, "Look I want you to go stand on a ledge, flap your arms wildly and fly," no one would really do that – and that's a great comfort in my life. I certainly wouldn't say it – I think there is a balance that's needed. But the argument is like a catwalk designer making outrageous fashions that no one is going to wear, but it makes you think about fashion in a different way.

'I think some of my fellow talk-show hosts are like that right now. Most of them won't have me on as a guest because I will say things like "You're kidding, right?" and there's not a whole lot of interaction. Up until a couple of years ago I was viewed as the specialty act at best and it was viewed as interesting that she got good ratings but she's not really one of us. And then all of a sudden I'm the fourth most-listened-to broadcaster in America so they think ... ummm.

'I hope that people realise they are bigots but that they should keep quiet about that and realise too that that is not the best part of them – learn not to brag about it.'

The clock is ticking and the almost-on-air lights are already on ... Dr Joy has one more thought for me before the red light makes her public property.

'And you know what – so many people look at the TV and now at the radio as a way to be famous. I have a policy of never talking about people who are up in court over crimes, just in case that is one of the reasons why they're there. If they think they can make themselves famous or whatever by their crimes – that's just not going to happen on my show ...'

The red light flicks on

'Good morning. Well, what can I say? It rained all holiday weekend but yup – come Monday it's sunshine. Let's get to it – Mike hello – this is Dr Joy Browne ...'

'I can't believe I'm talking to you ... I listen every day and I can't believe I have got through now ...'

'Well, Mike – let's see what we can do for you ...'

I leave Dr Joy to it in the studio and go and sit behind John to see just how this show is put together. John has a screen in front of him that connects to one in front of Dr Joy. He types in who is on which line, with a few bits and pieces about why they have called.

Mike is up on the screen as:

Line 1 – Mike/M/35 doesn't know what to tell people when he returns to work with HIV.

John uses shorthand: M for male; F for female; age – obvious; xwf – ex-wife; dtr – daughter. They have a code between them for just how important each call is. So a caller named Bob gets an 'old old old' after him, because although only 55 he sounds a veritable pensioner and that is not what John wants to open the show with.

Dr Joy is firm but fair with Mike.

'You don't have to tell people at work anything at all. It's none of their business – if you think it's going to make life hard for you then just say you were away for something else ...'

Mike is worried that eventually people will just find out – or guess.

'Well, Mike, if you go to work wearing a pair of sunglasses to hide a black eye, then no matter what you tell people they'll think they know why – but it's your choice what you tell them the reason for the black eye is. They'll gossip no matter what – but they won't have heard it from you.'

'OK, Dr Joy – it's great to talk to you – thank you.'

John has stacked the calls up and has some time to talk. He's been doing this for five years and wants the Dr Joy Browne Show to creep up the rankings to number one. A lot of thinking goes into choosing who makes it on air from the thousands of callers.

'Callers equal records – you'll get more of whatever people hear,' he says. 'If I put on lots of old people, we'll get more old people. If I don't put a couple of men on in the first chunk then we don't get the men phoning in ... hold on a sec.

'It's a very difficult show to get on – please call again tomorrow,' he tells one caller who he simply doesn't feel is right for the opening half hour – even though there is plenty of room on the screen and the call-holding system.

'It's difficult to screen calls – it's a knack. You've got to think male–female mix, quality of voices, quality of phone-line timing. You see this one here,' he points on the screen to:

Mary/F/53 how to get her dad to take her mum to be evaluated for Alzheimer's?

'I don't want to squeeze that one, so I won't put it on until after the next ad break.'

He stands up to count Joy into the ad break – using his hands – 5, 4, 3, 2, 1 ...

'This is Dr Joy Browne. We'll come back after these.' Cue the ads.

'Gerald you're on the air.'

Now Gerald is 42 and John says he sounds black, which is a good thing, because 'if WOR ruled we'd have white suburban housewives – so I like to play around a bit ...'

Gerald wants some advice on how to get his wife back after a big bust-up and some time apart.

Dr Joy deals with him pretty quickly with some advice about not just doing it because he's lonely but making sure it's worth all the recrimination. Judging by the number of lights now flashing there are higher-carat problems coming up.

'Does anyone ever lose it on air, John?' I ask in another quiet moment. 'Do you have to use the seven-second delay a lot?'

Every talk station is meant to have a delay button, just in case something untoward or slanderous gets said. The idea is that the presenter or producer just presses it and the output will jump to cover up the problem. It is rarely used. Slanders can often slip out without anyone noticing them at the time, and it's just as quick to flip someone's fader up on the mixing desk to cut them off.

John screws up his face a bit. 'Mmm ... only about twice a year and that's usually because some word just slips out that they didn't mean to say on air ...' He answers another series of calls and types into the screen:

> **Simone/F/26 gay, has a child from a rape, married now. How to let her husband down easy?**
>
> **Becky/F/36 how to discipline dtr 11 who is accusing someone of child abuse?**
>
> **Bob/old old old/55 when to tell 'son' that he is adopted and 'sis' is real mum?**

And it's only 9.25am.

We're out of the ads and the news, and the stations across the country pick up with Joy again. It's only in New York that I would be hearing this set of ads – that is why the countdown is so crucial to Dr Joy. She has to pick up at exactly the right time so that the stations across the country don't cut off the last bit of the ads they have put into the gap. She goes straight to Simone. Now Simone is in all kinds of shit. Just think of the number of Jerry Springer shows she could go on.

I'm a Lesbian but I'm Married to a Man
I'm Gay but I Have Kids
I was Raped but I Kept the Baby
My Kids Don't Know I'm Gay
I Married to Make Things Right but They Are Wrong.

Or perhaps just the season's finale entitled:

Bloody Hell – I Bet British TV Will Buy This One.

'Hi, I'm Dr Joy. How are you doing, Simone?'

'Well, I am seriously depressed. I have been on medication but that's just masking the underlying cause and it's not really working. I'm 26 and I'm married although I'm gay. I got married because I thought it was the right thing to do for my son. I was raped in 1994, so I thought when I was pregnant what is the right thing to do? The right thing is going to be being straight, so I married and now I've got two kids and I'm miserable and—'

Dr Joy butts in, 'Wait a minute – how old are your children?'

'One is five and I have a girl who's just two ...'

There is a pause.

'So one is from your current husband?'

'Yup, that's right but he knows that I am gay, his family knows it – I am totally out. I don't hide anything from him.'

'Simone, hang on a minute – you're looking for credit from something I don't think you should get credit for. Let's get this straight. First of all you've obviously had sex with him because you've got a two year old by him ...'

'Correct,' says Simone quite matter of factly.

'This is very confusing to me. Who raped you?'

'A friend – someone back in college. It wasn't him.' That is, it wasn't her husband. 'I tried to do what society said was right—'

'No, no, no – don't give me that. All of us have to run our lives in our own different way. Now if you had been 12, that would have been a different thing but you must have been 20 when this happened so you had a choice ...'

At this point the phone lines crumbles away and Simone disappears into white noise.

'Simone, Simone, I can't hear you properly – can you get to a different phone – can we get her number and call her back?' Dr Joy says this to John and the studio engineer. There is some frantic redialling going on in the outer studio while Dr Joy talks to thin air about the need to use a wire phone not a cell phone if you call in.

Within about 30 seconds Simone is back.

'OK, Simone, now what good does it do to be gay in a marriage with two kids? ... I'm a bit lost on this – what is your question for me?'

Simone sighs. 'OK, I think I know what I want to do but I need guidance so I can do it with less feelings getting hurt.'

Dr Joy asks her bluntly. 'What do you want to do?'

'OK. I'm not happy in a straight relationship.'

'Are you willing to lose your children, because you very well might?'

'Erm ... I don't want to but I don't think I'll have to.'

'I think you're kidding yourself. Take a deep breath for a minute – why would you have a child with a man if you thought you were gay?'

'Well, that was while we were in therapy. I guess we were trying to work it out or maybe I just thought that one day I would wake up and be straight.'

'Is there someone you're in love with right now?'

'No.'

'Do you love your husband?'

'I love him but I'm not in love with him.'

'OK, Simone.' A long exhale of breath follows this. 'Are you on anti-depressant medication and are you seeing a therapist?'

'I was, but nothing really came of it – they just wanted to deal with my preferences ...'

'OK. Now let's see if we can separate things out for you. Huh. You were pregnant long before you married this guy. You can't do the society thing because this is about you and your head. At one point you thought you could be happy with this guy. At this point I think there is some possibility you could lose your kids. Do you feel that you can raise your children?'

'Yes.'

'What is making your marriage so intolerable?'

'I feel that I don't want to be here.'

'OK. If you're saying you feel that your marriage has broken down irrevocably and you can now live by yourself and support yourself then that is good. Whether you're gay, straight or at it like cocker spaniels, what you don't do is start dating until after you're separated or divorced, OK?'

'Right.'

'Get a legal separation, get an agreement to co-parent – do it for six months and don't date during that time. It may occur to you that you're not gay and it's just this guy. If after a year you both think "let's divorce", then fine. After that, date whoever you want – at least it gives you a sense that you're behaving in a responsible way and that you're being a moral human being. Your children don't need to know about your sexuality – neither does anyone else – broadcasting it is really unfair.'

Simone agrees with all of that.

'As for the depression, well, one of the nice things about depression is that it really is treatable these days. In fact it's the only nice thing about depression – so just take some time and know what you want. But I am very impressed that you can get from a cell phone to a landline so quickly.'

Simone laughs.

'It's going to take some time, OK, but eventually you'll stop feeling like you're shadow-boxing yourself – and that's just crummy, isn't it?'

'Yeah,' says Simone.

'Good luck.'

'This is Dr Joy Browne.'

And in come the ads.

What an extraordinary story. I am gripped by Simone's many dilemmas. All of what she has just aired on national radio is so personal and private. To me and millions of other people listening, it is some form of entertainment. To Dr Joy it is some form of qualified work. To Simone I hope it helped. And I do hope her kids weren't listening.

In the studio something has just gone horribly pear-shaped. All the lines go dead – all the encouraging flashing buttons on the phone system go out at once.

'What the fuck is going on with this!' screams John. He buzzes through to Dr Joy. 'They've all gone again ... you'll have to chat.'

'Does this happen a lot?' I ask.

'Way too much,' John squeaks through rather gritted perfect white American teeth ...

Joy buzzes back, 'Just how do they expect us to do a phone-in show without any phones?'

It's a good point.

John turns round and talks with his back to me while pressing all the buttons in the vague hope that they might come back.

'She'll just have to vamp.'

'I'm sorry? Vamp?'

'Yeah, you know, just chat to herself until we get someone up.' He's hitting the buttons in rather a scary way now.

'Look at this – now I have no control – *no control!* I'll just have to put the first caller on that we get – no screening no nothing.'

In American lingo, John is pretty pissed.

So off Joy goes on a bit of vamping, mainly at the radio station's expense. 'Well, you know it's a busy programme and if you've been trying to get through for the past month then now is your time to do it ... Just give us a call and you're bound to get through – no we didn't cut you all off, the phones just went down ...'

Saved by the ad break and sure enough the phone lines all go bonkers with the detritus that John usually tries to keep off the air.

Within about two minutes the screen is full again:

Pam/F/38 midlife crisis

Suzy/F/40 procrastinating with finances

Sara/F/26 worried about church and teaching about guns

Mark/M/39 addicted to chat lines

'None of these are particularly good but we'll just have to go with them until we get some more.'

It's the bad callers' lucky day.

Once his blood pressure has reached normal New York levels, I ask John if there have been any real corkers in terms of the calls over the years. He ponders this one for a while, I imagine because he has quite a lot to choose from.

'Yeah there are some real touching ones – we had a guy who phoned years ago because his wife had just died of cancer and he just couldn't cope. He was really young – we all got upset by that one. And then he called after a couple of months, just to say that he was getting there and he keeps calling from time to time to kind of let us know how he is now. We all remember him. It's really touching to think he still listens now.'

'There must be funny moments too?' I can't believe that Dr Joy makes many cockups of her own accord.

John smiles. 'Oh there was the mafia call ... that was funny I guess. We put this guy on air 'cos he was having problems with his marriage. He didn't know how to tell his wife what he did for a living. Well, of course Dr Joy says, "What do you do for a living?" and it turns out that's he's a mafia hit man. So she's asking him all about how many people he might have hurt and the kind of things he's got up to. That was so strange – but of course this guy didn't think it was odd that he was talking about criminal activity, because he'd just phoned to talk about emotional stuff … our ears were popping out of our head. But she's good with the guys – she really gets them to talk …'

'Will she get to be number one? Can she ever beat Dr Laura?'

'Well, I think she will – we'll just keep at it 'til we do. But you know, it's hard here now. American radio is so controlled. You know that Dr Laura and Russ work for the same syndication network, so their shows get pumped out to 340 stations automatically. The real problem with that is no young talent can break through. If you're running a station in Idaho and you've got some young guns who want to do the mid-morning show, why are you going to give it to them if you can just plug into Russ Limbaugh? Why would I want Dr Sally from the local town when I can have Dr Laura or Dr Joy? It's just not going to happen – so is it going to change? No. Will it get worse? Yup …

'Sorry I've got to get back to these …' and he straps on his Madonna-style earpiece and is off again.

'This is a busy show – we can't take your call right now – do try again tomorrow,' he tells Line 1.

'Hello, what's your question for Dr Joy?' he asks Line 2.

Now unlike Fred Dineage my big question was still Why? Why would you phone a radio station and confess the innermost problems going on in your little world? Wouldn't you feel that your voice would be recognised? Wouldn't you have the mickey taken out of you for days? Wouldn't your local paper be round like a shot to pay your neighbours for snaps of you when you were 14 and wearing braces before your love triangle of different sexual orientations and animals?

On one of the only problem phone-ins in Britain, one poor guy found out about the lack of true anonymity the hard way. He had phoned Dr Pam on Heart FM in London to talk about his addiction to porn and how he liked it more than he liked doing it with his wife. Halfway through the conversation on air his mobile went off. It was his wife and she was listening to the radio too. All he could say was 'This is a nightmare.' I ask John if that's ever happened to Dr Joy.

'No, never – but that's why we don't say where people are calling from. You know this show is going out all over the States so really if you're listening in Wichita, population 3,000, you're never going to think that someone in the next-door house has phoned up – you'll always imagine it's someone miles away. And we can change people's names too ... you should talk to some of the callers though. A lot of them go on Dr Joy's TV show.'

Dr Joy's very nice assistant Deborah had fixed it for me to go along and see Dr Joy's TV show the next morning. I hadn't realised that it was a psychological show too – I imagined that Dr Joy was a chat show queen as well. So I was going to get the perfect opportunity to see the kind of people who did genuinely think that the good doctor could solve their life problems. It was a chance to make a direct comparison between TV and radio. Although it wasn't a competition, I knew which one I wanted to win.

In December 1922 John Reith, the then manager of the thing we now know as the BBC, said the following momentous words:

> Broadcasting is a development with which the future must reckon and reckon seriously. Here is an instrument of almost incalculable importance in the social and political life of the community.

He called it broadcasting: his words were spoken before the advent of mass television. But he was right, obviously. Broadcasting changed the world in a way not seen since the printing press arrived. I find it impossible to imagine a world without it. But although TV and radio both fit into that massive B word they don't always sit that comfortably with each other. Just think Chris Moyles. It's a shame to include him in the same paragraph as John Reith – although I may be helped out by the fact that neither men would know who each other are ...

Anyway, the only point of mentioning Moyles is that he may be good on radio (a matter of taste), but he certainly doesn't work on TV. The two media are different animals. For a start, TV relies on stimulating a completely different sense. It has none of the intimacy of radio, but it can be just as entertaining in a big bold way. It doesn't seem to have the spontaneity either, although when I do see someone on TV who can be spontaneous then it makes my heart sing with joy and it makes them very, very rich.

The money thing is the bit that can really piss off people who work in radio. The money that TV gets is extraordinarily large by comparison to radio – and exists in nearly every strata of the business. From channel controllers to presenters to studio managers to reporters, I'd be prepared to bet Carol Vorderman's salary that the pay is worse for radio. I will have to ask her first but I'm sure she'll be cool about it. There isn't so much money sloshing around in the coffers of radio, which I think tends to make radio people nicer. But ask me that again in 40 years time when bitterness at life in a small bungalow in Bognor has set in.

Carol Vorderman would work quite well on radio I think – nice voice, bright girl, she'd certainly be able to count the 30 seconds up to the news every hour. Whereas Richard Whiteley – lovely bloke and all that, but I'm not sure the stumbling, bumbling sentences would really work. Richard and Judy? God I don't know about that one. I think you have to see Richard to believe him, don't you?

I was interested to see how Dr Joy could make the change from radio to TV. I thought she was a very, very good radio presenter and I liked what she said about clearing thoughts from her mind and just letting the voices she heard create her focus. Watching her at work in her studio she really did look into the middle distance while listening to the callers and her concentration was obvious. No doodling, no fidgeting, no sending emails to other people in the building. Not that I'd know about any of those things. So what would happen when she was in a TV studio with a floor manager waving at her, lots of people staring at her and the visual distraction of her guests being right in front of her?

Up on 9th Avenue between 56th and 57th Street the crowds thin and the taxis make the most of the lack of traffic by sweeping down the wide street as if being chased by Steve McQueen. The dry cleaners and laundromats give the place a chemical smell and on the front of a blackened theatre is a huge white awning: 'Dr Joy Browne shows recorded here – 3pm CBS'. The black door has a piece of paper stuck to it saying 'Audience Entrance'. It opens and a guy waving a security wand ushers me in. The studio is already packed – these people are obviously even keener than I am.

You know what the studio looks like without me telling you. Think

American talk shows. Think a little raised stage with a couple of chairs on it, with a background that tries to make you feel at home with flowers and bookcases and an audience squashed into several tiers in front of the stage. Dr Joy Browne's studio has a pastel theme. This presumably reflects the fact that hers is not a shouty, shouty show with security men ready to prise apart fighting vixens – this is more of a self-help group which just happens to be on TV. The carpet on the stage could do with a Hoover.

I'm in the front row next to a group of ladies from North Carolina – in New York for a couple of days and packing in the shows. After this they are off to see *Jesus Christ Superstar*. Have they come because they like Dr Joy?

'Ohhhh yeah,' says one of them. 'I listen every day – and every day I learn something.'

'Do you know how long it will take us to get to the Imperial Theatre? The show starts at 1.30 and we don't want to miss it?'

As much as I hate musicals, I don't want to lie to them and pretend to be a native New Yorker so I suggest they ask someone else.

The rest of the audience is a very mixed bag. The girls behind me, who look very much like TLC, are comparing the studio set to Geraldo's so they obviously make a point of going to TV talk shows as a pastime. There are a few whole families in, lots of very made-up middle-aged ladies and a group of unruly black guys at the back who, with their huge puffa jackets and glinting gold jewellery, aren't really what I expected from Dr Joy Browne's demographics.

So we're all sitting there fidgeting and eyeing each other up, when on comes Jimmy. Jimmy is the warm-up man and he has a great future ahead of him.

He puts on some loud disco tracks and announces that we are all going to have a warming-up dance competition, so he drags a couple of the audience up on stage to do some dancing and break the ice a bit. Carl, part of the loud boys at the back, is more than happy to do this. It turns out they are a posse in from the Bronx. I imagine that there is a classroom missing some pupils today. Then there's a joke-telling round and Jimmy races round the studio getting people to stand up and try and make the rest of us laugh. It works and, by the time the lights are set and the cameras are ready to roll, the whole place is gagging for some raucous television.

On comes Dr Joy. Today her trouser suit is bright pink, well cut and her hair seems even blonder. She tells us that we mustn't boo people when they come on, even if we have heard bad, bad things about them. We all promise that we won't.

'It's not that kind of show, OK ... people have come here to sort things out and there are two sides to every tale – so no booing please.'

And on come the participants.

First up we have a couple. The woman is in a black T-shirt and leggings and has the strangest mullet haircut I've ever seen. Sadly her hair is so mesmerisingly bad that I don't quite catch her name. Her husband, who has a short back and sides, is called James. Dr Joy asks them what the problem is. Mrs Mullet explains that she is being made ill by the actions of her daughter Kristi. Kristi has come back to live with them, bringing her two-year-old daughter with her after her marriage failed. She is not doing enough to help around the house and Mrs Mullet is suffering from so much stress that she has ended up being hospitalised.

'I regressed to 1976,' she says through teary eyes and a shaky voice. Her husband James clasps her hand a little tighter. TLC make slight cooing noises of sympathy.

Dr Joy picks up on this.

'You regressed to 1976? What do you mean by that?'

I thought that was rather obvious and that she meant that her stress-induced illness had got as bad as it was in '76. I was wrong.

'I thought that I was living in the year 1976 ... all my actions and stuff were based on 1976.'

Blimey. Imagine that? The queen is still wandering around trying to pick an outfit for the Silver Jubilee, the world had yet to know John Major, Vanessa Feltz and Steps. Let alone Tony Blair, Bill Clinton and the fall of Communism. And Pop Tarts hadn't been invented. What a monstrous illness to have visited upon yourself. I'm not surprised she's angry at Kristi.

'Let's bring Kristi on ...' says Dr Joy. People are already booing.

Kristi does not look happy. She is rather a large girl and has trouble fitting into the seat and looks about as pleased to be there as Anne Widdicombe at Miss Universe.

Dr Joy got really rather angry with Kristi – or as angry as she could in two minutes as the multi-talented Jimmy was already winding her up to go into the first ad break.

But you could feel the hatred going on in that family. I have never seen a human look as bolshy as Kristi. Dr Joy's advice was to tell Kristi to go out and get a job and stop fannying around at home all the time. Kristi pulled her miniscule denim skirt over her stay-at-home thighs and gave Dr Joy the kind of look somewhere between loathing, self-loathing and a lobotomy.

And that was it. End of Part One. I felt a little vindicated – this wasn't nearly as good as the radio show. Dr Joy had no time at all to get to the bottom of these people's lives and she had approximately two minutes to solve it all. There was none of the intimacy, none of the pathos. But there was still a lot of Dr Joy adulation going on – the people on the stage seemed as transfixed by her as I was by their hairstyles.

Why was everybody else there? To sympathise, to learn a bit, to get their faces briefly on TV, to fill the time before a musical? I had no idea. Quite a few of the well-made-up ladies seemed to be concentrating very hard on what was going on. The Bronx boys were whooping it up and doing some very loud stage whispers and over-dramatic 'ahhhs' and 'ooohs'.

The show revved up again. And on came another stream of problem people.

April and Eileen were next, a daughter and her mum. Even though we had all promised Dr Joy again in the ad break that we wouldn't boo right away, no one could help themselves with Eileen. She was calling her daughter fat and trying to take too much control of her life. April said something that I thought was not allowed outside of a *Sons and Daughters* script: 'But I am a beautiful person.'

And at that the crowds were on their feet ... One of the boys from the Bronx let slip a 'fat old bitch' which seemed to go against the grain a little bit, but maybe they were getting confused with whichever show they went to see the day before. To be honest – and quite mean – you could have shouted that at any point during the show and have guaranteed that someone on the stage would think it was about them.

Dr Joy's pronouncement on the lives of April and Eileen was for the mum to leave her daughter alone for a week. She asked April what she would most like from her mum and she said movingly, 'For her to hold me.'

I thought Eileen was going to lose it then but she kept her hard image up and when April went in for the emotional magnum of a hug, she remained as frostily rigid as a board. TLC were on their feet again. 'Hug her! Hug her!'

But whenever Dr Joy gave out her advice the participants on the stage meekly agreed to give it a go. No one answered back.

There was a guy who said his mother was too controlling. She said she thought she was too but she didn't have anyone else in her life and had had some 'nervous' problems.

By this time the group from North Carolina were very fidgety and were almost rising out of their seats in preparation for *Jesus Christ Superstar*. Possibly this was just an intermission for them – a simple tale of friends dobbing you in, mothers who claim they never had sex and hearing voices from above may well be a little disappointing. But hey! It's a musical! It's got rhyming couplets! And as Jimmy had pointed out in his warm up, it's not like you don't know the ending to *Jesus Christ Superstar*. The group looked a little bemused when the guy's mother said that she had some nervous problems – they had to think about it for a while.

The half an hour flew by – possibly because it's not a full half hour by the time all the ad breaks have been put in. In fact Dr Joy only had about 18 minutes of the 30 in which to do her stuff. She was cool in front of the cameras though – having the odd joke with the audience about her bright trouser suit in the ad break while adjusting her hair and being shouted at by Jimmy.

We all gave her a standing ovation at the end and for a moment I thought we were going to have to shout Joy! Joy! in a Jerry! Jerry! Springer type way. We stopped short of that. Maybe the producers had thought it would make the show look a little too evangelical. After the participants had traipsed off the stage, Dr Joy came back in to sign autographs and have pictures taken. I sidled up for mine. She asked if I'd enjoyed the show and had got what I came for. I turned the question on her: 'Which do you prefer? The radio or the TV?'

She weighed this up for all of three seconds and said, 'Radio, I have more control – but there's an appetite for this kind of TV. I think it can help.'

That was all Dr Joy had time for as the musical crowd wanted snaps and signatures too. Dr Joy was definitely the star of the show. No one was even talking about any of the people who'd sat on the stage – but I was.

I saw Mrs Mullet in the foyer of the studios. She was dragging a large brown plastic suitcase behind her with tears splattering down her face and trying to get through the mob as they pushed towards the exit. No one was giving her a second glance.

I thought now was not the best time to try to ask her for her thoughts on the most successful medium with which to solve deep psychological problems – so I went for my alternative question.

'Are you OK?'

'No ... my daughter won't talk to me at all now ...' she spluttered.

'Could I just ask you what you thought coming on the show would do for you?'

She looked at me in the kind of helpless way that kittens in pet shops do. 'I thought Dr Joy could sort it out for us ... I've talked to her before and she's really good ... but I think I've made it worse ...'

'Wasn't it fun being on TV – you know, famous for fifteen minutes and all that?' I said, trying to cheer her up a little.

Mrs Mullet looked at me through the stream of snuffles and tears. 'No – I didn't do it for that.'

And you know, I felt a bit ashamed of myself for asking her that.

'What will you do now?'

'I don't know – Kristi won't even come in the car with us.'

Kristi was standing by the door glowering at us.

'Do you think Dr Joy's advice was good?'

'Oh of course – she is always so right. I love her show. I learn so much from it.'

Kristi swept past us making a loud snorting sound.

'Oh what am I going to do?' her mother wailed after her.

I gave her a hug – it seemed like the only reasonably human thing to do. Perhaps 1976 was a better place to live in after all and I know it may be of little comfort to the lady but at least it'll be twenty-five years before she reads this.

When Gideon and I were doing the Breakfast Show at GLR we did a link-up one morning with a radio station in Chicago when the Windy City was experiencing one of its hottest summers ever. People were literally dying from the heat of the Midwest and for some reason this caught our eye as the kind of news story that Londoners would be greatly interested in. It's quite possible that there was a slight dearth of any domestic news that day. So we phoned up the main station in Chicago – WGN, run by the *Chicago Tribune* newspaper – and asked if any of their journalists could do us a piece over the phone about the heatwave.

A couple called Steve and Johnnie offered because they were actually on air at the time. We linked up as a ten-minute simulcast and GLR's Breakfast Show went out to the midnight listeners across the Midwest, while Steve and Johnnie went out to the early morning listeners across W1. We learnt that the city was dripping with sweat, the authorities were caught on the hop and that Steve and Johnnie are a married couple broadcasting six hours of chat overnight every weekday night. Steve is the boy and Johnnie is the girl.

I have no idea what they learnt about us but probably that Gid and I had both failed our technical radio exams – there were lots of pauses and the wrong pieces coming in at the wrong time – and that there was no news to speak of in the whole of London that morning.

I always promised to look them up if I was ever in town and found myself doing just that a few months later when my sister enrolled for part of her degree at Chicago University. I went to stay with her for a couple of weeks and on the last night we thought it would be good to go and say hello to Mrs and Mr Late Night AM. What we didn't realise was that probably because they have to chat for six hours a night they would put us on air.

By the time we got to their studio we were what can only be described as pissed, having said our farewells to each other in the form of quite a few large ones at a bar in town. Going on air under the influence is never a good idea. I can't remember much of the hour-long chat we had but I do remember taking calls from their listeners about the current state of indie music in Britain – having explained that GLR was a towering influence in the whole country's music industry.

The calls were really specific and I ended up having to tell large fibs about what had happened to the bassist from Fleapit who had split from the group in 1987 or whether Shirley Manson from Garbage had been in any other bands before. It culminated in a call from a listener in Detroit who wanted to know what had happened to Marc Almond from Soft Cell.

'Oh,' I said. 'Marc? Yes the last time I heard of him he was living in Oxford and just about to get married.'

At this point, my sister motioned that it was really time to go.

9

Gene Hackman has a jackal of a day

Chicago

Five years on – and at the beginning of the end of my journey I found myself once again sitting in their studio in the midnight hour. This time I was sober. The following ad for the station is going out on air while I sip coffee and let my eyes get accustomed to the studio light. You have to imagine this being delivered at breakneck speed in a deep bloke's breezy Chicago accent over a music bed of bouncy rock:

Breezy Voice 1:
There's an all-new 720 Saturday now available in Technicolor sound ... Wake up to the great outdoors with Charlie Potter at six, followed by Mr Fixit at seven and at nine o'clock the all-new Steve Bertram show will fertilise the heartlands ... Cubs game – pre-game at 12.45, then we're heading for the locker-room in Sports Central, Let's Talk Gardening at 7.30 and David Lawrence with on-line tonight at 12.30 ... Phew!... boy, that's more than humans can really stand, isn't it?

Breezy Voice 2:
What number on the dial is it?

BV1:
720!

BV2:
Thank you!

BV1:
WGN.

The red light comes on and we're all on air.

Steve:

That's it, that's us Steve King and Johnnie Putman here on WGN ... evening to you all – the weekend shift starts here for us. We're hoping to do things a little differently tonight kids, because we have a special guest with us and we have some phone lines free tonight so if you wanna jump in ... Our studio guest is Fi Glover. She's with the BBC and she's writing a book about radio – so be thinking about great moments in radio. What makes you listen to us right now ... anything to do with radio, we would like to hear from you. What do you want our audience to help you with tonight, Fi?

Me:

Anything at all to do with your radio here, what you like, what you don't like – what all the Ks and Ws stand for would be a good start – but you know your listeners better than I do, so I'm in your hands ... It's good to see you both again, by the way ...

Steve:

And it's great to have you back, Fi....

The Comfort Inn in New York hadn't been the kind of hotel you'd want to stay too long in – this was not where my sister and I would end our days with our wigs and pooches. For a start it would get tedious having to walk up and down the stairs all the time with a lift that was permanently 'under repair'. The view of the air-conditioning units from the office block behind was only ever going to be inspiring if you were an air-con engineer and the absorbency of their towels suggested that I wasn't even among the first hundred to use them.

Do you ever wonder when you see that little sign in the bathroom that says 'Because we care about the environment and how much detergent is used on a daily basis we would ask that you only leave your bath towels on the floor if they do need washing'? Do you ever have a teeny weeny thought that says 'Why, if they care so much about the environment does this whole country throw away so much food and drive so many cars?' Do you ever think, meanly and I'm sure wrongly, that perhaps they get to save a lot on the laundry bills too?

Maybe I have spent too long checking in and checking out and I should be thinking of starting my journey home. So I called Steve and Johnnie from New York and asked them if I could come and wallow in their show with their listeners. With the same hospitality they had shown five years ago, they positively insisted that I do just that. Johnnie promises me that tonight's show'll be a good one ...

Johnnie:

Working at night and talking to people you get them a little more open, a little more willing – if they're sitting in their bedroom at midnight talking and the house is dark, they do start saying different kinds of things. And we find ourselves looking at each other going, 'Mmmmm, haven't heard this kind of thing before!'

Steve:

There is a real intimacy that occurs at this time of night and I think there are two reasons for that. Because of the nature of the show we are not as structured or fast-paced as other shows, say, in the morning or afternoon and we have the choice – our guests can stay for half an hour or three hours. We have a game plan but that can go out of the window at any time...

Johnnie:

Sure we had a game plan for the three o'clock hour last week but then suddenly we get a call from a woman who has a quiver in her voice ... She says, 'I can see a light in the sky ... I'm sitting here in my truck and the sky is blazing ...' So we say, 'Is there anybody else out there who can also see what this dear woman is seeing?' And boom, boom, boom, the lights on the phones go and there are all these people saying, 'Thank God you can see it too.' And I mean the hairs are standing up on the back of our necks by now ... It was so creepy and you hear the fear in people's voices and it was really up to us to find out where the UFO had landed ...

Steve starts laughing.....

Johnnie:

No, we really had to find some things out about what was going on. So we call the authorities and they say, 'Light? What light are you seeing? We don't see any light?' which made it even more intriguing. Anyway it turns out it was a power plant that was doing some kind of testing and the flames were visible in the clear sky ... nothing more than that. But we were sitting here thinking this is great radio because if you're driving along or lying in bed listening to that – all those different callers phoning up to share what they are all separately seeing – well, where else can that happen?

I suppose it could now happen in an Internet chat room. Within a few years most radio stations will have one as part of their website. It'll become another forum for discussion and chat and spotting UFOs. Having thought when I started this journey that the Internet was going to change the face of radio (and I know that sounds daft), I have come to the conclusion that it won't. People just aren't going to give up on the power of sound that easily.

Johnnie is right. Where else will you get that suddenness, that immediacy and that sense of community? The chat rooms will only add to that – I don't think they will create it. And if they do, I still believe there will be a huge market for the box in the corner that you don't have to log on to, or sit down at a keyboard to see, or pay a subscriber to use. You can't concentrate on a chat room if you're just driving along, letting the dog out for its late-night pee, having a fag on the veranda – whatever it is that you do when the radio happens to be on like wallpaper in the background.

Would Simone have logged on to a chat room to talk about her tangled life? Perhaps – never having met her, I can't really say. But you're never as close to your emotions as you are when you're telling someone something. If you're writing, then you are separated from that gushing nature of revelation by so many nerve endings that have to tell you to type, to frame a sentence. What would be an er or an um in conversation will have been edited out by the time you write it down. I truly hope that radio may always remain the spine-tingling medium for people's angst. It will help Steve and Johnnie no end.

Steve:
Another example of that kind of thing that I'll never forget – and I wish the gentleman would call us back some time soon – we were on the air a couple of years ago and we got a call from Pat ... where was he from?

Johnnie:
It was somewhere on the East Coast ...

Steve:

It must have been about two in the morning and he was calling us because he needed some help – he was a …?

Johnnie:

Paramedic.

Steve:

Yup, paramedic and during the course of his work in having to give someone mouth to mouth, he had just found out that he had contracted HIV. And what was he going to do? He was engaged, only recently engaged – should he tell his fiancée? This was just before Thanksgiving … Should he tell his family? He was calling us because he wanted to call a radio station a long way away from his home base …

Steve says they could just picture him parked up in some lay-by thousands of miles away – with that sudden need to just blurt it out.

Johnnie:

For about the next two hours the phones lit up with wonderfully compassionate people. They were calling from phone booths – it was a freezing night, wasn't it? – and some of them had pulled their trucks over to make a phone call to say, you know, just hang in there. And we were in tears and the callers were in tears and the dear man was just desperate to talk to someone. So we called a friend of ours who at the time was an AIDS educator, for some facts, and together we tried to help him out.

Steve:

We talked to him with our callers for about two hours and we wished him well and he said he'd check back with us. And he did check back with us – was it right after Thanksgiving? Yeah, it was, wasn't it … and he said he had told his fiancée and her reaction was so wonderful because she had said we'll find a way to work through this. And she had been tested and she was not HIV positive … And we haven't heard from him again … But that's just an example of what happens right out of the middle of nowhere, when you get a call that completely changes the show. You realise that people want to use the show to reach out to other people who they could never normally just walk up to on the street and talk to …

Johnnie:
To this day we'll go out on a public appearance and people will come up and say: 'I heard that show – I remember the guy ... Is he OK?'

Me:
But what still amazes me is that your psychological phone-ins are so popular – and nobody ever seems to question the advice that is being given. Don't you think it's strange that in the space of two or three minutes with so little detail known about their case history, people want to talk to these problem shows so much?

Johnnie:
Sure – it remains a mystery to me.

Steve:
I think often they just want someone with an authoritative manner to say, 'Right, dumbo, go and do this. Your life is a mess but you will sort it out.' And there'll be more people with worse things coming up. Now you know – having said that we don't have to stop every couple of minutes and we can let things flow – we are going to stop for some ads. Weather first though ... current temperature at O'Hare is 14, Lakeshore 14 too ...

Steve and Johnnie met through radio. Both of them worked for a station called WIND-AM. It was talk radio and I imagine that many people before me have cracked the obvious joke about the call sign. Before that, though, Steve used to play in a band with Peter Cetera before Peter went on to become part of Chicago – the band not the place. A love of music brought him to radio and a variety of stations including WIND. There he met one of Chicago's first female talk-show hosts – Johnnie Putman. They started doing promotional events together for the station and the rest is part of Chicago's radio history. Both of them moved over to WGN, where they have been broadcasting the overnight show from 11 'til 5am for 15 years. Yes, 15 years.

They have got to the stage in their relationship where I think that their brains have short-circuited together and they don't just finish each other's sentences, they begin them, punctuate them and add bits in the middle to them. And they have a very loyal listenership who treat them like old friends ...

Johnnie:

I was just reading a letter last night – snail mail – and this woman said she has an eight-bedroom house and in every room she has a radio which is tuned to WGN so she can hear it wherever she is.

Steve:

We have done surveys that have indicated we have the largest number of PWPs listening to us of any radio programme ... You know what PWPs are?

Me:

Nope.

Johnnie:

Well, the joke comes in because people think we mean Parents Without Partners but of course we mean ...

Steve and Johnnie together:

People Without Pants!

Steve:

We welcome people with prostate problems – if you get up in the middle of the night and happen to hear us, we welcome you!

Off air I ask them if their strange nocturnal life doesn't get them down.

Steve says they're used to it and in fact they have two days for everybody else's one.

'We go to sleep as soon as the show is done,' says Johnnie, 'and then we get up again in the middle of the afternoon to do chores and sort things out and then we go back to sleep and have a kip before we come in here.'

'Don't you find that it puts a stress on your relationship? Being with each other all of the time?'

Steve looks at me and puts his fingertips together and says quite matter of factly, 'Why get married if you don't want to be with each other?'

Steve:

We should get to these calls – Dave has been hanging on since Marconi first invented the radio – Dave, hi.

Dave:

Not quite that long but ... I wanted to make a couple of points about listening to radio on the Internet. You know that probably is the future of radio. Last year at LBC in London when Nick Abbott and Carol McGiffin did that weekend talk show, I would listen to them on the Internet.

Me:
What made you listen to them?

Dave:
Apart from being a nut I'm not quite sure ... I also do a local Thursday morning oldies show for a college station here – and all of a sudden I get an email from a woman who is listening in Washington and from a woman in New Zealand.

Johnnie:
So it's changing your life too? I just get so tickled – it's like flying in a plane ... Stick with me on this ... I'm fine about flying until I get up in the plane and really think about the fact that I'm in a Thermos bottle 30,000 feet up. I'm fine with this Internet thing until I really start thinking about it ... My mind just doesn't expand this far. They're sitting in Jerusalem in a kibbutz – we know that some of our listeners are doing that right now – listening to us. I think that can't be true, but they tell us that it is ...

Me:
So Dave, when you were listening to Nick Abbott and Carol, why did you choose to tune into a London station?

Dave:
Well, really for Nick Abbott – I found his website and it had lots of clips of him on it and I just started listening to him ...

Me:
Isn't it strange hearing lots of London news, though, that you don't really care about?

Dave:
Not really, I just like Nick Abbott ... I want to move on to something else if I may before I go.

Johnnie says feel free – with six hours to fill every night, the longer your point the better. Dave has a quite a long story about the origins of WGN which is too specific for me to grasp at this time of night. I'm so glad that Johnnie says she is spooked by the power of the Internet too.

Because it is spooky to be sitting in a studio in the middle of the night in Chicago talking to a man who spends his weekend mornings listening to Carol, Nick and a lot of ads for the Carphone Warehouse and travel problems at the Hanger Lane Gyratory System.

It's spooky because it's new. It must have been even spookier all those decades ago when radio first began and you went to the shop to buy a big wooden box, came home and put it on the table and suddenly voices started coming out of it. Dave's right – radio through your computer probably is the future. No longer tied to which frequencies you can pick up in your area, you can choose the nature, language, style and content from hundreds of thousands of stations. I've been doing it all over the place over the past few months. Logging on and listening.

The only thing that makes me odd is the fact that I'm then bothering to actually go to the places I've heard snatches from. It's hugely exciting once the spook factor starts to diminish. It means that back in Dalston I can wake up every morning to a different station. If it's a pissy North London day in the gloom of November I could wake up to some of the fresh audio air of New Zealand. If I could only find that site again for Peninsula Radio coming from Hong Kong, then I could wake up to hear what time someone would be round to place a chocolate on the guests' pillows. It means that if Nagi wants to log on in his house in Tiri to hear what the latest American slant is on the politics of his own region, he can just click in and hear Ehud Barak talking live on *Morning Edition* in Washington. That's if he can get the electricity supply connected. And if you just fancy a change – it's all there on your search engine. An enormous sweet warehouse is just opening up for business.

In the studio off Michigan Avenue, Steve is saying goodbye to Dave – so I have to pull back up to the bumper of consciousness.

'We'll be right back after these ...'

The ads are for a product called 'Joint Right-Us' which promises to give you more pain relief than you know what to do with, followed by an invitation to attend the Rehabilitation Institute of Chicago if you have a sports injury. Chicago is in pain tonight. No wonder George Clooney was kept so busy in the Emergency Room.

Johnnie:
You know only last week we were talking about the Easter weekend and what everyone was doing and we go to the email and I'll be darned if we haven't got an email from someone who

says that she is looking out of her window at a shepherd tending his sheep on Mount Olympus. She had no connection to Chicago but she had just found us on the Web and listens to us every night now. And the next email we get is from a guy in Italy who is just about to go out to work and he has us on his computer speakers too – I mean it just blows you away ...

Steve:
You know, Fi, you were talking off air before we came on about something that is really one of my hot buttons – learning about a place from the radio station that broadcasts to the local area. You know, when I was growing up I would love to do this – I grew up on the south side of Chicago and late at night I would do what we call DX-ing – you know, just spinning the dial and picking up things like Little Rock Arkansas which would have things on that I had never heard. The first time I heard Wolfman Jack he was on XERB, which was out of Texas but the transmitter was across the border in Mexico and because it was, they could exceed the 50,000 watt limitation that we have in this country ... I was playing in a rock band at that time and I'd got home from a gig, must have been about five in the morning, and I'm watching the sun come up in my car over Lake Michigan just listening to this guy going 'Can you dig it ...'

And this is what I love about Steve and Johnnie. They are two people who truly adore radio. Even if you offered them a big job in TV I doubt they would take it. I ask them if they too are a little worried by the consolidation of American radio. It's a bit precious of me to be overly concerned, given that I can go back to a country that is still offering a pretty wide choice.

Steve:
It may sound a bit self-serving to say this, but WGN is one of the very, very few that doesn't take syndication ... There is one show here – a Saturday night computer show – that I think comes from Cleveland—

Johnnie:
Washington.

Steve:

Yup, you're right, Washington.

Johnnie:

And you know we are one of the last live all-night shows – most places now you'll be driving through and you'll hear a traffic report and think, gosh that doesn't make any sense to what I'm seeing now, and then you realise that they are just putting out the daytime shows on repeat ...

Me:

Isn't that lazy, not to even bother to cut out the traffic reports in a show?

Steve:

Sure. Lazy but cost-effective. At least it doesn't happen here.

Me:

So why is it called WGN?

Steve:

It stands for the World's Greatest Newspaper – that used to be the tag line underneath the title *Chicago Tribune* on the newspaper so when they started the radio station they called it WGN.

Me:

You know what I'd really like to hear about Steve – why the Ks and the Ws?

Steve:

I don't know the specific history of call signs but I know what a lot of them meant. Like here in Chicago, at one point there was a radio station with the call letters WCFL which stood for the Chicago Federation of Labour ... erm ...

Johnnie:

A lot of our listeners probably thought that a couple of guys got together over a beer and came up with WGN ... and all the rest.

Steve:

Let's see if we can get Dick Sutcliffe our newsman in on this.

Johnnie:

He is a walking history of radio – I know that he's a little busy right now.

Dick pops up in the booth just to the left of the studio. He's a well-built guy who looks like he should be your favourite uncle – ruddy face and kind eyes and quite fond of the pies.

Steve:
What were some of the other ones Dick? We've done WGN ...

Dick:
I thought that stood for We're Going Nowhere ...

Johnnie:
Hey, Dick – we've got to keep some things a secret round here!

Dick:
No seriously ... I'm not all that familiar with the K stations ... but you know that some of them are a little mixed up – you can find the odd K in among the Ws no matter what side of the Mississippi you're on. I think I'm right in saying that when the Federal Radio Commission came along in 1934 they let those that had already named themselves stay but all the new ones had to tow the line ... but other ones, let me see ... WMAQ that stood for We Must Ask Questions ... There was WBBM – We Broadcast Beautiful Music ...

Steve:
Let's bring in one of our callers – the phones are busy – obviously a lot of you out there know a lot about call letters ...

Frank's on the line first.

Frank:
Yup, good evening WOPA – that was the Oak Park Arms Hotel – they actually broadcast from the hotel there. And there was one that had the name of the car lot it broadcast from as their title too ...

Frank has a lot of other ones – this must be his speciality. Many were named after their founders.

Steve:
WVON originally stood for the Voice of the Negro ... Now that will place the kind of time that we're talking about ...

Frank:

Young Negro Radio as well, that was WYNR ... You don't hear that said much more do you?

Steve:

Let's jump to ... is that really your name, Hiawatha?

Hiawatha:

It sure is – I'm a native of Chicago and can I start by singing the praises of this station? We don't often get the chance you know ...

There follows a paean to WGN but Hiawatha has a barbed point which has prompted him to call in – he fears that the BBC is dumbing down. He says that the news bulletins he picks up, presumably World Service ones, are being delivered in a more racy fashion with a kind of tabloid style to them. This, he says, is not what the BBC is for. Isn't it amazing how even people who don't pay their licence fee feel that they own some part of the BBC and that it owes them something in return? I say I'll try to fix it for him. There is something about this studio that makes me tell lies.

We chat quite happily during Dick's news. Steve tells a story about one guy who went on air at a new station and played only one record just over and over again. He then took out an ad in the local paper saying that someone had kidnapped all the DJs. The powers that be – the FRC – noticed this and came down on him like a ton of bricks pointing out that he couldn't play the same record over and over again, because that wasn't really the point of a radio station. But of course by that time the publicity job had been done – everyone was talking about this station that just played the same record – and everyone had tuned into it just to see what would happen.

Quite by accident, Classic FM back home hit on the same vein of publicity. Before the station officially launched they played a tape loop on their frequency to check that it was going out and to make people aware that, if they were flicking through the dial, something new was going to arrive in that slot. The tape loop was of bird songs – occasionally interspersed with a voice saying something like 'Classic FM begins on Sunday' or whatever. People became incredibly fond of the bird song, which probably was the most soothing thing you could find on the dial. Letters were written to newspapers asking the radio authorities to keep the service going; people said they didn't want the station, they wanted the nightingale to carry on twittering. Managers from the station wrote back. Publicity was garnered. Classic FM was a huge success. I'll grant you that other factors may have been at stake and that the station didn't do it deliberately, but it makes you wonder why they didn't apply for another licence for Bird FM.

Steve:
We've got only a few minutes left with Fi ... Anything you want to say or anyone you want to put her in touch with – now is your chance.

Me:
Before I go, can I ask you a question? What is your worst cock-up?

Johnnie:
Ooooh – worst blooper ... Mine would have to be my first day as a professional broadcaster in Aurora back in 1977. I was actually given the job by the general manager. He looked at me across the table and I said, 'Here, have a listen to my tape.' He said, 'I don't have to listen to a tape, the government said we have to have a woman broadcaster, so you look like woman.' I said, 'Oh my gosh, I'm only being hired because I'm a woman?'
So I walked out of there and I was kind of deflated, but then elated too because I'd got my first big break in radio, right? And I was given a pep talk by my father that evening. He said make him realise that you're not just any woman. So that next day I was really prepared. I had a four-hour talk show but we were allowed to play music. I thought that would be a bit safe – you know, you always have something to fall back on ... So I had lined up a theme of music in movies – people would call up with their favourite moments and I'd play a bit of the soundtrack.
Everything was going fine 'til I decided to share one of my favourite musical moments – it was meant to be Barbra Streisand from *A Star Is Born* ... but my hands were shaking so much because I was so nervous that I cued up the track before hers which was Kris Kristopherson ... that song is 'Go To Hell'. And he's screeching it out – 'Go To Hell, Go To Hell' and this is back in 1977 and I'm just there as the little girl at the station – and they'll all be thinking she's making some kind of a statement ...

Dick:
I've just had a call from someone saying, why don't we play the Chairman Dong tape ...

Steve:
It's around here somewhere ... Can we find it?

Dick:
Sure we can. I've already got it here.

Johnnie:
Oh, you know that shoe problem we had too, Steve.

Steve:
Oh dear ... That's a good one.

Johnnie:
You know that we have to read out some of the ads here – they pay more if we read them ourselves. Well, we had one for some shoe fitters and it came out very wrong – as soon as I'd said foo instead of shoe, I knew I was in trouble and, of course, once I'd started I had to finish it – I was mortified. But the client was delighted because it got on all the blooper programmes and got twice as much coverage.

Steve:
So we have to say goodbye to you now, Fi, but you'll be back at WGN tomorrow watching the Steve Cochran show – that's right, isn't it? Steve you don't know this yet but Fi wants to watch you in conversation with Gene Hackman – yup, it's a superstar in the studio tomorrow with Steve.

Johnnie:
You know I'm going to bet you, Fi, that Gene Hackman is going to be all business – you know the kind of guy that you'd just like to goose just to break him up a bit?

Me:
Right. I know what you mean but ... I reckon that's he's the kind of guy who's got quite a good sense of humour ...

Johnnie:
You think? Well I'm going to say all bizz ... Steve what are you going to say?

Steve:
I think he's going to be pretty businesslike too.

Dick:
Hey, guess what I've got lined up, guys? It's Dong ... the quality isn't brilliant but do you wanna hear it anyway? What do you think?

We all nod enthusiastically – there's nothing like a bit of someone else making a fool of themselves to round the evening off nicely. So this is how it goes, picture the scene of Dick – stalwart, responsible newsreader at Chicago's finest talk station:

'A leading China watcher says Deng Xiaoping no longer runs China and President Jiang Xiang Kung has taken responsibility for the country's day-to-day affairs. David Shamber, a political science professor at London University, told foreign correspondents that Kung has the second largest power base in the country after Dong. Shamber says that Dang ... sorry, Dong ... no ... it's Deng—'

There is the sound of a large grown-up man trying very hard not to think of the mortgage repayments.

'—has genuinely retired ... phhhhheeeee ... and that should Dong die ... the 84 year old Zing who also controls China's military ... I'm sorry ... that's Xiang ... would be supreme leader ... teeeee. Money after this.'

You may have had to be there for that, but believe me, by this time we all have tears in our eyes we're laughing so much.

Johnnie:
That should be the title of your next book ... Does Dong Die!

Despite the fact that Steve and Johnnie reckoned Gene Hackman was going to be dull and businesslike, I was not going to pass up on the opportunity to meet an enormous movie star. Apart from sitting in the front row of a Kiri Te Kanawa press conference way back in Beirut, my celebrity quota was really rather low. So, bleary-eyed from the late night before, I crawled back into WGN to watch Steve Cochran's show and see a big Hollywood star at work. Steve is a plump smiley kind of guy who you imagine is a great dad and takes his kids to all the Cubs and Bears games and buys his wife flowers every week. Gene is in to talk about a novel, the *Wake of the Perdido Star*, that he has co-written with Dan Lenihan, a friend of his who shares his love of diving. Piece of piss you'd think, wouldn't you?

Gene and Dan walk into the studio. Gene is doing that slightly menacing, narrowing of the eyes when he comes in – very much *The Day of the Jackal* look. Steve shakes both men heartily by the hand and motions them to sit down across the desk from him. Gene Hackman gets up to throw his gum in the bin, which is a shame because if he'd just put it under the desk like most people I would have had a souvenir.

Things get off to quite a slow start. The usual 'how are you?' and 'how did you meet and why write a book together?' Basically they both did some diving together. Dan is a qualified diver and Gene was just starting to learn and they got on very well. Both had a love of the sea and they decided writing a book with an underwater theme would be fun.

Steve is having quite a hard time prising any other details out of the two. I have a sneaking suspicion that Steve has not read the book. Supplementary questions on the plot are a little bit lacking. The ad break is over and there's a WGN trail that Steve picks up from:

'Did you get a chance as a boy in Danville to get to Wrigley much?'

This is Steve doing a neat trick as WGN have a Cubs game coming up later in the day, so having just trailed that, Gene must know that if he can talk a little about baseball it will all sound smooth and glorious. He doesn't seem to want to play ball.

Gene:
No – I was kind of more interested in a burlesque show over the road ...

Steve:
You could have done both – after all, they are all afternoon games!

Gene:
Laughs a little.

Steve:
The book is very well reviewed so congratulations on that. What happens next, because you know the publishers will be wanting

another one?

Gene:

Yeah well – that's kind of up in the air. I think we might have exhausted that area but Dan doesn't share that view. But we'll probably write again – whether that is a sequel I am not sure.

Steve:

But you enjoyed the process enough to ...

Gene:

Yuh yuh.

Steve:

It's a major time thing to write a book like this – I guess you probably have to plan about six months ahead to get the time off?

Gene:

Well, actually the book took us three years, you know because Dan had a full-time job. We think we should do another one in maybe a year or less ... so ... um ...

Steve:

How does it compare at this point in your life to making movies?

Gene:

I enjoy it but I'm basically a performer – I like to be out there doing what I've been trained to do. Writing the book was very satisfying, but not like acting.

Steve:

And what were you doing, Dan? What was your full-time job?

Dan:

Underwater archaeologist for the National Parks.

Steve:

First stab at writing?

Dan:

I had written some non-fiction before.

Steve:

Certainly different to writing a full novel?

Dan:

Very different. In fact I had written some non-fiction about shipwrecks up in the Great Lakes. Technical reports and that kind of thing. We had one of them published.

Steve:

You seem like a regular kind of guy, Dan, but before you started writing with Gene Hackman – when he just turned up in your diving class, were you starstruck at all?

Dan:

Well, he was a regular guy too.

And so it goes on – not exactly a free-flowing conversation. Steve ditched the questions on the book and tried to get them both talking about whether there is a 'Mid Western' thing going on in terms of personality. They all managed to have a bit of a laugh but I got the feeling that Dan was a bit nervous and that Gene was just very bored. I think Steve got that feeling too …

Steve:

Do you guys enjoy going out and talking about the book or do you think this is just a pain in the butt? Do you wish that the book would just go out and sell itself?

Gene:

It would be great if that happened.

Steve:

I know that, Dan, you're probably not used to sitting in front of a microphone talking about how great you are as a writer …

Dan:

You have guessed?

Steve:

Over the years, Gene, I could probably count on one hand the number of times I've seen you jumping for joy when you're doing another junket for a film.

Gene:

Well, it's tough – the press junkets that you do for films nowadays. They put you in a hotel and they bring in these people every seven minutes and you do the same interview over and over …

Steve:

I get the sense – and I hope this is an easy process for you because

I try and make it easy from my end – but I get the sense that this is just not what you care to do and you're thinking 'It's a nice book and come and see us at the bookstore' but that's about it ...

Good on Steve. Gene Hackman was being less than effusive. He must know by now that if he just drops in a couple of anecdotes about the film world for the punters listening and if he and Dan had planned who talks about what bit in the book, then the interview will sound smooth and lovely and people will warm to them. My heart went out a bit to Steve because it wasn't like he had said anything offensive or prying. Gene wasn't playing the game. But I'm very glad that Steve pointed this out to him because at least Gene was honest about why:

Gene:
Well, you know it's easier talking about books than it is about films – 'cos in some strange way it's kind of abstract. I'd always wanted to write – my grandfather and uncle were writers in commercial news in Danville – and that was always attractive to me but I never got around to it. You have to sell all the time in movies, and I don't feel that I have to sell this.

Steve asks him if that ever stops – having to sell, sell, sell all the movies, every time.

Gene:
There's a kind of implied agreement if you do a film – if you commit to it then you're going to have to do press junkets at the end of it – maybe only for a couple of days ... but boy, it's tough.

Steve:
It's not your favourite thing.

Gene:
No, it's not my favourite thing.

If Steve and Johnnie had put some money on their bet last night then I would have been a much poorer girl this morning.

But interviews always surprise you, the best people turn out to be the worst and vice versa. PR people push their clients around studios too much and by the time you get someone on air they've done 14 interviews with the same questions within the space of two hours. It can't be that much fun to put yourself through a grilling, but then if you are the one that is going to reap the rewards from it courtesy of a book or a film then, call me old-fashioned, but you should behave yourself accordingly.

I interviewed Ned Sherrin at GLR once, years ago. He greeted our producer with a hearty guffaw and a warm shake of the hand. He spurned the hand of our researcher and barely acknowledged my presence in the studio. This can be unnerving when you have twenty minutes to fill. But as soon as the red light went on, Ned went off into a hilarious medley of anecdotal splendour involving all his celebrity chums, a small incontinent dog and all three books he was plugging. During the travel he ignored me. During the record he ignored me and during my questions he ignored me. So I stopped laughing at his jokes.

At the end of the interview he stormed off in a huff (which was a pretty impressive huff), for exactly that reason. Although he stopped to have another guffaw with our producer. We had quite a few complaints that afternoon and no one phoned up to find out what his book was called. I vowed to one day to get a publisher to commission me to write a book about radio and travel all round the world on a pitiful advance simply to get the opportunity to say to a wider audience that I thought he was nasty to me. These little things can eat away at you, can't they?

Sadly he was not the worst either. John Barnes came on the programme while he was manager at Celtic – and the night after they had been beaten by Motherwell. He had also just published his autobiography which was well written and contained some interesting points about racist abuse and some well thought out arguments about why things weren't changing very quickly in that regard. It should have been a great listen. It wasn't.

I started off by asking him what went wrong last night at the Motherwell game.

He said they had lost.

I said, 'I know that, but why did it happen?'

He said, 'Because Motherwell scored a goal.'

I said, 'Yes, I know that, but why couldn't Celtic get it together to win the game?'

He said because they didn't score any goals.

It got worse. I asked him if he thought that sectarianism came from the same place within people as racism. He said he had never experienced any sectarianism. I'm not sure that you even have to know that much about football to realise that whatever deep dark mood you are in, or however stupid you want to make the interviewer look, saying that there is no sectarianism in Glasgow is a bit of an own goal.

Excellent. Now I've got that off my chest too.

I had lied when I said that Chicago would be my last stop before heading home. Something about Steve and Johnnie's love of their jobs had made me feel very humble and full of renewed vigour about the power of radio. Coupled with that, I just didn't want to go home yet. I could just about squeeze one more station into my schedule before I had to return to London and get behind the microphone myself. That station was going to be Radio Montserrat.

Montserrat is a teeny-weeny island just over 11 miles long and 7 miles wide. It's a British dependency, although if a question about its status came up on *Who Wants to Be a Millionaire?* I think most people would have to phone a friend. For this reason I'll give you a brief history of the place. It is a sadly familiar tale of European invasion and greed: the island's sugar plantations attracted the avarice of merchants and masters, who farmed the land and the people for their own means.

Although it is now linked constitutionally with Britain, its nickname is the Emerald Isle of the Caribbean. This reference comes from the dissident Irish settlers who arrived in the seventeenth century from the neighbouring island of St Kitts. Over the centuries Montserrat's main industries changed from sugar and limes to tourism and for a while, at the tail end of the 1990s, it used the slogan 'the Caribbean the way it used to be'.

Thankfully that didn't mean slavery and persecution but a drug-free, crime-free paradise for visitors. Brochures and guidebooks from before 1995 talk about it being 'free from over-commercialisation' and having a 'gentle and genuine warmth' to its way of life. Its musical heritage is pretty impressive given the tiny size of the island – it is the home of Arrow, the worldwide ambassador of soca and the man who gave the world 'Hot Hot Hot'.

When Sir George Martin set up Air Studios on Montserrat, a stream of overseas talent headed to the island to record albums in a laidback place where the sun always shone and the hassle factor was very low. So what if Stevie Wonder just walked down the high street in the capital

Plymouth, and what's the big deal if that bloke doing tantric yoga over there is Sting?

This 'pre-1995 brochure' thing is important and if you know your vulcanology you will know why. If you don't, then you have about a paragraph of suspense to get through first. In the glossy pages produced by the Montserratian Tourist Board, the island's capital Plymouth looked like the kind of place you could happily lose a day in.

There are photos of streets painted in glorious Caribbean greens and yellows with the inevitable shops selling 'locally made carvings, jewellery and resort wear'. I've never quite got resort wear. Peter Jones used to have a department called 'Cruise Wear' in the days before you could go on a two-week boat trip for less than 500 quid and wear whatever Lycra-based leisure wear you liked.

Cruise Wear included things like wafty kaftans and blue and white striped jumpers with brass buttons with nautical knots on them. It also had something billed as a 'day robe' which presumably you wore on deck while chatting to the captain and playing quoits. They looked a bit like the kind of robes that you can wear during the day if you are in a plush private hospital or you're just rich and daft and never have to go outside.

The Cruise Wear department was just behind the lingerie section and while my mother was buying sensible underwear I often used to go and gawp at the latest kaftan ensemble. There was something so Luxury Poppet about all the clothes. It just yelled Rich! Tanned! Bored! – which were three things I longed to be at the pale and pasty age of 12. I was therefore heartened that somewhere in the world Cruise Wear had merged into Resort Wear and the traditions of lightweight frivolity had been kept alive. However, if the Peter Jones Cruise Wear had fallen victim to a change in tourist tastes, the Resort Wear of Montserrat had fallen prey to something far, far worse.

Hundreds of wealthy retirees from North America and Europe set up home in the breezy sunshine. The Montserratians called them Snowbirds – they came in search of the sun every winter. In the pre-1995 days perhaps the owners would suggest to their house guests and visitors that if they were a little restless one day they might like to go and take a look at Galway's Soufriere – a hot sulphur spring up in the hills that dominated the landscape of the south of the island. There they would be able to marvel at jets of steam coming out of the side of the mountain and could also pick up some bright, yellow-coloured sulphurous rock as a souvenir of their visit. The volcano that caused this natural phenomenon was deemed to be dormant.

You may well be ahead of me here, because in 1995 the tourist attraction-cum-volcano in the Soufriere Hills sprang to life and showered clouds of ash over the south of the island. The quiet and fascinating hills became angry and unstable – and the eruption of July 1995 was only the beginning of two turbulent years for the people of Montserrat. Over the course of those next two years, life on Montserrat would change irrevocably. It's tempting just to say that the volcano started to erupt and never stopped, but this would be a lazy layman's way of describing what was happening.

The proper way to describe the thing that started coming out of the top of the mountain is a pyroclastic flow – a mass of red-hot gas, ash and rocks which tears down the mountain at enormous speed, destroying everything in its path. The flows could be accompanied by great clouds of ash billowing from the volcano that blew across parts of the island – some so thick that they shut out the sunlight at midday.

After the volcano started spewing pyroclastic flows down in the direction of Plymouth, the scientists decided it would be safer to evacuate the capital. Thousands of people now faced the prospect of living in shelters in the north of the island or finding accommodation with friends or family. Exclusion zones were created, whereby people were not allowed back to their homes at all, and daytime exclusion zones for people who could go back to tend their land but could not stay overnight.

Many people left the island. Its population went from more than 10,000 to under 2,000 at the worst point of volcanic activity in 1997. The Soufriere Hills turned from a verdant green to a scarred grey. In the worst pyroclastic flow on 25 June 1997, the life of the island was changed forever as a massive splurge of lava and rocks spewed out of the volcano and down the eastern side, covering everything in its path. Whole villages were submerged in frighteningly hot lava and rocks. The flow didn't stop once it reached the sea and a new coastline was created by the lava, which poured over the airport's runway and out into the ocean. Nineteen people lost their lives in that eruption.

I knew none of this until I came to visit the island for a day while on holiday on St Lucia. I had wanted to meet the legendary Rose Willock –

the station manager of ZJB Radio Montserrat. I first heard Rose on the radio back in Britain when she popped up on a BBC programme as part of a simulcast with Radio Montserrat. It was August 1997 and Clare Short was the minister in charge of International Development and overseeing the amount of help that would go to the island following the devastation.

The British Government had been monitoring the situation throughout the volcanic activity, with varying degrees of success from the Montserratians point of view. Let's face it, if you are a British dependency that has been ticking along quite nicely for years and then through no fault of your own a volcano goes off on your island, you'd be pretty peed off if you didn't get an awful lot of help. The islanders had got used to cramped conditions, living in shelters away from their homes or camping out with friends and relatives in the north. But it wasn't a situation that anyone would want to consider permanently.

Clare Short had been given a shopping list of things that the Montserratians needed in August 1997, which included a new hospital, new roads in the north and more housing to ease the cramped conditions of people living in the shelters. During the simulcast Rose Willock asked her very politely and respectfully about the amount of aid that could be sent and how soon things could be put into practice. Rose has the kind of voice that makes you pay attention – slow and purposeful, with fully formed sentences. Clare Short and Rose Willock had a full and frank discussion about the issues. Clare Short said the Montserratians would 'be wanting golden elephants next'.

It was, with the benefit of hindsight, something that Miss Short would come to 'completely and utterly regret'. And those were the words she used after the quote was picked up and reported on both in Britain and the Caribbean. It was a throwaway line that was interpreted as arrogant and showing a lack of care for the people suffering in a British dependency thousands of miles away. To put some of Clare Short's side of the argument, she had found herself in charge of a budget stretched to its limits by the needs of some of the poorest people in the world – Montserrat was one of a number of places that desperately needed funding from Britain.

Aside from having watched all of this go on in the political vacuum of Westminster, I had learnt quite a bit about the role that ZJB Radio Montserrat had played in the volcanic disaster of the last five years through reading Cathy Buffonge's books about the volcano. Every major twist and turn in the life of the volcano seemed to have been managed and reported and explained on ZJB. It was the only way the islanders could be warned of impending seismic events – and then helped through them and comforted afterwards.

Cathy describes one terrible couple of hours when ZJB fell off air just after the 25 June pyroclastic flow, 'but thanks to the cooperation of Voice of Nevis Radio (on a neighbouring island), Radio Montserrat's dynamic manager Rose Willock was able to get a message over and let the anxious community know what was happening.'

So I could hardly go to St Lucia on a tanning festival for two weeks and not make the effort to get over to Montserrat and see for myself the devastation of the volcano and meet the legendary Rose. However, getting to Montserrat from St Lucia for that day turned out to be quite an eventful and expensive experience.

There are many phrases that I thought I would never use in my lifetime, things like 'Isn't that Jonathan Aitken a marvellous man?', 'I'd like a mullet haircut' and 'Today I'm going to charter a helicopter'. But life throws funny things at you sometimes and sitting in my hotel room in breezy, sunny St Lucia, I found myself using one of the above for, what may be the first and last time in my life.

Although on a map Montserrat and St Lucia look like they are nestling in the same tiny Caribbean paddling pool, it's a tricky business getting from one to the other, mainly because the volcano's contents put paid to the air strip on Montserrat in 1997. So I spent a morning phoning round various helicopter companies trying to book a flight that would get me to my pre-arranged appointment with Rose who was off to Barbados for the weekend. I had just the one day to get there.

I tried every single number in the phone book listings under the words 'Flights'. Eventually I got through to a man called Peter who was recommended to me by a very helpful lady at a company with the words 'helicopter' and 'charter' in its title that did neither in practice.

Now Peter was the kind of guy who you don't think exists any more – he had an accent straight out of a 1950s film and I imagined that he was sitting on a balcony sipping his first large gin and tonic of the day while quite possibly wearing tweedy plus fours in the heat of a Caribbean afternoon.

'Oh you work for the BBC do you ... maaarrvellous thing the BBC, isn't it? – listening to it as we speak – never have anything else on. Now do you know that Martine girl – the one who does the news?'

'Mmm, no,' I told Peter. 'It's quite a big place and we don't often meet people from the World Service.'

'Well, she's just lovely you know – she looks very like my daughter … same colour of skin … very, very light …'

I was a bit lost for words at this so I tried to steer the conversation back to getting him to fly me to Montserrat.

'Do you have a plane, Peter? Someone said you might be able to help me out?'

'Oh yes, plane … yes … got one of those … not in use this week though … being flown by someone else … Conrad is who you need to talk to – looks after the plane's interests – huge bloke, six foot four – built like a tank, he's quite dark you know …'

Peter seemed to view the world like a human Dulux colour chart.

'Yes, now what did you say? Where do you want to get to? Montserrat, was it? … Well, we can't fly there anyway you know … No airstrip any more. Gone in the volcano – could fly you to Antigua though … Not at night though. Got no licence for night, but you must talk to Conrad and there's lots of sea, you know … Can you hear someone else on the line? Hello hello … are you still there?'

'Yup, I'm still here, Peter.' Peter didn't hear this though because he'd put the phone down, presumably to go in search of whoever it was that he could hear on the line. Two clicks later and he was back.

'Sorry about that … thought I could hear someone on the other phone – now where were we? Yes, Montserrat – no, can't help you there but you should talk to the new High Commissioner here – lovely wife – very attractive lady – breath of fresh air you know … yes give them a call … always arranging bridge dates … yes …'

I didn't know what the exact remit of the High Commissioner's job was but I suspected that fixing me up with my own private flight to Montserrat was not really among them. Peter thought it was and, as he knew more about the workings of the Caribbean than I did, it turned out that he was right.

A highly efficient lady called Alison at the British High Commission put me in touch with Greg, an assertive-sounding Canadian who promised to pick me up the next morning in his chopper on Antigua and whisk me off to meet Rose at the radio station. The price Greg quoted was non-negotiable and was frighteningly high, but I didn't feel I could back down now that I had got so close to chartering my helicopter. It was unlikely to happen again unless I changed careers and became a backing singer for Phil Collins or got Kate Adie's job. I didn't intend applying for either.

I had no idea really of what to expect from an island devastated by one of the world's most explosive natural forces. Greg had done the trip over to Montserrat on a regular basis, taking curious tourists and well-qualified scientists over to the island. I tried hard to pretend that chartering helicopters was something that I could just take in my stride but I don't think I fooled him at all.

It was the little squeaks of joy and trepidation that I kept emitting that might have given my novice status away. That and the fact that I had to have my picture taken with him standing to attention outside his chopper before we embarked on the trip. It is one of my favourite photographs of all time.

You can see Montserrat from Antigua as a small island shimmering in the distance in the Caribbean. The helicopter zoomed over the resorts on Antigua's beaches and within minutes there was just the sea below us. As we got closer Greg pointed out the volcano. It was an unnecessary thing to do. On the left-hand side of the island – or due south to give it a better geographical description – there was a huge mountain, topped in cloud with screes of pale rock scarring the hillside in front of it.

I could see quite clearly where the whole perimeter of the island had been changed with that massive flow of lava into the sea. It looked like the mountain had been sick down its side. We couldn't see the dome at the top of the volcano because of the cloud, but Greg skirted towards it to show me where the airport used to be. The runway was now partly covered at one end in solid rock. The volcano rose up behind it with this huge slide of rock in between it and the sea. It was quite simply an awesome sight. And I use that word in its true sense and not in the way American tourists attach it to everything they see in Englandshire.

The clouds were buffeting the chopper around so Greg said he'd fly me over the capital Plymouth instead of trying to get any closer to the volcano. We skirted round the mountain and suddenly there it was – a huge scree of pale rock running all the way down to the coast with what was so obviously a town caught in its path. There were office blocks and houses stuck with only their top floors protruding from the mud. You could hardly make out the streets near the sea front as the lava flow had consumed them all.

Nothing moved.

Greg tried to point out various buildings of interest but I just couldn't take it all in. My squeaking had stopped. Greg positioned the helicopter so that I could take some photos of what we were seeing but it seemed a waste to try to look at that devastated town through the lens of a camera. I just gawped.

Up in the hills behind Plymouth there were huge villas with pools. I could see the lines of people's gardens and the huge satellite dishes people had put up next to their houses. These villas were untouched by lava or rocks – they looked like you could walk back into them at any time. There was a cow drinking water out of one of the swimming pools. It was surreal.

'They're in the exclusion zone now,' said Greg. 'The owners can't go back to them ...'

'Will they ever be able to?' I asked.

Greg said he had no idea.

He seemed a little disappointed by the size of camera I had brought with me and by the fact that I didn't want to take that many pictures. I had told him I was a journalist when I chartered his chopper and I guess that he was expecting me to have the kind of equipment to bear this out. I explained I had come to visit someone at ZJB Radio Montserrat.

'We'll fly over that in a couple of minutes – it's just by the new airport. You can hear it on Antigua, you know,' he said. 'Yeah – I like ZJB, its funny sometimes – you'll be listening to a programme of music or something and they'll suddenly do an announcement. Yesterday it was about one of the islanders who'd died and they just talked about him for an hour or so with lots of people phoning up to pay tribute. And you'll get them announcing births in the middle of records and stuff – it's real home-town stuff ...'

As we left the wreck of Plymouth behind us we hovered above scenery that changed from rock to greener fields with more houses dotted up the hillsides. Greg pointed to another great mudslide that had coursed down the mountainside and through what used to be a river out to the beach and then into the sea. On the other side of this was the safe zone. The hills in the centre of the island were green and lush and I could see little groups of houses. We were flying close enough to see that these were inhabited – cars parked outside, people in the gardens, life going on.

We approached the new airport with Greg now in constant chat mode to air traffic control. We appeared to be trying to land on an old cricket pitch – a couple of large army-style tents were being buffeted by our chopper blades down below.

'This is it ... welcome to Montserrat Airport.'

I spent an incredible day on Montserrat with Rose who gave me the fastest induction possible into the life of a volcanic island and the part the radio station had played in it. Rose Willock is the kind of lady you should describe as imposing or statuesque, she has a wide smile and a direct gaze that you daren't look away from when she is talking to you. She was standing on the porch of ZJB waiting for me. The radio station is only a few minutes away from the airport and is in a building that once must have been a house. It has a wide balcony that you can imagine you'd want to have a swinging chair on and drink very, very cold beer of an evening while the sun sets and your memory goes a bit cloudy.

Rose took me on a whirlwind trip of the station while telling me the story of ZJB. When it started in 1952, it was a private hobby of a real estate developer, Frank Delisle. Frank is a big figure in the Caribbean, being not only a property developer but also the founder of LIAT airline and Carib Aviation.

'It began with some friends of his who would go to the basement of his house,' said Rose. 'It was just a small transmitter, his friends came and for one hour each night they would broadcast. Then they started to order programmes from the BBC and they formed a committee and set up in a different building in the botanical gardens.'

Rose gained a lot of her experience on another station in the Caribbean but came back in 1990 as station manager of Radio Montserrat. Frank gave the station to the government. 'And that', she says, 'is when we started putting in place the task of building a proper radio station.'

With the help of $4.5 million from the government, some spanky new state-of-the art studios had been built in the delightfully entitled Lovers Lane in the south of the island by 1993.

As we talked, Rose was pointing out the container parked outside that would one day be the record library and the strength of the building that would hopefully protect them from future earthquakes and hurricanes and eruptions. It struck me that of all the radio stations I had ever been in, no one had talked about the buildings – because no one would give a second thought to how long the walls would stay standing. Everyone was more concerned about how long their careers would last rather than the radio station itself in literal terms. She told me about the independent spirit of the people on Montserrat and the problems of communication that the government and the scientists had in letting those people know what was about to happen to them.

That was when Radio Montserrat came into its own. Rose said that there simply wasn't another way for people on the island to be kept informed of what was happening in the mountains.

'Radio Montserrat has always been the vehicle when it came to preparation for disaster and emergency information,' she said. 'Everyone automatically tuned to Radio Monserrat for their information.'

Rose seemed completely unfazed by the fact that I had turned up for a day just to ask her lots of questions about the radio station she was running. She did it all with very good grace, although I'm sure she had better things to do. She told me about her early career at Radio Antilles and how she had come back to run ZJB and she talked of the emergency operations that had gone on and how people wouldn't do things until they heard it on the radio.

'We had to get people mobilized in terms of whatever orders were being given, in terms of getting out of the danger zone, getting packed up, getting the right information out about what was happening in the Soufriere Hills – and news and current affairs. We had to put out how we were all reacting to the emergency. Up against all that we had to make sure that the authorities were actually giving out information – were they giving enough so that people would know how to respond to the emergency?'

She talked of the psychological help that so many on the island now needed and how the radio station would initiate debates and phone-in programmes so that people could share what they were feeling. Just before I had arrived that day, the first convoy had been organised to take people into the unsafe areas – some of the places I had seen from the chopper. Rose said that the emergency services had allowed people to go back to their homes that were abandoned four years ago to retrieve basic bits and pieces which they needed for their new homes over on the other side of the island. Rose had been allowed to accompany the convoy to cover it for the radio station.

'This morning you would have heard a discussion on it,' explained Rose. God, I always miss the best stuff.

'People called in – those who went on the expedition – they talked about how they were feeling and what it meant to go back. Some people, when they had been told to leave their homes in 1996, they had just three hours' notice. So they had to pack up their things in just a bag. Some people have not been able to get back to their homes at all.'

I could have kicked myself that I had just missed what was obviously a corker of a show.

'They were saying that today they could not give rein to the full extent of their emotions because they only had a limited amount of time. You had to concentrate on trying to get into your house because of all the volcanic activity. You know some people could not even get into their homes, they had to use crowbars, but they were only focused at the time on getting a few things out. They couldn't give time to how it felt to be going back in after four years – *four years* ... They couldn't think about that until after they were back on the safe side.'

Apart from the terrible sadness of going back to your home and having to crowbar your way in, it's hard even to contemplate the frustration that people must have felt during that time. Montserrat is a tiny place – the whole island no bigger than St Albans – which means that you would always know that your entire house and possessions were never more than a forty-minute drive away. But for four whole years you just had to get on with life with whatever essentials you had taken with you that day.

Rose said that some people gave examples, such as the only thing that they had left were the keys to their property – everything else had been lost.

'They treasure those keys because it is the only thing that they have left of their entire life's work, you know? This is what comes out when we talk on the radio – but you see how tremendous the impact has been and how we all focus on different things.'

I couldn't imagine just having a set of keys and nothing else left of your home. The keys would be useless – they'd never fit another front door, but you would hang on to them, wouldn't you? Maybe you'd pin them up in your new home as a reminder of a whole lifetime of possessions and treasures locked away by a flow of lava. I honestly couldn't tell you what my house keys look like. I think maybe one of them is a Yale-style key, I think one of them is brass in colour – but apart from that they are just the annoying things that I lose all the time or occasionally leave in the front door when I have too many bags to drag in from Sainsbury's. But apart from that, they mean very little.

We chatted for an hour or so sitting in one of the basement studios of the station. Rose told me how ZJB Radio Montserrat had insisted on putting the scientists from the Montserrat Volcano Observatory on air so that people on the island could be kept informed about what was happening in the hills. She explained about the fear that the community felt about the British government letting them down. We talked about the power of radio and why people trust it so much and she told me stories about her own times on air when she had talked the listeners through some of the worst crises of the past five years.

I found her mesmerising. Here was a radio station doing so much more than just entertaining and informing people. It was quite genuinely keeping people alive too. I felt stupid that I had assumed I could take in such an extraordinary place in less than the time it took to watch *Grandstand*. We'd only just got started really when I had to explain that the chopper was waiting and I had to get back on it.

'Well, you will have to come back, Fi – you can't come to Montserrat for just one day.' Rose had a way of saying this that was halfway between an order and an invitation.

As she was showing me out, back on the wide veranda of the house, she said, 'You know, Fi, Montserrat is a tiny island which is still existing with a live volcano on it – people are coming to see how we manage to live like that – until you've come and seen for yourself you have no idea. We want people to come because they can take away an accurate message.'

I felt that she was probably suggesting that I could not possibly be taking away an accurate message if I had only spared a day in my diary to come over.

'Even now we get tales of people calling in saying we hear that the volcano has blown again and such and such has gone – and we're like, "No, I don't think so." How can they call and tell us things that we would know were happening on our own island?'

There was a squeak of frustration in Rose's voice which was up there with my chopper squeaks of trepidation. Unfortunately the chopper was warming up its blades by this time and I knew that I was going to have to leave, or remortgage my house if I wanted Greg to wait for me any longer. But I did take on board what Rose was saying. And I had every intention of coming back.

Now that I am retelling this story it sounds daft that I ever chartered a helicopter for a day just to go and have a chat with someone. But I'm glad that I was so wanton with my holiday expenditure, because it meant that less than a year later I could phone up Rose and announce that I was coming back to Montserrat for a longer stay.

And I was going to arrive the day after tomorrow, just as soon as I packed up my things and said goodbye to Chicago.

10 Maybe I'll stay a while ...

Montserrat

I knew now that ZJB Radio Montserrat was going to be a fitting end to my journey around bits of the globe. Chicago had proved that there are still a lot of people in radio who truly believe in its value, even if Gene Hackman was a bit slow on the uptake. But Rose and what she had done at ZJB was truly a remarkable story of how those radio waves that Hertz worked so hard on came to do exactly what he hoped they would – save lives and put people in touch with each other.

It had struck me when I had visited Montserrat on my day trip that, given the size of the island, you could have put a loud hailer on most street corners for less than the cost of running a radio station. But what a loud hailer warning could never do is allow people to talk about the trauma they had been through, to ask questions of the authorities and to do all those things in between, like have a laugh and play some top tunes.

I arrived on the island from Chicago via Antigua and the last part of the trip was in a helicopter again. I hadn't had to charter it this time though – I just jumped on board the 8am departure from Antigua. This time there was no Greg and his running commentaries and my companions were two day-tripping Swiss tourists and a businessman from Montserrat. The day-trippers' jaws dropped as we approached the island and the volcano came into view. The businessman looked out of the window pretty nonchalanatly. I guess you get used to volcanoes after a while. I thought that the mountain looked bigger than before – at least a little higher, but with the peak still shrouded in cloud it was hard to tell.

There was a hire car waiting for me the other side of the airport tents and ZJB was there on the dial. Basil Chambers was my host and as I sauntered along the roads round to the town of Olveston to meet my appointed representative from West Indies Real Estate, Basil kept up a non-stop patter of enthusiasm in between the records.

'Nineteen minutes moving up on 9 o'clock this morning – and a gooood morning to you – it's a good-looking Thursday and we have to say gooood morning to all the nurses today. If you're a teacher we are saying good morning to you too. If you are an 8.30 worker and you have just got to work we say well done and let's have a round of applause ...'

And in comes a round of applause before Basil plays a track called 'Montserrat Lock Off' by a man called Pepper.

Eight in the morning ... Montserrat lock off ...

It took me a while to realise what Pepper was singing about and then it clicked that I had just been locked off myself – the helicopter leaves at 8.30 and the ferry goes at eight and until both of them come back at about four in the afternoon, there is no other way off the island. We are all locked off from the rest of the world.

It's only about a twenty-minute drive from the heliport to Olveston. Every few miles as the road winds round the coast there is a community made up of houses with perhaps a supermarket and a church. Driving round the island in the north you would never know there was a socking great big volcano less than ten miles away. The Central Hills – unsurprisingly in the centre of the island – protect the residents of the north from the volcano and mean that you can't see the Soufriere Hills from most parts of the island that are still inhabitable.

I've arranged to meet a lady called Carol from the real estate company in her offices in Olveston. The town, or village, is little more than a road with a few streets off it. The houses are a mixture of villas and wooden buildings, apart from the great big one called Olveston House, which sits behind a long wall at one of the junctions. It looks very private and the security-conscious residents of Palm Springs would be very fond of that wall. It is Sir George Martin's house. And very nice it looks too. Like ZJB, the West Indies Real Estate office turns out to be a house converted into business use. Needs must, I suppose.

Carol is a feisty lady who gives me a very warm welcome to Montserrat. While exchanging keys for dangerously open credit card imprints, I ask her if things have perked up at all with the rental business here. I didn't have too much trouble finding a place to rent for a few weeks at very short notice. She says things are OK with the villas – a lot of them are rented out to people from the various agencies sent over to work here – civil servants in other words. My, they must be delighted with a posting that gets them a private swimming pool and a view over to St Kitts and Nevis. As for the volcano, Carol says she is quite busy at the moment too. I hadn't realised that the volcano was thought of as being female.

Carol laughs. 'Oh, she is a woman, no question – she is a woman ... she's a flirt who likes to take all her clothes off when the men are looking ... she takes them off for the scientists and does a bit of a scene for them ...'

'Is she doing any flirting right now?'

'Oh, sure. She is flirting alright. The dome is growing – it's bigger than it has ever been right now.'

Having learnt a bit more about the structure and formation of volcanoes since my last visit, I have sufficient knowledge to be able to tell you that a dome is where lava has emerged from the top of the volcano but is thick and sticky so that it solidifies at the top rather than sliding down the outside. The dome gets bigger and bigger and eventually has to collapse somewhere, causing huge pyroclastic flows when it does. So when Carol tells me this I nod appreciatively.

Once the money side of things is complete, I am free to go and this time I have no rush to pack an island's life into a day. The villa where I'm staying is back down the road that I came in on, in Woodlands – a small community of no more than a dozen villas and a tiny beach down a dirt track at the bottom of the hill. If there was ever a competition to design paradise then whoever did Woodlands must have got a prize.

I had been wondering on the plane journey from Chicago to Antigua whether or not I had created some kind of a competition in my head about all the radio stations I had visited. Was I looking for a perfect one? Did I judge them all against each other? Perhaps that was why subconsciously I had saved Montserrat till last – maybe I wanted to find one station which I could point to and say, 'Now *that* is how it should be done.'

In all the changes with webcams and Internet streaming and audience chasing and advertisers running the show, maybe I was being a Luddite listener and was fearful of change just because it was change. Maybe I just wanted to convince myself that there was still a community of principled, warm-hearted, dedicated people making radio because they thought it mattered. Of course that would make it easier for me if I went back home and took a fat well-paid job on some shite commercial station just because I wanted to go and live in a luxury hotel or have minibars installed in my bedrooms at home. I could comfort myself with the thought that perfect local radio still existed and I had witnessed it, even though I had chosen the financially rewarding but cheesy version myself. I had a feeling I would never do that – but never is such a big word for its five little letters, isn't it?

What I did know for sure was that no one was ever going to say 'you must go and meet that legendary Fi Glover because you know her radio station has saved lives and kept a nation together'. For all the anecdotes that I could tell about the little bit of life I have had in radio, they are never going to add up to the ones that Rose Willock has. There, you see, I have said never again – although this time I really mean it.

The villa is enormous. And far too big for me. I could live in the pool house quite comfortably. And it has a kitchen and a hallway that doesn't have a lift in it and lots of people waiting to get into it. As much as I have enjoyed enormously the range of hotels that have acted as home for the past few months, the excitement is mounting about being able to open a fridge and choose what goes from the shelf into my mouth. I might even refuse to charge myself a 15 per cent service charge on taking the plate to the table.

Rose and I have arranged to meet the next morning at the villa and she has promised to take me on a hike up one of the hills to get a better view of the volcano. It was as if she read my mind when I called her – I didn't even have to say that in order to get my bearings I felt I needed to go up on something high. It was lovely that she remembered who I was and I told her that I was coming to the end of my travels with my radio and that she was going to be the pinnacle of broadcasting in my trip. I think I embarrassed her by saying that.

Since I last met Rose she has retired from her position as station manager of ZJB, having hit the retirement age limit for a public servant on Montserrat. Although this is good news for me, as it means that she has a bit more time on her hands, I wonder what that means for the station. Nothing bad, I hope.

Rose arrives early the next morning for our 8.30 appointment. She says that 8.30 is the time that the scientific report goes out on ZJB, so we both listen to it before starting our hike. It's given by the chief scientist at the MVO, Peter Drunkley, and this week it is a significant report, given that the dome is growing at the top of the volcano so fast. There has been a bit of a spat on the island led by the Chief Minister David Brandt, who was on the radio earlier in the morning declaring the BBC to be the public enemy of the people. Peter refers to this in his report.

It turns out that someone from the BBC ended a report on the volcanic situation on the island by inferring that the volcano was just about to erupt again with similar consequences to the eruption in 1997. Rose explains that things like this are irresponsible journalism, giving the impression that Montserrat is a no-go area and that even to step foot on the island is to jeopardise your life. I can see her point. I make a note not to hand out too many BBC business cards while I'm here.

We set off for the walk up the mountain. Rose promises me it will be a gentle climb and it's on a dirt track leading up to one of the farms at the top of one of the Central Hills. The walk is known as The Cot – which refers to the ruins of an old summer house which lies at the top of the hill. Rose points out the cinnamon trees and the bay trees and the huge leaves that are known as Forest Faxes because they are so big you can leave messages on them for people walking the same route as you.

It's a brilliantly clear morning and hot with it. After spending so much time in cities it's a joy to be outside and Rose is a great walking companion. I tell her a bit about the other places I've visited and why I wanted to come back to Montserrat – mainly because of her and to hear all the stories she didn't have time to tell me on my whirlwind trip before.

It's almost impossible to imagine the hardship and tragedy that befell the island three years ago on a morning like this one. All we can hear are birds singing and the occasional sound of a car passing on the road down below. We could be a photograph in that brochure of 1995. Rose has many tales of just how sad things were, though. She tells me about one young man who lost his mother in June 1997.

'That young man was 23,' Rose says. 'His mother returned to the island a week before she died. She had gone away for the three years of volcanic activity and he stayed with his aunt. He called the authorities at the airport to get permission to go to the ramp at the airport to meet his mother – she was expected back at 4 o'clock in the afternoon. And do you know what? He was at the airport at eight in the morning – he could not wait to welcome her back. He said when he saw his mother he thought he was in heaven, he was so ecstatic.

Just seven days later his mother was dead. And so was his aunt. This guy is normally a happy person, but even now he can't see a picture of his mother – he thinks he'll break down – though he thinks about her all the time ... He says it's so much easier to be happy, because if you think about how you're really feeling you'd be down all the time.'

Rose never left Montserrat, even when many others around her were taking the opportunity to get out while they could. The population on the island went from more than 10,000 down to 1,500 at its lowest, but is now creeping back up to about 4,500. I ask Rose if she ever even thought about going somewhere else just while the volcano did its worst. She laughs out loud.

'No, Fi – I could never have gone. I can understand why people did but this is my nation, this is my island. I have a job to do here and during the worst of times the radio station was a lifeline to people. No, I could never have gone. It still is so important – we had always been an integral part of the island, but Radio Montserrat took on an even greater role when it had to be the integrator. We were putting families in touch with each other – sometimes it was just simple basic information for the community. When people had to come on to this side of the island they had no telephone, so even if it was just stuff like "I want my family on Antigua to know that I am safe", then Radio Montserrat could do that. It might sound insignificant but I assure you that it wasn't – and it's what we continue to do.'

We pass a couple of farmers working on steep terraces along the side of the track. Rose explains that every bit of land in the safe zone that can be used, is being used. I ask her if people listen to any other radio station on the island.

'Sure, they might do from time to time, for a different type of music perhaps. But, you see, we have turned into a kind of Everything Centre for people ... so that if there isn't electricity in some parts of the island they call the radio station. Every single thing that happens that is out of the ordinary, everything that is a part of life here, we get the information and broadcast it. If there is a strange boat coming down here they'll phone up and say "What is that? Why is it coming here?" When there was the first cruise ship coming in to the island people called up to say "There's a big boat coming close called the *Mistral*, what is it?" That's what happens – for visitors who come here they find it fascinating because we can tell you everything. Each time the volcano sneezes someone will call and tell us.'

As we are walking, the track gets steeper. We round one bend and suddenly in the distance in front of us is the volcano. There are no clouds today. There it is in all its scary glory – a great big malevolent mountain. I know what I was expecting to see if I ever caught a glimpse of the volcano behind the cloud, and that is the kind of volcano you would draw in school. It would be a pointy hill with a stream of fire coming out of the top – and nothing like what I am looking at over the valley.

It has several craggy peaks with steam coming out of holes in the sides. It's enormous and a dark brooding brown. It looks like someone has thrown it down to earth and it has smashed open. The dome which is causing so much concern is obvious, with a gravity-defying skyscraper of rock coming straight out of the centre. Rose says this is called the 'spine', caused by the same lava as a dome, and built up in the same way by thick sticky molten lava clumping together until it tumbles down.

Rose says that we are lucky and that they don't get many clear days like this one. I am rendered utterly speechless. All down the sides of the volcano I can see only brown screes of rock. I can still clearly see the path that the flow took in 1997 – deep scars formed in the flow as it rushed towards the sea. Bloody hell. Imagine if you were caught in that.

There are still those villas nestling in the hillsides where the flow narrowly missed them. I can't see how their owners will ever be able to go back to them. Rose follows my line of vision.

'Something that we all realised was that we invested a lot in property. As you fly over the devastated area, you've seen the size of the houses. Now that we are so accustomed to living in a one-bedroom little place or sharing a two-bedroom and you see places like that – these huge homes on two or three levels where just two people lived and you think, my God! It's just amazing and it's only now that it's hitting us that it was just a waste. A lot of us come from large families and some of those families are abroad and so you want them to be comfortable when they come and stay. So you build and you build – but now, you can't afford to do that, maybe you build one more bedroom if you can, but that's it.'

I can't really imagine the fear that must have struck when the big thing in front of us started to blow. I ask Rose if looking at the volcano makes her feel scared.

'In 1995 when we had the first phreatic eruption, you could have cut the fear with a knife it was so intense. You have the lights on in your house and it is so black that you can't see a thing. That first eruption came down billowing like a cloud that shut everything out for miles around. And, of course, everyone panicked.

'I happened to be on the air that time. I was doing the morning show and by the time I had turned around everyone had gone from the station – I was alone just talking to a country in the middle of an eruption – but you had to do what you had to do and it was done.'

'What on earth did you say?' I ask.

'God knows – some of the things that they were telling me afterwards I can't even remember – I mean I must have been on the radio for about 12 hours but, you know, at the time you don't think about it. It has nothing to do with anything. All I know is that I remember it happened at about eight in the morning. The cleaner was doing some work and the early morning technician was there and the technician came in to see me. The studio was on the western side of the building – but from the eastern side you can see up to the mountain and he came in to me and he says, "Rose! Rose! This time the volcano blow!" and I say "OK" because in situations like that I try to laugh it off.

'I could see that he was visibly scared – so I say "I'll go and check" and that was the last I see of him for the rest of the day, right? So what I did, I put a record on and I didn't say anything about it on air and I go up to the eastern side of the building and look out and when I looked out I saw all of the vehicles going in the same direction – north-west – all with their blinkers on and yet you could hardly see the blinkers in this heavy thick black cloud.

'And then it struck me what he was saying was true, so I make sure that all the windows are closed tightly and I call the MVO and say, "Obviously this is an eruption, how bad is it?" and the scientist on duty says, "Rose, we are going to be coming up as fast as we can." Coming up to the station, that is. "Tell them that it's just a phreatic eruption [a steam or ash eruption] and we'll get there as soon as we can."

'So I say, "How long will that be?"

'"About half an hour, maybe forty minutes."

'So I went into the studio. I always had a pile of suitable music ready – you know, motivational stuff – always, always because anything could happen at any time and I don't like leaving my studio once I have started. I like to have everything with me. I remember saying, "God, give me the words," and I sat down, put the records on and opened the mike.

'I was saying things like, "OK, folks, we have just had word from the MVO that we have a phreatic eruption, I know that we are all feeling it and you can't see where you are. Just stay where you are – don't go outside, keep your radio on, keep listening to me and I'll tell you what it's all about. I know you're scared and that's understandable – but trust me in a short time you will be able to see again. If you have someone with you, hold your hands – if you want to pray, then that's OK – it's not going to be completely devastating ..."

'And I was talking and playing the music – and I was saying just stay where you are, it's going to be OK. I said it like I'm talking to you now but apparently it worked! It really worked! All you know in a situation like that is that you have a job to do and you have to do it right and it better work first time. You need to get the desired effect and that is what we have to do all the time ...'

I could see why Cathy Buffonge had described Rose in her book as being 'dynamic'. It was very odd to be standing in front of this incredible natural phenomenon and hear someone talk about a time when it was threatening the lives of so many people. I had watched a couple of videos taken by people on the island at the time of the ash cloud that Rose was talking about and you really couldn't see further than a hand outstretched in front of you. All you would have would be your ears to guide you. I asked Rose again if she had been scared – she just shrugged her shoulders.

'All I knew was that I was the person manning the thing – there was a national emergency and I had to do it ... What else can I say?'

By Monday morning I was famous on Montserrat. Rose and I had been to dinner at Ziggy's restaurant, a beautiful converted tent halfway up a road called Mahogany Drive and run by two lovely people called John and Marcia. I stopped short of calling them delightful because that was the description someone had used in the visitors' book at the villa and it sounded rather patronising. It's the kind of adjective that presenters of QVC use when describing fake gold jewellery.

John used to be an accountant and Marcia used to be a dental nurse and, although both were from the Caribbean, they had lived in London for years before coming back to Montserrat. I have no idea how well John used to be able to balance books or how good Marcia was with the suction hose but they can do extraordinary things with marinated lamb and jerk pork tenderloin.

Ziggy's was full that night with a party for the governor's wife

Margaret. Lots of civil servants looking a bit suntanned and wearing the full range of Marks & Spencer outfits did lots of guffawing at the next-door table. And as a special treat, two masquerade dancers arrived at the end of the meal. Rose explained that the masquerade was a dance that the slaves invented to mimic their European masters. It's danced to a fast beat and in bright red and white costumes not unlike Morris dancers (although obviously better). The mimicry involves flicking the tails of their costumes behind their bottoms as the slave masters would have flicked the tails on their coats before sitting down.

There were only two masquerade dancers, although Rose said there were usually eight. But one of the two turned out to be Basil – Mr Breakfast DJ at ZJB. He made a few of the ladies come up and dance with him. Margaret, the governor's wife, was really annoyingly good at the heel-toe movement. I was crap. Now there's a surprise. However when I told Basil that I had come to Montserrat to listen to ZJB, he did ask me along to his show on Friday which he said was an extra special day of the week. And the next morning he played a masquerade song on the show for me and gave me a name check.

So when I stopped for lunch at a roadside cafe called the People's Place, the owner's wife came over and said 'Hi, I heard you mentioned on the radio this morning.' And when I stopped by Carol's office to sort out something to do with the phone bill she said the same thing. I had arrived in Montserratian society. It was like being back in Sonoma County with the on-air backing of Brent and Texan Bob – I'd even had to do bad dancing in public in order to achieve my status, which was a spooky coincidence.

That lunchtime I was on my way from the MVO where I had had a tour from a lovely lady called Jill who was in charge there. She had shown me all the seismicometer thingies that register when the earth is moving below Montserrat. It was fascinating, not least because she had a map of where all the monitors were on the island and said that a cat had once made its bed on top of one of them. It had caused quite a bit of consternation at the observatory, with the graphs jiggling away every time the animal moved into a more comfortable position.

Having bought yet more reading material about the events on the island in their makeshift shop, I was on my way to do a bit more exploring. Rose had told me where I was and wasn't allowed to go on the island. The exclusion zones are there for a reason and although tourists do try to ignore the warnings from time to time I wasn't foolish enough to venture into places where even the scientists wouldn't go. Rose said the closest I could get to Plymouth on land was to get to the top of Garibaldi Hill which was the other side of the Belham Valley. So that was where I was heading for the afternoon.

A few weeks earlier some Venezuelans had landed on the shore by Plymouth in their yacht and had calmly started to walk up the side of the volcano because 'they wanted to see how hot it was'. Mmmm. Not too clever really. The police caught up with them and I hope showed them some hot tempers instead. I wasn't going to chance anything silly like that.

The road down to the Belham Valley winds away like all the others on the island. It crosses occasional ghauts – little ravines that run from the hills to the sea – and you pass through Olveston and the next little town of Salem to get there. It was a road that I knew quite well by then. You drive past the bars of Salem – big wooden huts with fantastic names like the Gary Moore Wide Awake Bar and the Desert Storm Bar. Then the road dips down steeply as you approach the valley.

Two enormous heifers are standing in the road on the bend down to the river. They take a while to relieve themselves before standing back. There are two handpainted signs saying 'Exclusion Zone – no unauthorised entry' and 'Mudslides are common in this area'. And then suddenly it all goes brown.

Round the final bend at the bottom of the valley, the greenery stops. In front of me is a river bed – dry now and stretching about two hundred yards in front of me. But it's not just a river bed. There are trees stripped of their branches and greenery and huge boulders scattered across the ground like someone has just dropped a bag of giant marbles. Great piles of rocks are jamming up against the dead trees and swathes of mud have dried into deep cuts in the ground.

This is the Belham Valley now. What should have been a river running down to the sea and down to a beautiful beach turned into a furious mudslide bringing down boulders from the hills, alongside trees and rocks and anything in its path. They have all congealed into this river bed, taking the bridge with them and stranding the people living on the other side. One house which must have boasted a fine riverside viewpoint is now knee deep in solid dried mud.

Further down to my right is where the beach was and you can see the line of the palm trees which, in pre-mudslide times, would have marked the end of the sand. They stand in mud now – with the beach all but gone.

I bump through the roughly made tracks on the river bed that will take me on to the road up to Garibaldi Hill. This is not in the exclusion zone, although it is the only part of the island south of the Belham River which isn't. Some of the other villages and communities not directly in the path of any previous volcanic flows and activity had lived in a halfway house called the daytime exclusion zone but, because of renewed seismic activity, that has been upgraded to full exclusion – just in case there is a danger when the dome collapses.

From the river bed road I can see villas and condos perched higher up and closer to the volcano, which have long since been included in the full exclusion zone. Great big splurging houses with pools and patios. I wonder how they look inside now. What happens if their owners can never go back? Will they be peered into by people like me behind velvet ropes in fifty years' time?

It has struck me enormously since I've been here that there are so many questions that can't be answered. You kind of expect science to have answers for most things, don't you? I want people like Jill at the MVO to be able to say that the volcano's dome will collapse next Wednesday between the hours of four and nine. Then the volcano will stop. A bit like a night out on the Cinzano when you are fourteen – eventually you just can't throw up any more and that will be that. Montserrat will then be able to open up the exclusion zones and people will be able to live under the Soufriere Hills once again. And Plymouth can be turned into a fascinating archaeological dig and site where crowds of tourists can buy lava key fobs and real phreatic ash snow storms.

But they can't say that. And if *I* want them to be able to say that as a tourist passing through, God knows how much the people who live here must want some kind of confirmation. I can see why it was so important to get the scientists on to ZJB every week – and more often, when things were too seismic.

The drive up to Garibaldi is scarily steep and I thought at one stage the car was going to roll over backwards, so I abandoned it and walked the last two hundred yards which stretched my calf muscles more than a year's aerobics classes could have done – if I ever went to any. The view was astounding. Rose had promised it would be.

There below me is Plymouth – just desolate with the wind blowing through it like a whistle. It's another one of those views where you just can't stop staring – at nothing in particular – just at the whole thing. A capital city sitting there – static like a sepia print. All brown and lifeless. Just buildings – the grain stores, the clock tower, the businesses. Empty. Dead. But still there.

I'm not the only one looking at the view. There are two men at the viewpoint on the hill. One is carrying a duty-free bag and a camera and the other is pointing out various things to him. Eavesdropping on their conversation, it is obvious that this is a tourist and a guide. The tourist wants to know about how much the properties on this side of the island might go for now – I suspect that he is a speculator. It seems churlish not to have a chat.

The guide may well be having quite a long day. He points to where his family used to live – one of the villages now gone in the flow. He shows me where the river would originally have widened before the lava came down. And he points out the clock tower in Plymouth, now with only its top poking through the debris. As the wind sweeps down the side of the mountain, it turns from more than a whistle into a right royally spooky kind of hum. Apparently this is nothing compared to the sound of some of the rockslides, which are like a jumbo jet going overhead.

He asks me what I'm doing here so I tell him I've come to see Rose. I have stopped using her surname in conversation with people on the island as it's obvious that everyone knows who she is. He says he listens to ZJB all the time, which comes as no surprise to me now either. I tell him that I'm finding it hard to comprehend quite how important the radio station has been to Montserrat, as I've never been somewhere where people have been so dependent on the wireless.

'It kept us safe,' he says while looking out over the view. At least I think that's what he said, but the wind was carrying his voice away from me and for a moment I thought he had said, 'It kept us sane.' I think maybe the two phrases are interchangeable.

I saw Rose nearly every day that I was on the island and never tired of her company once. There wasn't an inch of the place she didn't know. She was pretty busy with meetings and committees and trying to help organise an impending gathering of the heads of the Caribbean states, so I also spent a lot of time doing what you do on a Caribbean island. It involved a fair bit of lying down in the sunshine.

This was a pretty enviable two weeks in a very enviable stretch of weeks. I left ZJB on the stereo in the villa and in the car all the time. I heard lots of warnings about the heads of the Caribbean states coming to the island and the fact that I should make way for their convoy on the roads. I heard Margaret, the governor's wife, ask me if I'd like to take part in a raffle for seats for the new Cultural Centre. I heard lots of requests and times of Red Cross dinners and Jump Ups down on Woodlands beach. And I sadly knew everyone who had died, as ZJB did weekly announcements of the deaths followed by an ad for the local undertakers.

Basil was an addictive listen every morning. Each day of the week seemed to be dedicated to a different lot of people on the island. Not just the teachers and nurses, but a whole Wednesday dedicated to the Ladies. It made me feel proud of my chromosomes. I'd say that at least one record in every five was made by a Montserratian artist too – not just Arrow (although there was a lot of Arrow), but Pepper, some guy known as Darkman and a whole host of others. More often than not the lyrics were about the volcano, or about the evacuations, or living in shelters or just in celebration of the island. If it was propaganda, it was working.

The station took the BBC World Service news and the Caribbean Service news but had its own news programme at six which thundered in with a huge set of jingles and covered everything that had moved on the island that day. On the whole it seemed very balanced – and the smaller the community the harder that is to do. Rose had told me that, because the station is a public service broadcaster and takes money from the government, it has to work hard to ensure that it isn't seen as a mouthpiece for the authorities.

And obviously in such a small place you have to be very careful about saying who is doing what – and to whom. In that respect it was quite unlike the *Montserrat Reporter*, the local newspaper that I took as my chosen piece of reading material one evening while having a few beers outside Gary Moore's Wide Awake Bar in Salem. With a name like that you just have to stop and have a drink.

On the front of the *Reporter* was the headline 'Chief Minister Angry, Calls Media Distortion Wicked Lies'. I could understand the anger about people saying that the volcano was going to blow; I had kept my employers rather secret since getting here. That wasn't the problem though – it was the back page that made my eyebrows rise up at a speed that would make Angus Deayton jealous.

On it was a weekly column called 'Jus Wonderin' in which whoever it was who wrote it did a lot of wonderin' about everyone else on

Montserrat. It included things like: 'Jus Wonderin' why the cost of living is so high in this land.' This was a fair point: the supermarket prices were fearfully high given that many people were still paying mortgages on houses they could never live in and rent on new ones that they had to live in.

But 'Jus Wonderin' went even further: 'Jus Wonderin' who's that Big Girl living in Salem who still pees her bed' (this seemed awfully cruel) and 'Jus Wonderin' if a certain young educator from the northern primary school doesn't understand the meaning of morality.' Given that there couldn't be more than a dozen teachers at that school, everyone would know who that was, even if I didn't.

It had all kinds of stuff about married women making phone calls to men late at night and who was sleeping with whom. It suggested malpractice in most public services. It 'Jus Wondered why the lady without work experience and some sort of qualification is head of that Health Office'. It was unbelievable. Every kind of Chinese whisper and rumour was reprinted alongside quite admirable wonderings about general school standards and why civil servants get given plush villas when they wouldn't be living in that kind of style back home.

Peter Carter-Ruck would have a field day if he ever chose to up sticks from London and set up his libel practice on Montserrat. Inside the paper among the pieces on the important meetings coming up was an advert which caught my eye. It was for a reporter on the *Montserrat Reporter*. I re-read it about three times. I had all the qualifications. There wouldn't be a lot of money in it and obviously you had to have an interesting interpretation of libel laws – but it set me thinking a bit about exactly what I was going home too.

I was prevented from reaching the end of my thought process by the arrival of Jerry at my table. He invited himself, which wasn't a problem at all, and he was keen to chat. His idea of chat was quite novel though, as it involved him telling me a lot of things and ignoring my questions – he was very tiddly, as my mother would say. Having gone back to London during the worst of the volcanic activity he had managed to sire 19 children with three different ladies in what must have been an exciting, if not tiring, life so far. I would say Jerry was probably in his fifties and he said that he was missing his current girlfriend.

'I'm like a bull in a pasture,' he kept saying to me. 'A bull in a pasture, me.' We had a couple of drinks together and I attempted to tell him that I had fallen a bit in love with Montserrat and was thinking about the possibility of staying. Jerry attempted to tell me that he had sent back quite a bit of money to his ladies in the UK but that he needed some of it back now. I think that was what he said.

The only really consistent thing was the fact that he was a bull in a pasture. I should imagine that before the beer Jerry would have been very good company – as it was, the evening was somewhat ruined by the arrival of another man called Jim who was intent on telling me to stop smoking. He was so drunk he could barely stand and I just thought that was a bit rich. It doesn't matter how many high-tar cigarettes I get through of an evening, they never make me shout at people while standing very close to them in a slightly threatening way. Before I let slip any other bad habits – or developed BSE – I folded up my *Montserrat Reporter* and headed home.

I managed to make it to the last hour of Basil's Breakfast Show on the Friday. It was very, very fast. He had a Caribbean track running in the background over which he talked all the time – flicking up the record fader to maximum decibels in his brief pauses. It was a non-stop flow of words.

'What happens once in a month, twice in a moment and never in an hour? What is it? What is that?' Basil throws the question out to the audience. He flicks on a caller just by touching a button on the desk.

'It's M,' says a voice out there in the ether.

'You sure?' shouts Basil

'Yes.'

'You're really sure?'

'Yes.'

'You're right!'

Up goes the music, but only for a few seconds.

'What can go up and down stairs without moving?' cries Basil before flicking a caller up.

'Water,' says a voice.

'What?' screeches Basil.

'Water.'

'You're wrong,' he shouts 'What can go up and down stairs without moving? That is what I am asking you. What do you say?'

'Handrail,' says a caller.

'You what?'

'Handrail.'

'You sure?'

'I am sure, Basil.'

'You are wrong,' says Basil. 'What do you say?'

Another faceless voice shouts: 'A carpet!'

'You're sure, you're sure?'

'Yes.'

'You are right!' shouts Basil with a great big grin on his face.

Up goes the music. This goes on for a whole half hour with no pauses, no whole records played – just constant questions and callers. It's manic and the fastest show I have ever seen done in a radio studio. Basil calls this his Friday Pappy Show and I don't have time to ask him why. In fact we barely have time to chat at all. He gives Rose a glowing verbal reference and says he will always be indebted to her because she got him over from Antigua to do this job. He says that people on the island phone him up at home if they don't hear him on the radio in the morning. Everyone on Montserrat now knows who he is and, yes, he loves his job.

Apart from being the fastest talker in the western hemisphere, Basil is the only DJ I have ever met who has en suite facilities in his studio. Because the station used to be a house, this studio we are in was probably the master bedroom suite so it has a bathroom off it. Usually in radio stations, toilets are built without any recognition of the fact that radio is one of the few jobs where you can't just saunter off and have a pee whenever you feel like it (that and those jobs in medical emergency rooms where you have to hold arteries together for hours).

The simplest thing when building new radio stations would be to pop in a handy en suite facility just off the main studio, thereby avoiding the need for the person presenting to have to pee within a three-minute 45 record or a five-minute news bulletin. A five-minute news bulletin may sound like an eternity but it's not when you have to get through two locked and coded doors and run halfway down a long corridor, pee and do all of that in reverse. God knows what happens if you develop prostate problems.

It doesn't really matter that Basil has so little time to talk because I feel I know him already, having listened to him every day now for over a week. I have to stay till the end of the show just to hear his sign off which, as far as I can gather, is the same every day. Just before ten o'clock Basil gives his listeners a little aural hug.

'If you have love in your heart, don't keep it there – let it out. Remember to be moderate and keep your head on – this is B-A-S-I-L Chambers wishing you all a good-looking day. I'll be back on Monday.'

That probably sounds a bit happy clappy to you now but whenever I have heard it, it's always made me smile. It's so much better than 'And the news is next,' which is what I invariably end up saying just before the hour.

ZJB hasn't changed at all since I first visited Rose here, except for the fact that Rose is no longer here. Her office is now occupied by a nice, calm-looking young man called Herman who is the acting station Manager. He is fielding endless phone calls too, although they are probably of a different nature to Basil's. But he does have time to make rather an important point. Herman says they want to keep ZJB how it is.

'Montserratians coming back – they want to hear ZJB is still the same – they like it that way – we are a constant. It's not about change for us, it's about keeping the station as good as it is now.'

And Herman has just put his finger on what I've been trying to work out about Monsterrat all week. I don't love ZJB because it's small and quaint and does things that a big city station never could. I like it because it does it very well. It's not chasing the tail of a new millennium, not seeking out a wider reach or audience. It's not hiking up the ad rates, not bringing in the big stars. And you really couldn't come here and not put it on your dial. You simply wouldn't know if the volcano was rumbling dangerously again. You wouldn't know if a hurricane was on its way. You would certainly have no idea of what to do at the weekend. You couldn't come to Montserrat and not listen to ZJB. Well, you could, but it wouldn't work. Like a pie without the crust. Yippee! Local Radio Works!

This evangelical zeal was partly what led me back to the offices of West Indies Real Estate to take a guided tour of some of the properties available for sale on the island. I didn't want to go home. Montserrat had turned into a very appealing place to settle. Not just because of the climate and the beauty and the constant volcanic curiosity. I promise that I hadn't been swayed too much by the sunsets and the pool.

I wasn't just being daft. Quite often on these travels I've met people who have settled somewhere, people who first visited as tourists and just decided not to go back. Don and Elizabeth in Palm Springs – they'd only taken two weeks to move their whole lives to the sun-drenched valley of golf carts.

There was an extraordinary woman called Julia whom I met when we were filming for *The Travel Show* in Mallorca. She had fallen in love with a bonkers aristocrat who lived in a tiny castle up in the hills. He had a king's emblem flying on a flag outside his castle and a dragon painted on the bottom of his swimming pool. It seemed like a charmed life but I think Julia was a bit lonely – they both seemed very keen for all of us to stay and play with them.

There are only so many parties you can have where your happiness is dictated by the fact you have nothing to do the next day. Perhaps work is a bit like broccoli on your plate – not instantly appealing but quite good for you and if you do manage to get through it, the chips taste even better. But I really fancied it in Montserrat. If I could have got a job on ZJB or worked my way up on the *Montserrat Reporter* then I could have the best of both worlds. I asked myself all the sensible questions, though. Would I feel the same after a long hot winter? Would I end up having to learn how to play bridge with the ex-pats just to fill the evenings? Was it a bit like buying an album because you like the single, then finding out that all the other tracks are rather poor?

For one day at least I wanted to think like I could. Mrs D who runs West Indies Real Estate showed me round a few places. I have no idea what her surname was because everyone just referred to her as Mrs D. She was a kind lady with a big bouffant hairdo who had come to Montserrat after the break-up of her first marriage. She was either Canadian or American – I always get the two accents confused and I know that Americans feel insulted if you ask them if they are Canadian, and vice versa, so I avoided the question altogether.

Mrs D showed me round some very plush places with pools and hot tubs and decks and views. All of them were out of my financial reach, apart from her own house, which I think she had placed rather reluctantly on the market. I didn't quite get to the bottom of why it was up for sale, but I sensed there might be a sad reason – she had lost her second husband the year before.

It was a beautiful house on the coast in Old Town – the main area for villas now on the island. It had a small swimming pool with a huge shady area next to it and a garden full of bougainvillaea. At the end of the pool was a raised dining area which looked straight out to sea in the direction of the sunset. It was all dreamy. Mrs D was a potter in her spare time and one bedroom was full of unglazed pieces and a kiln. I could use it as an office. I could plug in my computer and through the Internet I'd be able to listen to Five Live, if I wanted to. I could send Nicky Campbell those emails saying nauseating things like 'Just come in from the pool and thought you might like to know what I think about the European Defence Force.'

Mrs D was after a quick sale which was why her villa was going for a song. It really was a viable option. I kept thinking that if I had found such a lovely radio station on such a beautiful island then what was I going home to? A job filled with insecurities, judged by ratings and focus groups? A miserable sodden winter in Dalston where they have a wipe-clean crime board on the Balls Pond Road so they can appeal for witnesses to whichever monstrosity has occurred that week? Why shouldn't I just stay?

Rose has come round for dinner at the villa and inevitably we are having a chat about radio again. Her face lights up when she talks about her former job.

'It's so immediate. I could go on air and I was just as likely to learn something as the people are who were listening. I always did. Someone would call up and tell me something – you can't get that on TV. I find TV rather boring. It just does the same thing over and over again. I remember when I was at Radio Antilles in Antigua – it was when I had just started. And this lady came up to me in a shop one day and said, "Heey, I love listening to you because when I do I feel that I am the only person you are talking to." And I just thought – that is it! That is what I want to do. Every time I go on the radio I want to feel that I am talking to one person. It's just conversation – but conversation that tells you something – conversation that always surprises you.'

I told her I was thinking of buying a place here, which she looked delighted at. But I didn't get around to saying that I wanted to get a job on the island. I don't think she would have approved. After all, I would be taking the place of a Montserratian. I asked her if she had ever thought about upping sticks and moving somewhere else. I didn't mean just because of the volcano and all the problems that had caused. I meant doing what I was considering doing.

'You know, Fi, it's very simple. I love my country – my country is my child. I love the people in it. What more can I say? I'm a broadcaster and a journalist, for heaven's sake. I have never met a journalist who'll walk away from a situation like we have had here – no way, no way ... so that's why. It is our country. Where else in the world can we call home?'

At that moment I put Mrs D's house into the box marked 'Unlikely' and decided that I really did have to go.

I too had a home and it was in London. I would never really be able to latch on to the patriotism of Montserratians because I hadn't lived through what everyone else had. Even if I spent ten years watching the sunsets from Mrs D's balcony and even if I could get a job on the island, it wasn't my home. If I tried to stay then I could guarantee that the *Montserrat Reporter* would have something to say about it – it would go something along the lines of 'Jus Wondering' why that British journalist has got a Montserratian journalist's job.'

And they would be right.

---

11 I haven't forgotten the chutney

Somerset Sound

Coming back to my home was a jolt. For a start I was having to do my own washing. My bedroom didn't have an en suite. In the bathroom that I do have downstairs, there were no mini toiletries. If I hung my towels up after using them, it was because there was no space for them on the floor – not because I wanted to preserve the environment. I had arranged the pile of stolen stationery by the phone and it looked good. But if I nicked anything else then I would only have myself to chase up. The mini bottles of mayo and tomato ketchup from Las Vegas were in the cupboard where they would stay until they exploded some three years after their sell by date. And I had the photos printed.

I scared myself when I saw the picture of me and Mystery Mike from Las Vegas. Where did that look come from? I didn't know I had a stalker side to myself. As well as all that, I had to go back to proper work at Five Live. When the red light went on I actually had to say something.

The strange thing was that I sounded different to myself. I don't know if anyone else noticed it – in my headphones I just sounded perkier. There was no way that I could ever compare myself to someone like Rose; I didn't have the dedication that Steve and Johnnie had either – and I would never be able to talk up to the lyrics like Fitz did, but I was very content to live in the same radio solar system as all of them.

I realised that pride – as a sentiment – wasn't something that I had felt all that often before. I'd been chuffed to get jobs before – and the Cheltenham and Gloucester Mortgage Department had been chuffed for me too – but I'd never felt truly proud to work in a business that is usually slighted as being a bit on the luvvie side of normality. But sod anyone who says that radio is stuffed full of egos. It's simply not true.

Since sitting outside the line dance in Petaluma all those months ago, I'd met so many people who were a million miles away from Simon Bates' vision of what success is. That thing he said in his autobiography, the mentor he quoted as saying 'if you don't know what the fuck you are talking about, speak loudly and with great conviction', that had bugged me a lot. I think it's rubbish. All the people I'd met who I thought were talented had, in fact, been doing the opposite. They thought quite carefully about what they were saying, who was listening and what they would make of it. Except perhaps for the Broil Their Dogs episode in Vegas.

And as for the Internet – it *will* revolutionise radio. Webcams and websites with all their visual stimuli will take away much of the mystery of radio. But it will just evolve accordingly. Maybe it will grasp back some of the attention TV has got, as it will be a truly interactive medium. Books didn't die a death simply because people put pictures in them. And now you'll be able to listen and log on and sit in a chat room and talk about what's on air and maybe if, like me, you aren't brave enough to phone a problem show, then at least you can meet on-line the people who are.

We will soon be able to buy portable digital radios with their clear-as-a-bell sound quality that will take away the crackle of the medium wave. We'll be able to log on in our cars and chortle away to Howard Stern even if we're in Slough. But I bet that a lot of people will still use radio in the way it's been used for the past eighty years – as a fantastic tool for information and pleasure that just wafts into your brain through your ears. I won't stop taking my little wind-up radio with me wherever I go. I might listen to more international stations at home in Dalston, but it won't change the fact that I like to listen, on site, when I'm in a foreign place. I hope not anyway.

A couple of weeks after getting back from Montserrat I decided to go the full circle and go back to where I started working in radio. Really to see if my gilded vision of local radio had, in fact, been swayed because I was abroad and staying in luxury hotels at the time. So that meant going back to Somerset Sound, the smallest BBC local radio station in the country.

I've picked a bugger of a day to do it because some cheeky little sod has turned the colour down on the whole of the south of England. Driving through Hampshire and Wiltshire is a monochrome experience with a thin layer of snow and ice covering the fields and roads. By the time I can see the sign for the South West, the snow is coming down thick and fast. I made the same journey in the same kind of weather from London to Taunton in 1993, when it was my appointed task as a young and entirely inexperienced trainee to spend three months at a tiny BBC local radio station, in order to hone my chosen craft as a radio journalist.

So I packed up my sexy girl-about-town, three-door Volvo – the 340, bright red with a slight smell of cat's pee – and prayed for backwind to make up for the loss of Swedish acceleration technology. It worked and I arrived. We had spent a mere eight weeks in a classroom just above the Euston Road learning shorthand, how to report trials and courtroom sagas, what constitutes libel and how to chop up pieces of black magnetised tape with a razor blade and stick them together with little pieces of white tape.

This process was called editing and meant that you could turn your err-ing and umm-ing interview into a sleek masterpiece. You literally did it by cutting out the bits of tape with the ers and ums on. This very laborious process died a death when computer technology advanced and I'm sure that many people rejoiced at its demise. But sadly it meant that you could no longer recognise radio trainees by the Masonic missing fingertip.

The eight weeks of that training course were fantastic. We were suspended in this aspic somewhere between the heady excitement of being allowed in a radio studio with proper microphones and everything, yet at the same time we weren't really broadcasting – so if you cocked up it didn't matter. For the purposes of making our training as close to reality as possible, our tutors had created a fictional radio station called 'Radio Grafton' – named after the building we were in on the Euston Road.

Radio Grafton rolled into action every afternoon towards the end of the course, as we beavered away pretending to be newsreaders and editors and producers. One day we had a Commentary and Live Action seminar where we all had to go and hide round the back of doors and behind tables, and pretend that we were commentating on an armed siege that was taking place in Classroom 4. It really was almost like being in Sarajevo, bar the fact that occasionally mid-flow, when your voice was straining with the adrenalin, fear and excitement, one of the coffee ladies would have to tread over you on the way to the loos on the first floor.

Someone came to talk to us about the NHS one day and managed to explain the whole process of internal markets in under half an hour, which we thought was rather suspect. We had trips round the Magistrates Courts and the Old Bailey ,where it was tempting to go the whole hog and hold hands in crocodile fashion while taking the piss out of the teacher and eating all the nice things from our packed lunches, like Wagon Wheels, before eating the sandwiches.

It was a blissful introduction to local radio. We were all full of excitement and ambition about where our jobs would take us. Our tutors were encouraging and annoying in equal measure, which was a perfect combination, because on the one hand your enthusiasm grew and on the other you were anxious to leave. We spent hours doing vox pops on the Euston Road about whether or not London had enough cycle lanes. Invariably you had to stop a cyclist in order to ask this question so the results were *No!* – with a couple of expletives you then had to cut out with those razor blades.

We were expected to do a lot of shorthand practice in the evenings – most of it done at the pub round the corner. We learnt how to turn boring local council reports into ear-catching stories with top lines like 'Dog Fowling – Grafton Council Slips Up!' and 'Planning Applications – Really This Story is Interesting!' And we learnt basic things about the legal system – like you can't go on air and say 'That woman looks guilty to me ...'

It all went swimmingly – except for one event. One day towards the end of Radio Grafton's magnificent 1993 run, we found out that, by chance, Jeffrey Archer was in the building for the day doing a training course that would enable him to slip into the slip-ons of Jimmy Young for a couple of weeks. We thought it would be a great idea to go and get an interview with the man and put it out on our fictional station.

That morning we had been playing around with a computer programme that assessed our grammar for us, just to make sure that we were using nouns and verbs in the right places – unless you wanted to work on Radio 1's *Newsbeat*, in which case you could drop the verbs altogether. Some bright spark suggested that we put a bit of one of Jeffrey's novels through the computer to see what assessment it would give out. This would provide the blinding final question in an interview that would surely surpass any the little Tory had done before. I was sent up to do the interview .

No one had been *really* nervous on Radio Grafton because we knew that even by local radio standards the audience was very small – just our tutor's office next door. The coffee ladies didn't play it – not even when there was a siege on. I was shitting myself with Jeffrey though. I piped out the usual stuff about what motivated him and some other bollocks about why he chose the Tories and did he really think John Major could carry on. Then I came out with the striking evidence that our computer had printed out.

'Mr Archer, we put one of your novels through a computer programme this morning that assesses how good the grammar is and it came up with the answer that it was actually worse than that of the *Sun*'s leader column. And that is the lowest comparison it could make ...'

I didn't even bother to turn it into a question and left my statement hanging in the air.

Now Jeffrey had been quite charming up until then, but he looked at me with astonishment following this statement and paused a little longer than was necessary before fixing me with a horrible stare.

'I don't need some snob from the BBC telling me how to write my novels ... What would you or a computer know about grammar? What did you say you were training to be? A BBC journalist? Well, best of luck with that.'

I was speechless and I could feel little tears pricking up just behind my eyes as I fumbled to switch off the UHER machine that was spooling the tape around. The very nice man who was training Mr Archer up for the Jimmy Young Programme came through from the studio next door and attempted to make a joke of Jeffrey's rudeness. Mr Archer then put his hand out to shake mine and gave me a rather slimy smile, complete with the raised eyebrows that always made him appear so sincere.

'That'll make your training a bit more interesting, won't it? ... Good luck with it all.'

And I realised that he'd just been rude for the sake of it. As I left the studio I could hear him laughing. I felt about two inches tall. It was just his way of making a journalist out of me.

A couple of days after all this high excitement – and it was exciting by comparison to doing daily vox pops on the Euston Road – we all had to gather in our classroom to learn our geographical fate for the next year. The deal on the BBC scheme was that you got paid a very basic wage while the BBC trained you, and in return you were sent off for a year to work in the regions at no cost to the local radio stations.

We weren't allowed to go to places that we had spent any time in before, so earlier we had filled out a form saying where we had been brought up, been to school, attended university or had close connections with – in my case Slough, Winchester, Kent and any branch of Miss Selfridge or Oddbins. We would deliberately be sent to places far, far away from familiarity. Basically we would have to turn up in a place we didn't know and use only the radio station as a means of getting to know the place. Now where have I heard that idea before? Anyway there were 12 of us on the course and an awful lot of worry was now packed into that dozen.

There were all kinds of preferences being aired – it was generally accepted that the big cities were at the top of the most wanted list – Manchester, Birmingham, Leeds and Newcastle all had big newsrooms and a lot going on in their patch, which meant a steeper learning curve and less likelihood of being sent out to cover council meetings about planning applications. I was hoping the exact opposite though – the idea of being slung into a huge city was far too daunting.

I also had my driving disadvantage and big cities mean big one-way systems and road signs that deliberately mislead you and send you into multi-storey car parks when in fact you want to get to the ring road. This would mean hours of frustration and endless missed deadlines and lots of news editors who would only remember me in future as 'that idiot girl with no sense of direction'. So I was secretly hoping for everyone else's nightmare – Radio Cumbria – which was right down at the bottom of the list, just because it was such a long way away. No one wanted to go to Somerset Sound because it was still an AM station and only had a staff of three people. Northampton and Hull were other black spots for reasons like 'What's the point?' and 'Shit it'll be cold' respectively.

And so our tutor Sarah read out our fates. We would be sent to three stations each and spend three months in each place and hopefully at the end of it, we would have proved ourselves so damned talented that the last placement station would want to keep us for ever and start paying our wages. I should imagine it was a bit like playing bridge, where you had to remember which stations had been taken and which were still available and search the faces of your opponents to see if they were happy or disappointed. I can't remember everyone's fate but I know that my best mate Jenny got Leeds and Berkshire in her lot and Annabel who all the boys fancied got Cumbria. She had a look of horror on her face when that was read out – and so did most of the boys. I got Somerset Sound, Hull and Northampton.

So six years later I am driving down the same icy roads with slightly less trepidation than I had first time around, but the same addiction to twiddling through the dials on the stereo that had got me into all this trouble in the first place. Or DX-ing, as Steve would say. And all that lovely, lovely British choice is there on the dial.

I've never been one for cassettes on car journeys – I think Ruby Turner was stuck in the Volvo 340's stereo for years, but I can't say that I noticed. You know what's on a tape and I find that slightly dull. Just like a key change in a song (particularly the Nolans' 'I'm in the Mood for Dancing'), radio can lift you all of a sudden out of one mood and into the next. It's that little feeling like driving over a humpback bridge – when your tummy just goes a little bit 'whooah' – that's what I love about the beginning of a top track. If you're really lucky, the DJ will have introduced it as just that – 'heeeere comes another topppp track ...' It's the way you can slip from the comfort blanket of Jenny Murray's *Woman's Hour* to the very itchy flea-ridden blanket of Derek Hatton. The sheer kaleidoscopic pick 'n' mix works for me every time.

Tonight, over on medium wave, Peter Allen and Jane Garvey are battling with the buildings that preclude many Londoners from enjoying Radio Five Live – and, although I could listen to their combination of curmudgeonly humour and brainpower quite happily for hours on end, the perils of being on the medium wave mean that every couple of seconds it sounds like Peter is using an electric shaver on his microphone.

GLR's signal is surprisingly strong as far as Fleet – surprising given that the L stands for London. You can recognise GLR, or London Live as it now is, because it's more than likely someone is playing a Travis album track, something by Squeeze or trying very hard to slip in something by The Clash without the new management noticing too much.

As I turn off the M3 towards the South West the London signals have finally crackled away and I'm in new untried local radio territory. One station proclaims itself to be 'All Across Basingstoke', which is a boast you don't often hear.

WAVE 105.2 has a good strong signal that might just get me as far as the West Country and tonight the presenter appears to be a lady called Michelle Horn. The station's slogan is 'Better Music: Great Talk'. It seems that 'better' music means Phil Collins and Robbie Williams. In fact a clearer description would be 'saddish, ballady, invariably in a minor key but you'll know all the words'. But you can understand that it may not have been easy for Michelle to keep saying that in between every record.

She is doing little bits of 'great talk' in between 'Sussudio' and 'Angels'. It includes her sharing with me the trials of Christmas shopping and why her mother wanted talcum powder. It seems that nothing else this Christmas is good enough for Mrs Horn and such is the detailed account of her need that I am left dearly hoping that the itchiness of her condition has got better by now. If not she should really see a doctor.

Radio 4 news had a report about why smokers get so lardy after they've given up – this is brought to me by Corinne Podger who is presumably an appropriately named Fat Correspondent. You can imagine the morning BBC News meetings.

'Oi, Simpson – we have a war for you to cover today – get on to it ...'

'Paxman – you're on shouting duty in the *Newsnight* studio ... and Podge, we've got another fatty one for you – leap to it, girl ...'

But it was BBC Bristol that got the gong that evening; it was indulging in exactly the kind of broadcasting that I should imagine makes the BBC governors' buttocks swell with pride. The programme was called *The Century Speaks* and was a finely honed collection of local voices talking us through little bits of their lives.

There was a Druid who had had a gay 'hand-fastening ceremony' at Stonehenge and who spoke movingly about what it meant to be able to feel married and have a relationship accepted, even though some would say it's not the norm. There was a Jewish man who said that, after much consideration and thinking about how society now worked, he wouldn't mind if his daughter married outside the faith. There was a woman whose status as an unmarried mother had brought shame on her family. It sounded like it had ruined her life.

The pieces all floated off the back of one another with gentle pauses where a sharp-scripted presenter would usually be. Silence is a superb radio tool – and we had had that drummed into us at Radio Grafton, where the lesson was often put into practice by mistake, sometimes for up to four minutes on the trot. But when it is used as a bit of punctuation it can make your brain pause for a moment too.

Sadly everything changed at 7 o'clock. I couldn't quite catch the lady presenter's name because she said it with such speed but it sounded alarmingly like Sarah Gonads. Hers was the kind of show that cleverer and sharper comedy brains have turned into classics now available in cassette form in all good music shops.

It was a music and chat show and Sarah wanted people to phone her with all kinds of things. She wanted to hear people's special Christmas noises – things that made them feel really Yuletidy. It was tempting to phone up and say 'carols' with more than a hint of irony in my voice, but I was beaten to it by a man who suggested singing wreaths and ho-ho-hoing Santas. You could have added children crying and turkeys pleading – but that would have been taking the piss.

Her programme was addictive though – mainly because of her main competition of the evening. It was called 'Who is in my cupboard?'

Whoever it was who was in the cupboard, he or she was squashed into a corner by innuendo. It was a simple competition – Miss Gonads gave a clue and you phoned in to see if you could guess it right. This was clue number one:

'It's a famous person who has done something remarkable.'

It was going to be a long night.

All this had brought me to the outskirts of Taunton – there was a huge new bowling-alley complex that I didn't recognise but apart from that it all looked reassuringly familiar. They were bound to have changed the one-way system though – just to fool me. It had been bad enough all those years ago. Despite hoping for the comforting single roundabouts of a small market town, I had soon realised that size doesn't matter when it comes to road planning. Whoever those buggers are who do all those one-way systems and car park flows, they can make it equally gruelling in a town like Taunton as they can in a city like Birmingham. Even though I lived in a village not more than a mile outside Taunton when I worked there, it would still take me 40 minutes to find my way to the car park opposite the radio station.

When we were all beavering away across the country for the Trainee Reporter Scheme, I think that our accommodation allowance was about fifty quid a week. There is no reason why the BBC should have splashed out more for us and it would have been a crime against the Licence Fee Payers if we could have afforded to stay in Realistically Named Hotels.

But even in 1993 it was pretty hard work finding somewhere to stay for £7.50 a night. I got lucky in Taunton and found a B&B just outside the town which had a tiny single room that the proprietors were more than happy to let me have on a three-month cheap rate. It had one single bed, a basin, a TV and a hospitality tray which I would work my way through every morning and night. Two sachets of coffee in the morning and two cups of tea and the shortbread biscuits in the evening.

It was a no smoking establishment, which at first I thought was a bit of a drawback, but in fact turned out to be a bonus and not only for my lungs. If I did need a fag late at night I'd get in the sexy Volvo and go for a drive, thereby finding my way round the endless little hamlets and villages tucked away in the hills about Taunton.

Even back in 1993 I had a thing about hotels and I had looked on enviously at the Castle Hotel with its huge draped wisteria on the front and constant row of shiny Rover and BMW 7 series round the back. It looked like the kind of hotel that you should go and spend your 10th wedding anniversary in and order really pricey bottles of champagne and get a bit pissed because you don't have the kids with you. And it got maximum points for naming itself correctly. It was once the castle for the town and has the thick walls, fortified ruins and mentions in historical books to prove it. For example it has been recorded that in 1685 the Duke of Monmouth's officers were heard roistering at the Castle Inn. Hopefully soundproofing will prevent you from hearing the couple with the Rover 7 series doing the same.

I'd gone a bit homecoming queen and walked around the town centre that night reminiscing, while the Rotary Club singers pumped out Christmas carols to a dejected-looking bunch of people hurrying home in the sleet. Some of the shops had changed – but not very many. I thought that perhaps the road layout had been made even more complicated but I wasn't certain. I walked up to the radio station to check that it was still in the same place.

The fascia on the building had changed but it was still just behind the high street and opposite the multi-storey. When I arrived all those years ago, it used to have the logo of a green apple instead of the full BBC bollocks. I had been rather impressed that it had escaped the corporate image machine. Perhaps it also showed that not many managers ever bothered to visit. Now the BBC branding department had caught up with it and it had the same big three letters in the same font as the rest of the corporation.

None of the lights was on so I assumed that there wasn't a live programme coming out of the station. In a similar way to the opt-out station at Euro 2000, Somerset Sound doesn't broadcast live all the time ... Tonight the listeners of the town would be getting Sarah and her cupboard pumping out from Radio Bristol. I wondered if anyone had guessed the occupant yet.

To be fair to Sarah her competition was by no means the worst that radio can supply. BBC Manchester used to do a similar thing on their Breakfast Show – but their question was 'What's in My Hand?' Apparently this was a staple of humour for students in the city because sound effects were used as the clues in this competition. And at 8 o'clock in the morning when the sound effect is rather a squelchy one and the male host asks 'What's in My Hand?' the answer is a lot of giggling and more innuendo than a cupboard can ever dream of.

Nothing much is stirring in Taunton at ten to seven in the morning. It's only a short walk from the hotel back to the studios of Somerset Sound and no one else seems to be up. When I worked there the station operated from two storeys of the building. I hadn't noticed the night before that they have been relegated to the top floor only, and a shop now rents the ground floor.

While I'm waiting for someone to answer the buzzer I can see a William Hague head peering down from the window above. This is the man I have come to see: Somerset Sound's breakfast host, Mr Simon White.

Simon White is 34 and presents what is the smallest BBC breakfast show in the country. Today it is just him and Becky who reads the travel, puts calls through and makes very strong coffee. Simon is playing a tape when I arrive which means that he has plenty of time to lean out of the window, let me in, offer me coffee and a seat at the table opposite his DJ's desk.

Today there isn't much news – it's only a few days before Christmas and not a lot is going on in the world. Simon says that doesn't really matter because they'll play a bit more music and they have a couple of guests coming in. One is a bouncer from a Taunton nightclub and the other is a policeman. Both are going to talk the listeners through 'How to Remain Safe this Christmas'. The tape is coming to an end – Simon says it's about the history of Christmas carols, which is why it has ended with an uplifting rendition of 'Hark the Herald Angels Sing'.

'That's my dad doing that,' Simon says as he lifts the tape off the spool – it may be some time before Simon gets the kind of computerised desk that every other DJ now has.

'What – singing "Hark the Herald"?' I ask rather dumbly.

'No ...! doing the piece about carols, he's a vicar. But you knew that, didn't you?'

I think I did, somewhere in the dark recesses of my mind, and I think when I was working at Somerset Sound I met Simon's religious dad. I have a feeling that we called him up quite a lot as he was obviously the easiest vicar to get hold of if you wanted an emergency Church quote.

Simon looks very, very tired.

'So how are things?' I ask him.

'Well, you know ... pretty much the same as they were last time I saw you, I think – we're still rumbling along.'

Somerset Sound still smells the same apart from anything else. A slightly musty, mouldy smell.

'And what about you?'

I tell him about my travels over the past few months – which is not an entirely fair thing to do to a guy who has been up since 3.30 and is now playing tapes out in a studio the size of a competition cupboard.

'So why come here?' he asks.

I explain that I wanted to check that local radio is still happening here – and that I had got a bit misty-eyed about how I first got hooked on radio. I ask him how many listeners the station now has and if the bosses are happy with it. I seem to recall that every week there was a rumour that someone was on their way to shut Somerset Sound down.

'About 10,000 people probably listen across the week,' Simon says. 'I don't think we're under threat right now – it's popular for what it does and it's not like it's costing a fortune to keep all this going.'

Simon waves his hands around the studio.

'And I think I've got a bit better too – there's a bit of Mark and Lard in my show I like to think,' says Simon. 'You know ... a bit sarcastic but really very friendly. Was I in my One FM stage when you were working here?'

I'm a bit flummoxed by this question. 'Errr ... yes I think so.' I don't know if this is a good or a bad thing to Simon. Turns out it was a bad thing – that was when he was being all Rock-On. Now he says he feels more secure about what he's doing so he's got a 'warmer tone'.

Right on cue, Becky the travel and producer-type girl comes in with the morning post which consists largely of Christmas cards addressed to Simon. One card from a listener comes with the message, 'I haven't forgotten about the chutney – it's on the way, promise.'

When I was here as a little trainee I don't remember seeing Simon all that much – mainly because he was finishing his daily shift as I was starting mine. Every day I'd arrive at about 8.30 for the daily news meeting where Richard, the senior producer, would decide where it was that I was going to spend my day. I was on perpetual 'Minehead Sea Wall Collapses!' duty and was often sent out to see whether the vicious tides were about to cause tragedy in the town. Fortunately for everyone that never happened.

The second most frequent story was sightings of the Beast of Bodmin. It's one of those stories that everyone just loves – the idea that panthers are roaming the countryside, or that a superbreed of feral cat comes out in the dead of night and savages sheep. There was a taxidermist in one of the villages on Exmoor who swore that he had seen it – judging by the look of some of his stuffed animals, they had seen it too in the moments before their death.

The highlight of my time in Somerset was when I got to go out with the elver fishermen. It was the first big piece that I was commissioned to do. These baby eels can only be caught at a certain time of year and there are strict licences for the fishermen – but there's an awful lot of poaching and I assume my boss hoped that I might stumble on to something criminal and squelchy in the dead of night on a riverbank.

It was an experience marred by the fact that I had had a tattoo done on my ankle that day and it itched like hell – I had waders on up to my thighs, a UHER, a torch, several spare tapes and a camera to carry. It was a long night spent trying to balance on a riverbank with a stick stuck down my waders trying to itch my ankle, while holding conversations about river flows and eel prices with a group of surly men.

I thought it was a triumph. I've still got the piece somewhere and I'm sure if I listened back to it I'd be able to hear the scratching going on in the background. It went down quite well with the management, though, and the next week I got to do another solo piece, this time about a fence builder in Taunton who had just got a commission to build a high wooden wall to protect the privacy of John Major's house. Mr Major wanted a certain kind of wood used and had chosen this Somerset fence builder above all others.

My piece was not such a success. I only managed to sustain the conversation for 1 minute and 50 seconds. After asking him what the fence was made of and how long it would take to build, I kind of dried up. I got a bollocking for that and it did teach me always to have some standard questions up your sleeve. I now know that there are five questions you can guarantee will help out most interviews:

1. Can you give us some more background to this case?
2. Were there any casualties?
3. What happens next?
4. How does this affect the peace process?
5. What happens if the wall falls down?

But apart from those momentous moments, which I'm sure the listeners of Somerset Sound remember vividly, I don't think I contributed that much to the station's output. In fact I probably did it more harm than good. I used to drive around in the Somerset Sound car which had a kind of radio attachment in it so that you could file back urgent reports about sea walls from any part of the county. Due to its signage, it also meant that loyal and health-conscious listeners could phone the station irately if they saw you stopping in a lay-by for a fag in between searching for big black moggies that people might have mistaken for sheep-torturing feral cats. They did occasionally call to complain.

While Simon is setting up the news and sports junction I pull back the curtains and peer out at what must be one of the least inspirational views you can have from a studio – floor after floor of a multi-storey car park. Simon follows my gaze.

'No one's done it during my show ...' he says, very matter of factly.

'I'm sorry?'

'No one has jumped during my show. That's where they go to commit suicide – happens rather a lot really but fortunately not during my programme ...'

'But that's awful – how many people have succeeded?' I ask.

'Two of them went during the afternoon show. We used to have a gag that they all jumped during Sheila's show ... it was that bad.'

Sheila was a lovely woman and still is, by the way – she didn't take the top floor multi-storey exit. Her show was a kind of Woman's Hour for Somerset and it was eccentric rather than depressing. I remember walking past the studio one day when she was doing her Exercise on Air class. This must have been very hard to follow at home. She's now running a glossy magazine for people who live in big houses in the Mendips. But that doesn't mean you shouldn't stop what you're doing and lie on the floor at three o'clock to stretch your pelvic floor muscles. I thought it was quite bold to try to do something so visual over the airwaves.

Simon seems quite reticent about the fact that he is still at Somerset

Sound, whereas ex-trainees like myself are touring the world. I'm not sure he is convinced when I point out that no one ever sends me cards promising bottles of homemade chutney and say that I admire the loyalty that he has found in his listeners. In fact it's not just the listeners who love Somerset Sound. Paddy Ashdown and David Heath both raised the issue in the House of Commons when managers suggested that the station might close down.

We've now got to competition time in Simon's show. The competition is just a simple question-and-answer one. The question is 'Which big structure other than the Dome has gone up in London to celebrate the Millennium?' Simon says on air that he will take the generic term for the structure (ferris wheel) as well as the actual name (London Eye). Someone hasn't been listening very closely though and has sent an answer in saying the Dome. Simon jokes it's from a P. Mandelson.

Simon ends the programme with an interview with a PR man who has done a 'turkey survey', which has revealed the not-so-startling fact that by the end of the festive season we all end up suffering from turkey fatigue. I wish that I could have told the PR guy about the turkeys who fell from heaven in the promotional stunt in the States – but I am playing a silent role in today's proceedings. Simon puts on one last track, Jonah Lewise and 'Stop the Cavalry'.

It's easy to take the mickey out of local radio and it's chutney-based links between presenters and listeners, but I'm truly heartened that nothing has changed much in Somerset. It's part of the choice on the dial, which would be a poorer place if everything was dictated by the agenda of big business and national news. I buy Simon breakfast to ask where he thinks I should go in the evening for my final radio-inspired excursion, using only Somerset Sound's *What's On Guide*. The choice is between a blood donor's session, a talk on 'Badgers in My Kitchen' or some carol singing in a place called Highbridge.

The Badgers in My Kitchen one sounds perfect to me, but Simon and I agree that if no one else turns up or it's really, really dull then I have little chance of escaping. The blood donor's session really isn't a goer at all and so it has to be Highbridge. Not only because it gives me the chance to sing my little heart out safe in the bosom of a close community bonded by radio, but also because Simon says that Highbridge was deemed the most miserable town in Britain last Christmas when they had only one Christmas light up in the High Street. It made the national news because when that light broke no one could be bothered to replace it, so Highbridge celebrated Christmas with no fairy lights at all.

I wished Simon a very Merry Christmas and asked him if he wanted to come with me to sing carols around what would hopefully be a better decorated tree than Highbridge had last year. He said he'd pass as he had a Christmas party to go to at the local newspaper and anyway he had to be in bed by 10 o'clock. I wished him the best of luck with his career and then realised that I sounded really patronising, which I hadn't meant to. I made a note to send him some chutney, should I ever get around to making any.

Without realising it I had timed my trip out to Highbridge perfectly and it was Sarah Gonad's time again on the radio. She may still have the same person as last night in her cupboard but the clues are just as tricky. Now the hidden person is 'a celebrity famous for an outfit'. Her listeners are straight in there – answers include Max Wall, Santa Claus and Lily Savage. None of them was right although Sarah wasn't going to make it any easier by giving us a perhaps more detailed clue. She seemed more than happy just to chat along with her merry Christmas punters about the hassles of buying presents for kids and the likelihood of having snow on Christmas Day this year.

I rather expected Highbridge to be some kind of massive glowing beacon on the horizon, such would be the town's desire to make up for the lack of Yuletide cheer last year. But Highbridge town centre didn't seem to be trying very hard – a couple of strung-out bulbs and some gaudy decorations straggled in the wind. The carol singalong was meant to be taking place 'around the Christmas tree', which you would have hoped would be the large conifer decked out with tinsel and lights as is the custom across the Western world.

Highbridge wasn't going to make the end of my journey that easy. I drove round a few streets looking for their equivalent of the star in the east, but I lacked the magnetic pull that the wise men had. One house on the road out of the other side of town had decided to rectify the problem all by itself and was covered in lights and sleighs and beaming Santas. But there was no huge tree in their garden either.

I stopped and asked in the newsagent's, where the shop assistants were packing up for the evening.

'I've come for the carols,' I beamed. 'You know, the singalong round the tree?'

A cross-looking lady pointed over the road. 'They're going to be there – outside the hall – but I don't think it's really the night for them.'

I said my thank yous in an over-ingratiating style that I adopt from 1 December through until 4 January and everyone in the shop looked at me in a way that suggested they had spotted I was a stranger in their midst and I should leave as soon as possible.

So I went and sat in the car to wait for the throng to gather. Three pissed blokes emerged from the pub carrying cans of lager. Ten minutes later a woman emerged from the hall, lumbering under the weight of a table which they carried round to the side. And only then did I spot the tree. Cunningly disguised as a normal tree, it appeared to be from the Shy and Understated school of conifers but when I looked a little closer it did indeed appear to have just a few lights twinkling on it. Maybe Highbridge had simply gone minimalist this year.

I was getting a bit hungry now, so I had a car picnic consisting of the only instantly edible things from the supermarket outside which I was parked. This consisted of a packet of TUC biscuits and a slab of Ardennes pâté. The pâté had as much chance of having come from Ardennes as the biscuits did of being made by the Trade Union Congress. And they all broke in the car, which gave the impression of a biscuit-killing spree.

I wondered what all those people I'd met over the past few months would be doing for Christmas. Maybe one year I could persuade them all to come round for turkey at my house. Rose could bring the inspirational tunes. Dr Joy could stop us all from arguing. Steve and Johnnie would get everyone talking and act as Mum and Dad – and maybe we could club together and buy Paul Lyle a small puppy for a present on the basis that he wouldn't then broil it later in life.

What would Art Bell be doing now? Christmas must be a tricky time with all those antichrists floating around. I doubt whether I'd be able to persuade Fitz to leave his sunlit paradise of Palm Springs, but I bet Mary-Anne and the rest of the Dusty Wings lot would come round for the odd Snowball. It'd be a fantastic evening full of radio anecdotes – I could ask Dickie Arbiter too and get him to relive his Oil Tanker hiccup as a party piece.

By 7.45 I'd had it. No one else seemed to have turned up – even the blokes with the cans of lager had disappeared back into the pub. To be honest I couldn't have cared less. I'd been twiddling my dial while I was waiting and been promised by Radio 2 that there was a programme coming up in half an hour hosted by Evelyn Glennie – now this is a woman who is deaf and still making radio shows. And if you think about that for just one moment, it is quite extraordinary. Evelyn can't hear any of the things that I've taken for granted across the world, but she must appreciate the power of sound to do what she does.

It seemed the perfect way to end a trip around bits of the world listening to the wireless. I stuffed another broken biscuit into my gob, muttered something slightly unChristmaslike to myself about Highbridge and started the car.

So I'd ended up in a car park in Somerset. It wasn't that bad. In fact, it was exactly where I had started out all those months ago in Petaluma, North California. I was still sitting in strange places with only the radio for company – thinking little thoughts about who the people inside the wireless were. I had travelled thousand of miles and met people doing all kinds of radio and I still couldn't get enough of it.

The search button was zooming through a variety of pre-Christmas ballads. If I was really lucky, someone would be playing 'Driving Home for Christmas' with that little twinkly bit at the beginning and Chris Rea's gritty voice singing about 'a thousand memories'. Or maybe I'd get a bit of 'Fairytale of New York'. I bet they had that tune out in Tibnin in the little white hut of a radio station. Perhaps the boys of the Irish Battalion had had a hard day's peacekeeping but would be able to put their feet up for just an hour or so and play some good old festive tunes that would bring a little tear to the eye.

And all over the world there would be millions of people just getting on with their daily lives with the radio on in the background. Just a little aural wallpaper that they probably wouldn't even be thinking about. What a poorer place the world would be without it.

Ho Ho Ho. Happy DX-ing.